How Press Propaganda Paved t

"Fake news and disinformation distorting public opinion from real, checked facts is one of the biggest threats facing today's democracies. In this must-read book, Rawlinson lucidly describes how emotions—sometimes unrelated to the real subject matter of the vote—gained the upper hand and brought an entire nation to a decision potentially harming its own interests."
—Enrico D'Ambrogio, *Policy Analyst, EPRS – European Parliamentary Research Service*

Francis Rawlinson

How Press Propaganda Paved the Way to Brexit

Francis Rawlinson
Ottignies, Belgium

ISBN 978-3-030-27764-2   ISBN 978-3-030-27765-9   (eBook)
https://doi.org/10.1007/978-3-030-27765-9

Cover illustration: Collage by eStudio Calamar based on the images Zerbor/shutterstock.com,
Landscape Photograpohy/shutterstock.com

This Palgrave Macmillan imprint is published by the registered company Springer Nature
Switzerland AG.
The registered company address is: Gewerbestrasse 11, 6330 Cham, Switzerland

FOREWORD

Frank Rawlinson is one of the many British officials in the European Commission, and other EU institutions, who has worked with integrity and competence to help build a constructive and collaborative relationship between the European nations. Because of his long career, he has been able to draft this book which gives insights into the motives which drove the development of the EU, and the motives of those who voice criticism of it, both deserved and biased. Anyone wishing to understand the background to the UK's participation in the EU and the political currents which led it to the Brexit negotiations will find in this book a clear, informative and objective analysis. His presentation of the realities as compared to the myths, such as the reliability of the Commission's accounts, is perfectly correct. It is odd that the UK should want to leave the EU when the Commission has adopted the British principles of good management, and applies these better than many UK public services.

FCA, Former Chief Accountant of the   Brian Gray
European Commission and subsequently
Director-General of the Internal Audit Service
Brussels, Belgium

PREFACE

Comment is free, facts are sacred
—C. P. Scott

Right-wing newspapers like the *Telegraph, Mail, Express* and *Sun* have helped shape British public opinion about Europe for over 20 years. Within the written press, anti-EU newspapers have been in a majority. Their influence has been strong, fostering distrust and animosity towards the EU, exaggerating its disadvantages, and denying its benefits. These newspapers have supported the efforts of a minority in the right-wing political Establishment to which they are closely affiliated to take Britain out of Europe.

The influence of the anti-EU press on public opinion has extended beyond its immediate readership, the older voters who still read newspapers and who voted overwhelmingly for Brexit. Television and radio tend to take up the main stories run by the print media and re-broadcast their headlines often without much challenge. The result is that negative reports about the EU are proliferated in the media as a whole, even though TV and radio stations like the BBC try to remain impartial.

The right-wing press also has a disproportionate effect on British politics, beyond the minority of politicians in Westminster, mostly Conservatives, that share its views. This is because its influence on public opinion, as amplified by the rest of the media, makes politicians pay close heed to the views expressed in such newspapers and adapt their policies accordingly.

I am a strong supporter of a free press. A free press protects people against abuses of power by their rulers and helps ensure democratic processes that allow bad rulers to be removed. But the press must strive to report events objectively and fairly. Persistent bias against particular policies, individuals or organizations, domestic or foreign, betrays the principles journalists should live by and is an abuse of the power of a free press.

On the issue of Europe, the right-wing newspapers in Britain have fallen short of the standards to be expected of a free press and been guilty of persistent bias and misinformation in their reporting. When maintained over a long period, such content can only be described as propaganda.

The real propaganda affecting Brexit was not the leaflet the Cameron Government distributed to every household putting the case for EU membership, which was hardly substantial enough to count as such, given the scarcity of positive information available about the EU. The propaganda was perpetrated through a long-standing, relentless campaign by a so-called free press which on this issue had laid aside its standards of fairness in order to pursue a political objective.

When Paul Dacre, the long-standing editor of the *Daily Mail* and passionate Eurosceptic, announced his retirement in June 2018, some commentators claimed that without him Brexit would not have happened. I agree, except to say that it was not only him, but the majority right-wing press more broadly.

As well as the biased content in the newspapers themselves over many years, other evidence points to the same conclusion that press propaganda paved the way to Brexit. Firstly, surveys conducted after the referendum found that the older and newspaper-reading voters were more inclined to vote for Brexit and that most newspaper readers tended to vote in accordance with the editorial policy of their newspaper. Secondly, in Scotland and Northern Ireland, the referendum produced majorities in favour of remaining in the EU. While there are clearly other factors at work as well in the pro-EU result, it is surely no coincidence that these are the two parts of the UK in which the circulation of English-based newspapers is least and the local press is generally more pro-EU than the English newspapers.

The lesson from the referendum is not to take for granted the freedom of the press and the responsibilities it places on journalists and editors in terms of truthfulness and objectivity of reporting. Freedom from government interference is not sufficient to keep up press standards. To fulfil its role in a democracy, a free press must not seek to manipulate public opinion towards an ideological objective; it should inform the public by reporting facts fairly.

The purpose of this book by a British former EU official is to correct the main false statements about the EU made before, during and since the 2016 referendum in the press and by politicians and commentators, which arguably affected the result. Whether my country leaves the EU or not, I hope the book will contribute to a proper understanding of Europe in Britain. The debate is to set to continue for years to come.

Ottignies, Belgium   Francis Rawlinson

ACKNOWLEDGEMENTS

Writing a book makes you realize how much you owe to others. I must start the list with my autodidact father and heart-of-gold mother and my six siblings. It was a crowded and noisy household but a welcoming and loving one. We played cricket in the yard (it was a farm), and the main London–Glasgow railway line was close by tempting me across the fields to watch the trains. The College sports ground was also next to the railway line, which was why I was never much good at football. I inherited my interest in newspapers from my father: he had a hen cabin full of them, back copies he intended to read again but never got around to. I was fortunate in getting into a school where they taught languages, lots of them, from Latin and Greek to French and German. My English, German and Latin teachers, Arthur Malone (a brilliant Scot), Kenneth Charnock, and F. Lyons (probably Frank, but he was "Ben" to us), were inspiring educators. At Manchester University, my fondest memories are of the Swiss German dialects specialist Professor R. E. Keller and the seminar on Rilke with Professor Idris Parry (a Welshman), not forgetting the visits to the Fox and Grapes with my flat mates in Mauldeth Road, Withington, John Vanston and Stephen Uttley. Four years doing a PhD in German linguistics in Marburg, Germany, followed, during which I met my Japanese wife, Hiroko. We were married in 1970 near Preston. At Marburg, I also met Bernd Dumke and his family, with whom we became related, as he married my wife's sister, Fumiko. My parents never appeared to have the slightest qualms about either my learning German so soon after the war or about my going on to marry a person from another of our former enemies, Japan. Nor did I ever encounter the slightest hint of racism on the Japanese side from my parents-in-law, Masahisa and Katsuko Kageyama, or their other daughter and son-in-law, Masako and Osamu Ishizaki. They welcomed me into the family with open arms.

After an interval in the German department of UCNW in Bangor, under Professor Keith Spalding, a refugee from Nazi Germany, in 1973, after Britain joined the European Community, it was off to Belgium to start what turned out to be a 35-year career in the European Union (EU), first as a translator, then from 1989 onwards as an economist in the competition and regional development departments; in the 1980s I had benefited from that wonderful institution the Open University to get a degree in Economics. In the European Commission, I was fortunate to work with Rolf Schäfer, Chris Dwyer, Gerhard Thies, Manfred Caspari, Claus-Dieter Ehlermann, Asger Petersen, Jonathan Faull, Kurt Ritter, Robert Shotton, Kurt Hötte, Brian Gray, Christina Borchmann, Catherine Day, Nicholas Martyn, Lena Andersson Pench, Androulla Ioannou, and Daniel Kahn, to name but a few. A highlight of this period was the five years I spent in Finland in charge of the EU-financed regional programmes, where I made many close and lasting friends including Kari and Pirkko Nenonen, Hannu Vesa, Pentti and Anne Bruun, Heikki Vesa, Esko and Sointu Elo, and Heikki and Eija Alasalmi. From Finland, it was a short way to Russia, where I first sampled the hospitality of that country, a truly exotic culture at that time, staying with the Jääskeläinen family (Finnish name and heritage, Russian nationality) in Petrozavodsk, Karelia.

At the end of my career, not wishing to stop working, I returned to my teaching roots to lecture in European studies at Kwansei Gakuin University in Japan. Apart from gaining immeasurably from colleagues and friends like Munenori Nomura, Holger Bungsche, Anna Schrade and Yukiko Nakamura, the probing questions students put to me about Europe—how we could possibly work together so closely with so many languages, how we coped with immigration, etc.—started me on the road to writing textbooks. But then Brexit intervened. As a lifelong newspaper addict, and dismayed at the bad press the EU had long been getting, I could see the result coming and, when it came, could not resist the urge to delve more deeply into this particular factor in the vote.

I am grateful to Palgrave Macmillan and Anne-Kathrin Birchley-Brun my editor for giving me the chance to cast a little light on this episode in recent British history and its causes. My thanks also go to Kari Nenonen, Mark Corner, and Nicholas Simoncini of the European Parliament for comments on the text; to Maurice Ffelan, Tom Massie, Luke Lythgoe of

InFacts and Steve Buckledee for helpful advice and suggestions; and to Enrico D'Ambrogio and Chiara Salvelli of the European Parliament, my daughter Monica and her husband Didier, and my son Ken, for suggestions and help with tables, figures, indexes, and copyright permissions. Many heartfelt thanks, too, to my wife Hiroko for her patience during the long gestation period of this book. My thanks also to the News Room at the British Library for their help in locating back copies of newspapers going back to the 1990s—an invaluable resource. The errors that inevitably remain in this book are naturally all mine.

I am also grateful to the Telegraph Media Group, News Licencing (for *The Sun*), *Daily Mail* and *Mail Online*, Express Newspapers, the *Financial Times* and *De Morgen* for permission to quote from their newspapers, to Councillor Alan Law and Dimitis Vayenas for letting me quote from their readers' letters to the *Telegraph* and the *FT*, respectively, to Roger Bootle for permission to quote from his book *The Trouble with Europe*, and to Sir Roger Scruton for allowing me to reproduce excerpts from a talk he gave on BBC Radio 4.

A final word to my dear brothers and sisters, their spouses, their children, our cousins and other relatives, many of them still living in the Preston area: Brexit can divide but not conquer.

Contents

About the Author

Francis Rawlinson was born in Preston, United Kingdom, in 1944 and attended Preston Catholic College, a Jesuit grammar school. After German studies in Manchester and obtaining a PhD in German linguistics at Marburg University, Germany, and working three years as a research fellow and lecturer in the German department of the University College of North Wales, Bangor, he entered the service of the European Union (the then European Community) in Brussels in 1973. He worked in the EU institutions from 1973 until his retirement in 2009. In the European Commission, he served as a translator for 15 years and then, after studying Economics with the British Open University in the 1980s, worked for 20 years as an economist in the competition and regional development departments. While at the European Commission he authored articles on state-aid control, co-authored with Ritter and Braun a book on EC competition law (*EEC Competition Law: A Practitioner's Guide*, 1991), and contributed the state-aid chapter of successive editions of the German law commentary on the EU Treaty edited by Otto Lenz, *Kommentar zum EU-Vertrag* (from 1994). After retirement from the Commission, he lectured on EU policies at Kwansei Gakuin University in Nishinomiya, Japan, from 2011 until 2017, as a professor attached to the Industrial Research Centre and as visiting professor in the Economics Department. During this period, he gave public lectures and contributed to books in Japanese on the euro crisis, competition policy, regional development, Brexit, and the Association of Southeast Asian Nations (ASEAN). He remains a Fellow of Kwansei Gakuin University and is involved in EU-related research and teaching projects with them. He is married with two children and three grandchildren and lives in Belgium. He retains close connections to Japan, where his wife is from, and Finland, where he worked for the European Commission in regional development from 1995 to 2000.

LIST OF FIGURES

LIST OF TABLES

PART I

Background

CHAPTER 1

Introduction

On 23 June 2016, the British people voted by 51.9% to 48.1% to leave the European Union (EU). Some 17.4 million people voted Leave and 16.2 million Remain. The turnout was 72.2% of the electorate, and the shares of the electorate voting Leave and Remain being 37% and 35%, respectively.

The voting figures show that the majority in favour of leaving the EU was small. While it was a clear result, it was hardly a "decisive," let alone an "overwhelming" one. The number of Leave voters, though a majority of those who voted, was a long way short of half the electorate, when non-voters are counted. However, no minimum threshold for a valid vote had been set either in relation to the proportion of the electorate voting or the size of the majority, so Leave won.

In view of the narrow majority in favour of leaving the EU over those wanting to remain, it is an exaggeration to say leaving was "the clear will of the people." Given the variety of ideas put forward by Leave campaigners as to what leaving would mean, claiming this or that form of Brexit—leaving without a withdrawal agreement, leaving the customs union and the single market, etc.—was the "will of the people" is absurd.

The proportions voting for Leave and Remain varied in the four constituent parts of the UK (Table 1.1). There were majorities for Leave in England and Wales and for Remain in Scotland and Northern Ireland. The Remain majority in Scotland was genuinely "overwhelming," that in

© The Author(s) 2019
F. Rawlinson, *How Press Propaganda Paved the Way to Brexit*,
https://doi.org/10.1007/978-3-030-27765-9_1

Table 1.1 Voting in EU referendum, by constituent part (country) of UK (% of voters)

Constituent part (country) of UK	Leave	Remain
England	53.4	46.6
Wales	52.5	47.5
Scotland	38.0	62.0
Northern Ireland	44.2	55.8

Source: Author's presentation based on data from *BBC News*. 24 June 2016. Referendum results

Northern Ireland clearer than the Leave majorities in England and Wales. This has led to demands for special treatment of Scotland and Northern Ireland in the settlement with the EU and the proposal by the Scottish government for a second referendum on Scottish independence to prevent Scotland being taken out of the EU against its will.

For the purposes of the referendum, the electorate was defined in the same way as for national elections: 16- and 17-year olds and long-term British expatriates were excluded. The former had been given the right to vote in the Scottish independence referendum, but it was decided not to repeat the experiment in the EU referendum. Long-term expats—British citizens living abroad who had not been registered to vote in Britain for 15 years or more—were excluded, despite promises by the government to extend the suffrage to them.[1]

Irish and Commonwealth citizens resident in Britain had the right to vote, but not EU nationals living in Britain. Many of the latter were long-term residents but because under EU free movement their and their family's right to stay in Britain was secure, before the EU referendum they had had no reason to become British citizens and few had done so. EU nationals had been given the right to vote in the Scottish independence referendum, just as 16- and 17-year olds had.[2]

Had the electorate in the EU referendum been widened to the 1.46 million 16- and 17-year olds, the result might easily have gone the other way, because polls suggested 80% might have voted for Remain.[3] If, in addition, all the estimated 1.2 million British expatriates living in Europe had been eligible to vote, a Remain victory would have been virtually guaranteed. Most of these, too, would probably have voted Remain in order to keep their current rights to live and work and retire to another EU country.

Over 3 million citizens of other EU countries were living in Britain at the time of the referendum. If even only those among them who are long-term residents—for example, those married to British citizens and with British-born children—had had been allowed to register to vote, the result

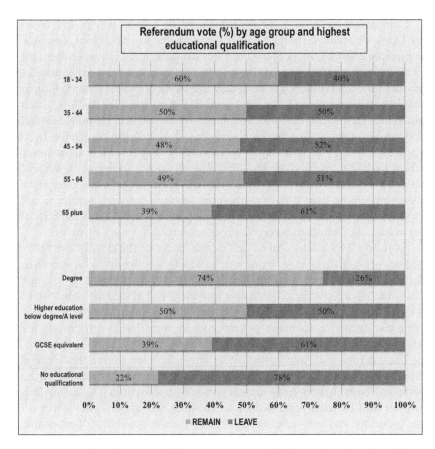

Fig. 1.1 Referendum vote (%) by age group and highest educational qualification. Source: Author's presentation, based on data from Swales, K. 2016. NatCen Social Research. Understanding the Leave vote[5]

would also have been different. Admittedly, under current EU law there is no requirement to allow citizens of other EU countries to vote in national elections; this only applies to European Parliament and local elections.

A.C. Grayling cogently argues that deliberate restriction of the franchise is gerrymandering: the EU referendum was gerrymandered.[4]

Figure 1.1 shows the different voting patterns according to age and highest educational qualification. In general, the younger the voter and the higher their level of educational qualifications, the more likely they were to vote to stay in the EU, and vice versa.

Considerable research has been done into the reasons why people voted for Leave or Remain. John Curtice[6] considers that as well as looking at the immediate explanation, people's attitudes towards the EU, it was important to examine the underlying reasons for those attitudes and the circumstances in which the referendum was held. In *Eurobarometer* surveys which look at attitudes towards the EU in the member states, the UK has long been unique[7] in having a majority of the population who feel exclusively British and not European at all, whereas elsewhere in Europe most people feel both a national and a European identity, in varying degrees. Britain has never taken the EU to its heart. I think this is largely down to deep cultural and historical reasons which have made the EU seem less relevant and more alien and remote than it does to the populations of other countries. I will explore these reasons in Chap. 3.[8] In my opinion—and this is the focus of my book—the British Eurosceptic press has reinforced such attitudes.

As John Curtice also notes, the circumstances at the time of the referendum—the financial crisis from which the EU was slower to recover than Britain, the euro and migrant crises which the EU struggled to manage but which hardly affected Britain, and intra-EU migration which had affected Britain significantly since the early 2000s—all made the EU look even less attractive to many people and so were hardly propitious for advancing the Remain cause.

The surveys that were done soon after the vote found that voters' immediate reasons for voting the way they did were mainly related to the perceived costs, benefits and risks of remaining or leaving. The calculation of costs and benefits pertained to sovereignty and identity, the effect on the economy, and immigration. The risks were the possibility of economic crisis in Britain or the EU, impaired security and increased terrorism, and uncontrolled immigration. Curtice concludes that the opposing assessments of these factors among Leave and Remain voters evened one another out and therefore produced a close result. This was particularly so for the economic costs and benefits, where opinions were most divided. Many Leavers were unconvinced of the Remain campaign's predictions of serious harm to the overall economy and to their personal financial situation. Indeed, people living in old industrial areas who were economically marginalized in any case and felt "left behind" by globalization and economic change tended to think things could not get any worse.[9] Emotional reactions of various kinds and reliance on cues from influential campaigners such as Boris Johnson were also important, especially for the large number of voters who did not have well-formed opinions about the EU beforehand. Britain's international standing was a bigger issue for Remain voters than for Leavers.[10] Curtice sums up the two extremes of the social divisions evidenced by voting patterns according to age and educational qualifications as the gulf between young well-educated, mobile professionals and older, less well-educated people "left behind" by economic change, along similar lines to Goodhart's dichotomy between "Anywheres" and "Somewheres."[11]

Voting in the referendum was not on party political lines. Both main parties officially supported Remain, but a majority of Conservative voters (58%) and a considerable minority of Labour voters (36%) voted Leave. Because of the low profile the Labour party leadership had in the referendum campaign, many Labour voters apparently did not know which side their party was officially on. The voting of Conservative voters in the referendum was close to the split between Brexiteers and Remainers in the parliamentary party, where 55% of Conservative MPs supported Leave and 45% Remain. Among Labour party voters, support for Leave was much higher than in the parliamentary party, where it was a small minority (4% as against 96% for Remain).[12]

It is frequently observed that in referendums voters that do not have well-formed opinions on the question asked will rely on proxy measures such as their evaluation of the overall performance of the government or of the state of democracy in the country. There can then be an element of protest against the government, politics, and elites in general in the result. With many voters being uninformed about the EU because of its remoteness and many of the "left behind" being dissatisfied with their economic situation, I think such proxy voting was likely in the EU referendum.[13]

The high majorities for Leave in the old industrial areas of the Midlands and North of England and of Wales suggest that the general dissatisfaction of people in such areas with their economic situation and a feeling of being overlooked by politics were indeed a factor in the vote. This took on a distinct element of protest against the Establishment and the political class, a desire to give the elites a "good kicking" and to get them to change their policies. Mrs May promised at the beginning of her period in office to respond to this dissatisfaction among the "just about managing" and continued later on to interpret the referendum result as a demand for change to improve the lot of the "left behind."

People in strongly Leave voting areas had justified reasons for dissatisfaction and protest: they had suffered more from the austerity policies of the government since the financial crisis than more prosperous city areas; earnings had stagnated and dependence on social welfare in such areas had been increasing since the financial crisis and the onset of recession; the bulk of investment had been in London and the South East, not in the Midlands and North of England or Wales; social inequality had increased; and Mrs May was quite right to pledge on the steps of Downing Street after becoming Prime Minister that she would tackle the "burning injustices" in society.

However, there must be some doubt whether the dissatisfaction with their economic and social circumstances that motivated people to vote Leave in the referendum had much to do with the EU. Economic policies are in fact little constrained by EU membership—especially outside the eurozone. Crises like the eurozone debt crisis excepted, member countries are largely the masters of their own economic choices. The EU did not ordain Britain's austerity policies, forbid it from investing in infrastructure in the Midlands and North of England, or stop it taking measures to reduce inequality or improve welfare. These were entirely national choices. Nor would saving the less than 0.5% of GDP the UK contributes net to the EU budget have made enough difference to public finances to finance all these desirable things like the National Health Service (NHS) that the British government had been neglecting.

The intermingling of motives for the Leave vote, some quite extraneous to the question on the ballot paper—membership of the EU—goes some way to explaining the refusal of Remain supporters to go quietly, shut up, and accept the—narrow—result as the "will of the people." Similar extraneous motives inexorably creep into all referendums and are a major reason why many countries reject this form of democracy altogether in preference to representative parliamentary democracy, or at least use it extremely sparingly.

Under the legislation, the referendum result was to be advisory but in a leaflet about the EU distributed by the government before the vote,[14] it had been stated that the government would take the result as binding. This undertaking was repeated by campaigners on both sides of the debate.

It was natural, therefore, that both the government and the opposition in Parliament, despite the pro-Remain majority among MPs, should feel obliged to act upon the result and take Britain out of the EU.

That the divorce of the UK from its over 40 years' relationship with the European Union should prove difficult has not been a surprise to those familiar with the depth of those relationships.[15] If many Leave voters have been disappointed that Brexit has not been easier, this is because their leaders downplayed the impact and difficulties of leaving. Britain's relations with the EU cover more than trade in goods and services but also numerous essential aspects of people's daily lives that the EU has made easier, ranging from travel and communications to health care when abroad and a safe environment.

At the time of writing (mid-April 2019) it was still unclear whether, when, and on what terms Britain would leave the EU. The government had concluded a withdrawal agreement with the EU, which included a transition period to maintain the status quo after leaving until the end of 2020. However, Parliament had rejected the withdrawal agreement three times, with the hard Brexit contingent of the ruling party and the Northern Irish Democratic Unionist Party (DUP) lining up with the opposition Labour, Liberal Democrat, and Scottish Nationalist parties to oppose the agreement. MPs of all parties had then taken the initiative to explore alternatives themselves and when that failed the Prime Minister had held talks with the Labour party to try to find a formula that could gain a majority. The original departure date of 29 March 2019 had been postponed once until 22 May and then again until the end of October 2019. An increasing body of support was building for a second referendum, or "People's Vote," pitting whatever withdrawal terms Parliament would be able to agree against the option of Remain. Opinion polls were showing an increasing tide of support for a second ballot and for remaining in the EU after all. The May government had conceded Parliament's demands to rule out the option of crashing out of the EU without a withdrawal agreement and transition period.

The Cameron government did not make any plans for Brexit because it did not expect to lose the referendum. On succeeding Mr Cameron after the referendum, Mrs May assembled a government carefully balanced between Remainers and Leavers. Leavers were put in charge of the main portfolios relevant to Brexit, namely, the ministry for exiting the EU, international trade, and foreign affairs. Initially, Mrs May leaned towards a "hard" or "clean" Brexit, involving exit from the Customs Union—in order to enable the UK to pursue its own trade policy and strike new trade agreements—and gradual divergence from European regulations governing the single market, competition, employment rights, the environment and consumer protection.

The UK gave the EU notice of its intention to leave on 29 March 2017. Mrs May then decided to hold a snap election to increase her majority and make it easier to pass Brexit legislation, but ended up in fact losing her majority and relying on the Northern Irish DUP for support to get legislation through. If this delayed the negotiations with the EU on the details of the future relationship and how close or distant that would be, so did the EU's insistence on settling preliminary matters concerning the withdrawal itself before turning to the end state of UK-EU relations after Brexit. The withdrawal aspects concerned the UK's outstanding financial obligations to the EU at withdrawal (the "divorce bill"), the future rights of EU citizens in the UK and British citizens in EU countries, and the future arrangements for the border between the Republic of Ireland and Northern Ireland, which the EU, Ireland and Britain all wanted to keep open after Brexit despite it then becoming an external EU border. All three are co-guarantors of the "Good Friday Agreement" which ended the nearly 30 years of sectarian violence in the province, of which the open border is a powerful symbol and a practical necessity for maintaining the island of Ireland as a continuous economic area, with a prospect of political unification at some later stage.

It was only in early 2018, after the settlement of the preliminary matters concerning withdrawal (and with the agreement on the Northern Ireland border question only being provisional), that the negotiations moved on to the question of the UK's detailed future relationship.

However, even by the second half of 2017, after the snap election, evidence was mounting that a hard Brexit and, even more so, a no-deal exit would cause severe disruption to the British economy. In addition, the government knew it would face a vote in Parliament on the final outcome of the negotiations and that it might not win a vote for a form of Brexit that would hugely disrupt the economy, as both the Labour party and many Conservative backbenchers would oppose such an outcome. The government therefore gradually began to shift its position towards a softer Brexit in which the UK would remain closer to the EU than under a hard or "clean" Brexit. This change came about amid increasing pressure from the business community to minimize the disruption to trade, and estimates by the government's own financial forecasting services of the severe impact a hard or no-deal Brexit would have on the UK and its regions.[16] There were also mounting warnings from particular sectors such as the automotive and engineering industries about their future investment in the UK in the event of a hard Brexit or an exit without a deal.

The new approach was formulated in a proposal pushed through at a meeting at the Prime Minister's country retreat, Chequers, in July 2018, against opposition from Brexiteers in the cabinet who wanted a harder Brexit, including Boris Johnson. Mr Johnson and the Brexit minister David Davis resigned from the government in protest.

Negotiations on a detailed withdrawal agreement and a non-binding Political Declaration setting out the framework for the future relationship between the UK and the EU after the transition period—this framework would be fleshed out after withdrawal—were concluded in November

2018. The Political Declaration took up many of the ideas for a soft Brexit option contained in the Chequers plan. The agreements were ratified by the other 27 EU member states at a special meeting on 25 November 2018, but at the time of writing the British Parliament had yet to do so. The main stumbling block is the provision intended to guarantee an open border between Northern Ireland and the Republic of Ireland, whereby Northern Ireland would remain aligned to some single market rules and the whole of the UK would remain in a single customs territory with the EU until other arrangements can be found to ensure an open border (the so-called backstop).[17]

The detailed "withdrawal agreement" comprises three parts. The first is the "divorce bill," the phased payment by the UK to the EU of around £39 billion to cover its outstanding financial liabilities to the EU. These are the country's shares of: outstanding commitments to fund certain EU projects entered into while the UK was a member; undisbursed payments on uncompleted projects; and the EU pension fund for officials and MEPs. The payment also includes budget contributions covering the standstill transition period until the end of 2020.

Secondly, the UK will grant a permanent right of residence in the UK ("settled status") after five years of residence to over 3 million citizens of other EU countries resident in the UK on the date of withdrawal or coming to live in the UK during the transition period. Similar rights to live and work will continue to be enjoyed by the estimated 1.2 million UK citizens resident in EU countries, the details being determined by each EU country concerned.

The border between Northern Ireland and the Republic of Ireland will be kept open without physical infrastructure or controls of goods crossing the border after the end of the transition period. Until an alternative way of avoiding a hard border can be found, this will be through the "backstop."

The UK has also decided that most current EU legislation will become UK law at Brexit where this is not already the case. It is already the case for EU directives, which had to be transposed into national law to become effective and so are part of British law already. The legislation that will expressly be made part of UK law at Brexit—under the British EU Withdrawal Act—consists of regulations and decisions issued by the EU institutions which have previously been directly effective in British law without transposition through a British act of parliament or statutory instrument. After Brexit Parliament will gradually sift through and to some extent will be able to amend or repeal the previous EU legislation.

The degree to which it will be able to do so will be constrained by whether or not it agrees in the negotiations on the future relationship to remain aligned with EU regulations in order to have access to the single market. Much of the current EU legislation will therefore remain unchanged. The process of repeal and amendment could take many years.

It is planned that some areas of EU law, covering in particular agriculture, fisheries, customs procedures and external trade, will not be taken over wholesale for possible amendment later on but will be repealed and be replaced after the transition period by domestic legislation passed beforehand. The country will then be able to pursue its own policies in these areas. The regulatory framework for business in many areas like competition including restrictive practices and subsidies, employment, consumer protection and the environment can diverge but will have to remain closely aligned to EU law in order to maintain a "level playing field" in future UK-EU trade.

All in all, the "bonfire of red-tape" promised by Leavers will not materialize.

The Political Declaration setting out the framework for the future relationship between the European Union and the UK is not legally binding, but a list of aspirations for arrangements that the EU and UK will negotiate in the period after the UK's departure which it is hoped will replicate or continue much of the cooperation that exists already but with less constraints on the UK's or the EU's freedom of action.

The introduction of the Political Declaration lists among the priorities of the future relationship from the UK's point of view that it should ensure the "sovereignty of the United Kingdom and the protection of its internal market" (presumably a reference to the UK's territorial integrity, in particular, the union of Northern Ireland with Great Britain), the freedom to develop an independent trade policy and the ending of freedom of movement for EU and British citizens.

The main provisions of the "envisaged" relationship include tariff-free trade for goods with "ambitious" customs arrangements "building and improving on" the arrangements under the "backstop" involving a single EU-UK customs territory—which obviates the need for checks on rules of origin—and regulatory alignment to avoid technical barriers to trade "as far as possible." The two sides might agree on the UK's cooperating with EU agencies such as the European Medicines Agency, the European Chemicals Agency, and the European Aviation Safety Agency. On services the new arrangements "should" include market access and "regulatory approaches" that are, "to the extent possible," "compatible." For financial services, the UK will have regulatory and decision-making autonomy but will seek market access on the basis of recognition of equivalence. The UK's future public procurement regime will be based on the WTO Government Procurement Agreement, but the EU and UK "should" provide mutual opportunities in their respective markets going beyond the WTO rules.

"Mobility" arrangements, to be negotiated, will replace freedom of movement. On air transport, the UK and the EU "should" negotiate a "comprehensive air transport agreement." Mutual access to one another's road transport markets is to be negotiated, as is a "wide-ranging" nuclear cooperation arrangement between the European Atomic Energy Community (a separately managed part of the EU) and the UK. The parties will establish a new fisheries agreement on access to fishing waters and quota shares. They will continue to cooperate globally on climate change and in other areas. The UK will have to maintain a similar competition law to the EU's. It is intended to continue security cooperation, including on law enforcement and judicial cooperation, some data exchanges for security purposes such as Passenger Name Records, and to respect commitments on human rights and data protection. The UK and the EU will work together to "identify the terms for the UK's cooperation via Europol and Eurojust" and to establish effective arrangements to replace the European Arrest Warrant. The future relationship will "enable" the UK to participate in EU-led crisis management missions and they will exchange intelligence for counter-terrorism purposes on a voluntary basis. They "should consider appropriate arrangements" for cooperation on space.

The entire future relationship will be based on an overarching institutional framework. There will be dialogue between the parties at summit, ministerial, technical and parliamentary level. For dispute settlement, there will be a Joint Committee type of arrangement, with the possibility of reference to an arbitration panel and, on matters of EU law, to the European Court of Justice.

It is said to be the intent of both parties that the agreements on the future relationship should come into force by the end of 2020.

That an entirely new relationship can be negotiated so quickly is wishful thinking. The work that needs to be done is as much as in an accession negotiation. There are bound to be major sticking points—on money for access and services, on dispute settlement (the role of European Court of Justice), and on complicated trade-offs between policy areas that the two sides would like to keep separate like trade in fisheries products and access to fishing waters but inevitably become linked. Free movement is bound to become an issue despite the UK's insistence on ending it. Such trade-offs are guaranteed to make the negotiations protracted and possibly acrimonious. There will be resource constraints both in the UK and the EU and it will be a costly exercise for both. Who will pay for it? Taxpayers, of course. The UK will divert civil servants from other tasks and recruit thousands more. Government ministers and civil servants will spend more time in meetings in Brussels than they do now. Both the government and Parliament will continue to neglect urgent domestic problems in order to negotiate the terms of a future relationship that are less advantageous that the current ones. The EU Commission will be similarly distracted from more urgent and necessary tasks and will quickly lose patience.

For the last three years, Brexit work has been all absorbing, to the detriment of everything else. Tackling the purely domestic problems that partly caused the Brexit vote in the first place like low labour productivity and wages, the NHS, education, regional investment disparities and widening social inequality has had to wait. The repatriation of some powers from the EU and the replication of EU agencies to "make Britain an independent country again" will not make solving domestic issues any easier; rather it will lengthen the logjam of parliamentary and government business unattended to.

All for the sake of unravelling decades of legislation and hard-fought compromise and replacing it with something hardly different and possibly less good, in order words reinventing wheels to the nth degree.

The consensus of opinion among economists, in business and the government, is that even this softer form of Brexit keeping the UK relatively close to the EU will have a negative impact on the British economy. Politically, too, opponents of Brexit fear that far from having a liberating effect on a "global Britain" the divorce from Europe will turn Britain in on itself and make it more isolated and less diplomatically engaged in helping to solve world problems when they cannot be linked to narrow financial advantage for Britain itself. There is a widespread feeling that Brexit will also damage Europe politically, depriving it of valuable British influence, expertise and diplomatic weight. There is a genuine regret among European leaders about the political damage to Europe from the loss of Britain as a cherished and influential partner—however much Brexit supporters may like to paint this regret as purely financially motivated.

So, if this is the outcome we are getting, with all the side-effects, the question must be, Is Brexit really worth it?

The book argues that press propaganda was one of the factors that tipped the referendum result to Leave. It shows that a large section of the press had put out misinformation about the EU over a long period before the referendum in order to sway public opinion against the EU and that in this it was serving a political agenda espoused by long-standing opponents of EU membership to get Britain out of the EU. This section of the press became the mouthpiece of a Brexit movement.

Part I continues with two chapters setting the scene for the discussion of anti-EU propaganda in Part II. Chapter 2 provides a short historical background to Britain's fraught relations with the EU, examines the place of referendums in democracy, and looks at how events in the run-up to the referendum and the conduct of the campaign itself influenced the outcome. Chapter 3 examines questions of national identity and attitudes to the world among people in Britain, the media landscape, particularly newspapers, and compares British newspapers to Continental ones which are arguably much more neutral on Europe and do a better job of informing and educating their readers about the EU than the British press has done.

Part II of the book, Chaps. 4–7, compares the misinformation put out by the Brexit press with the facts on three key issues which voters say influenced the way they voted, sovereignty, money and immigration, encapsulated by the Leave campaign's slogan of "taking back control of our laws, our money and our borders." Chapters 4 and 5 both deal with the sovereignty issue, the first examining the claims surrounding the democratic character or otherwise of EU legislation, the second questions of sovereignty, the extent to which the EU determines what goes on in Britain relative to the decisions taken by the country's own institutions. Chapter 6 tackles questions of the cost of membership, financial management, and the likely cost of Brexit, and Chap. 7 deals with the issue of immigration.

The conclusion in Chap. 8 is short: a plea for more investment in education and higher standards both in politics and journalism. The referendum showed Britain has a lot of work to do in all of these three areas.

Notes

1. The Conservative Party promised before the 2015 general election to extend the suffrage to all British nationals living abroad without time limit, but this commitment was not repeated in the manifesto and no legislation had been passed before the EU referendum. A renewed commitment was

made in the Conservative manifesto for the 2017 election, but a Private Member's bill to change the law and grant British nationals a vote for life failed to pass the Commons in March 2019.

2. See Grayling, A. C. 2017. *Democracy and Its Crisis*, 189–190. London: Oneworld.

3. *The Independent*. 2016. EU referendum: UK result would have been Remain had voting been allowed at 16, survey finds. 24 June.

4. Grayling, A. C. 2017. *Democracy and Its Crisis*, 192. London: Oneworld.

5. See also Lord Ashcroft Polls. 2016. How the UK voted on Thursday, and why. 24 June. The percentage of 18–24-year-olds voting Remain was 71%: Moore, Peter. 2016. How Britain voted. YouGov UK. 27 June.

6. Curtice, John. 2017. Why Leave won the UK's referendum. *Journal of Common Market Studies 55 – Annual Review*: 19–37.

7. With the exception of Greece in 2015 at the height of the euro crisis.

8. A recent book by Danny Dorling and Sally Tomlinson not only shows from exit poll data that numerically the result was much more due to middle-class Conservative voters in southern England than to working class Labour voters in the Midlands and North but also traces the strength of the Leave vote back to nationalist sentiment and nostalgia for England's past: Dorling, Danny, and Sally Tomlinson. 2019. *Rule Britannia: Brexit and the End of Empire*. London: Biteback Publishing.

9. Clarke, Harold D., Matthew Goodwin and Paul Whitely. 2017. *Brexit: Why Britain Voted to Leave the European Union*, 173–174. Cambridge: Cambridge University Press. See also Runciman, David. 2016. Brexit: A win for 'proper' people. *The Prospect*. 30 June.

10. Lord Ashcroft Polls.

11. Goodhart, David. 2017. *The Road to Somewhere. The New Tribes Shaping British Politics*. London: Penguin.

12. *BBC News*. 2016. EU Referendum Results. 24 June.

13. Curtice, 32–33, does not see a major protest element among (generally better-off) Conservative voters. I think, however, there was a major element of less well-off Labour voters registering a protest against Conservative austerity policies and welfare cuts through the referendum.

14. HM Gov. 2016. Why the government believes that voting to remain in the EU is the best decision for the UK.

15. The Leave campaigners Liam Halligan and Gerard Lyons acknowledge how big an undertaking it will be to unpick the intricate and far-reaching relations with the EU: Halligan, Liam, and Gerard Lyons. 2017. *Clean Brexit: Why Leaving the EU Still Makes Sense*, xi–xii. London: Biteback.

16. *BBC News*. 2018. Brexit will make UK worse off, government forecasts warn. 28 November.

17. *BBC News*. 2019. Brexit: What is the Irish border backstop? 5 April.

CHAPTER 2

The History of the UK's Relations with the EU: From Reliable If Sometimes Awkward Partner to Estranged Outsider

2.1   Love Match or Marriage of Convenience?

"Brexit—A Love Story?"—a BBC Radio 4 series presented by Mark Mardell—traced the history of Britain's relations with the European Union (EU), from the time before it joined the then European Economic Community until 2016 when it decided to leave the bloc now called the European Union.[1] The statements made at the time by contemporary figures, taken from the BBC archives, and the reminiscences of participants in this drama specially recorded for the series, were revealing. In the BBC tradition, the series tried to maintain a balance between different points of view for and against the EU.

But could anyone ever be tempted to describe Britain's relationship with Europe as falling in—and then out of—love? I think not.

The initial enthusiasm for Europe in the 1975 referendum and during the early years of the Thatcher era was hardly love, more a belief that being in the "Common Market" was in Britain's economic interest and there was no alternative. No doubt Edward Heath and other leading figures of the time believed in the political imperative of uniting Europe inextricably and integrating Britain into that structure as firmly as Germany and France were, but such Europhiles were in a minority and their enthusiasm did not stem from a short-lived infatuation with some European ideal but from a deep-seated political commitment to European integration. In this, they were no different from continental Europeans, for whom, too, progressive cooperation leading to extensive economic and political integration was a

© The Author(s) 2019   17
F. Rawlinson, *How Press Propaganda Paved the Way to Brexit*,
https://doi.org/10.1007/978-3-030-27765-9_2

hard-headed rational decision about a stable long-term future for a Europe free of war. The rational basis of European integration, both then and now as Europe faces new global challenges which it seems better to face together, is why the European Union is likely to endure in the future.

So for Britons as much as for continental Europeans attachment to European cooperation was never a love match. It is more correct to liken it to a "marriage"—a marriage in which, in Britain's case, as the prominent Leave campaigner Gisela Stuart describes it, each side was hoping that the other would change but decided to split when that didn't happen.[2]

Many people in Britain today fail to recognize the political rationale of European integration. Continental Europeans have always seen the European Community, and now see the EU, as a force for internal political stability and greater international influence. British people, on the other hand, seem to have a blind spot for the political dimension of European integration. They assume that only commercial interests are rational in such arrangements and that Europeans are irrational for pursuing political motives as well.

This misconception often appeared in the past when British politicians who became members of the European Commission were criticized as having "gone native" when they had become more convinced than before of the usefulness of the EU as a political institution and not just a commercial one. It is also to be seen in the exasperation of Brexiteers with Brussels for its alleged intransigence in the Brexit negotiations. Surely, they reason, the priority of the other EU countries must be to maintain their trade with the UK after Brexit. This appears to many Brexiteers as the only rational approach. After all, it is in the EU's commercial interest to grant Britain free access to the EU market in return for access to the UK market because they export more to us than we do to them. In reasoning like this, Britons easily forget that the cohesion of the EU is necessary to achieve its long-term political objectives. These will not be served by concessions to a departing member that remove the *raison d'être* of membership and cause the EU to disintegrate. This is not "ideology" but political reality for the EU side. Brexiteers also conveniently forget the largely political and ideological case they themselves advanced for Brexit: regaining sovereignty, although in a world that is increasingly interdependent it is rational to share sovereignty in many areas and these areas are precisely the ones where Brexiteers wish to regain it.

So the early enthusiasm for Europe in Britain and its later cooling was not a "love story" any more than it was on the continent of Europe. It was initially based on a rational, and in Britain's case—except for the political motives of a few committed Europhiles—largely commercial, decision. The gradual estrangement of Britain from the EU was a result of a divergence in the rational preferences of Britain and the other countries about the direction and speed of integration, not a dramatic "falling out of love."

2.1.1   Britain's Late Start

There were calls for European unity from both German and French statesmen in the 1930s to prevent the war that was looming on the horizon.[3] Then, with Europe in ruins after a second war even more terrible than the first, the calls became stronger and began to take concrete shape. The British wartime Prime Minister Winston Churchill advocated a "United States of Europe" in a speech in Switzerland in 1946,[4] but the idea was directed at continental Europeans and not intended for his own country. Britain, he believed, should continue to pursue its separate political destiny.[5]

It was the French, and in particular Jean Monnet, the head of the French economic planning office, who took the initiative to give the idea of European unity its first concrete form. Monnet's blueprint for common control of the coal and steel industry was presented in a speech in Paris on 9 May 1950 by the French Foreign Minister Robert Shuman.[6] The aim of what came to be known as the "Schuman Plan" was to remove the unilateral power of European countries to divert these industries from peaceful uses into the production of armaments, and thereby to prevent further wars in Europe. The Schuman Plan was enthusiastically supported by Germany, under Adenauer, and by the Americans. The European Coal and Steel Community (ECSC) Treaty was signed between France, Germany, Italy, and the three Benelux countries Belgium, the Netherlands and Luxembourg in Paris on 18 April 1951 and entered into force in July 1952 for a time-limited period of 50 years.

Britain was not a signatory. It had been invited to the negotiations from June 1950 onwards but had shown a less than keen interest in a treaty that would put two vital industries under virtually federal control and cede sovereignty to a supranational body, the "High Authority."

After the failure of attempts to set up a European Defence Community in 1954, the same six countries decided in 1955 to press on with further steps towards European integration by establishing a Common Market covering virtually all the rest of the economy other than coal and steel, and including atomic energy, which was seen as a replacement energy source for the declining coal industry. The "European Economic Community" (EEC) would establish a Common Market for industrial and agricultural goods; a customs union with common tariffs on imports from outside the community and a common trade policy administered by a new supranational authority, the "Commission"; a Common Agricultural Policy; and a competition policy, also run by the Commission, to maintain a level playing field in the Common Market. The negotiations led by the Belgian Paul-Henri Spaak, and with Monnet again instrumental in securing German and French approval, were completed in early 1957 and resulted in two separate treaties, one on the Common Market, or "European Economic Community," the other on the "European Atomic Energy Community." Britain took part in the initial negotiations but withdrew when its suggestions for watering down the supranational or federal elements of the agreement were not taken up. Again it doubted the new ambitious arrangements would survive. The EEC Treaty was duly signed in Rome on 25 March 1957 and entered into force on 1 January 1958 between the same six countries as the ECSC Treaty of 1951.

The European Atomic Energy Community (EAEC or Euratom) Treaty, negotiated in parallel, was signed in Rome on the same date as the EEC Treaty and also entered into force on the same day, 1 January 1958. Its purpose was to jointly control the trade and use of nuclear materials both with safety and security (non-proliferation of nuclear weapons) considerations in mind. Again a supranational commission was set up to administer the arrangements.

As a counterweight to the European Economic Community, Britain had in 1960 brought some of the remaining western European countries into a new, looser grouping, the European Free Trade Association (EFTA). However, seeing how well the EEC "Common Market" was progressing, in the 1960s—a period of repeated sterling crises—it began to feel that it would be better off joining the rival organization after all. Accordingly, in 1961 and 1967 the Macmillan and first Wilson governments applied twice to become a member. However, each time the application was refused by the French President De Gaulle, on the ground that Britain with its close links to the United States would not fit into the European Community. The humiliation felt as a result of De Gaulle's repeated *Non* caused considerable resentment in Britain and among some people strengthened their own conviction that the UK was ill-suited to intensive cooperation with Europe just as De Gaulle had said.

Britain finally joined the European Economic Community and the other two treaty organizations in 1973 after France under President Pompidou switched to supporting the British application. Ireland and Denmark, both also EFTA members, joined at the same time. In a precursor of difficulties with securing popular mandates for membership of supranational organizations, Norway had negotiated entry at the same time but failed to convince a majority to support it in a close-fought referendum and stayed out of the EEC but a member of EFTA.

2.2   THE FIRST 20 YEARS[7]

Britain's membership of the European Community began under difficult economic circumstances. The first oil price shock in 1973 set off high inflation and there was dissatisfaction with the Heath government's policies and industrial unrest which continued in 1974. The government's unpopularity paved the way for Harold Wilson to win a general election in 1974. The Labour party had taken an ambivalent position on membership of the European Community while in opposition and had fought the election on a platform of renegotiating the terms of Britain's membership and holding a referendum. In a preview of David Cameron's renegotiation in 2015–16, the Wilson government obtained some changes in the terms of accession in relation to the budget and imports of New Zealand butter, on the strength of which it recommended remaining in the European Community. The convincing majority of 67% for staying in the EEC in the referendum owed something to the comparatively poor economic situation in Britain and the hope for improvement from being in the "Common Market." It was facilitated by the novelty of membership and enthusiastic support from most of the media including the newspapers. Of the newspapers still in circulation at the 2016 referendum, only the communist *Morning Star* and the right-wing weekly *The Spectator* wholeheartedly supported a No vote.[8] The opposition of left-wingers to membership was partly on sovereignty grounds and partly based on the view that the EEC's ethos was capitalist and left no room for advancement of workers' rights. The young Margaret Thatcher campaigned for a Yes vote.

Common Market membership was not the panacea for Britain's economic ills that its more ardent advocates like Edward Heath had held in prospect. The country's economic malaise continued in the late 1970s under the Wilson and Callaghan governments and culminated in the 1976 bail-out by the International Monetary Fund (IMF). But European Community membership was definitely helpful to the UK during this period. There were no major difficulties in implementing Community policies and disputes like those over the budget and imports of butter from New Zealand before the referendum were settled amicably. Britain even led the way in pushing through the beginnings of a Community-financed regional policy. The European Regional Development Fund was founded in 1975 and the British commissioner George Thomson was the first to be in charge of this policy area in the Commission. It was a time when Britain often took a different approach to its partners on issues of the moment such as energy policy, pollution control, and working conditions—for example, lorry drivers' hours—but often succeeded in talking them round to its point of view. It was a sometimes awkward but always constructive and engaged partner.[9] For the Community, too, the troubled 1970s were a period of crisis management and consolidation of Community policies. The major political initiatives such as monetary union and border-free travel and the inevitable disputes surrounding them would come later during the Thatcher era.

During most of her 11 years as Prime Minister, Britain under Margaret Thatcher played almost as active a role in advancing the development of the European Community as Germany and France under Schmidt and Giscard d'Estaing and Kohl and Mitterrand. For example, at the 1984 Fontainebleau European Council (summit) meeting the UK Government put forward its own proposals for the future of Europe, calling for liberalization of the internal market, including air transport, and relaxation of checks at borders.[10] For most of the 1980s, Britain was genuinely at the heart of Europe, a position to which Tony Blair could later only aspire to return the country after the acrimonious battles around the Maastricht Treaty and Monetary Union in the early 1990s. The contrast with the later period was stark: at the beginning of the 1980s there was still a Europhile British President of the European Commission, Roy Jenkins, and in the second half of the decade a British commissioner Lord Cockfield was driving the programme to remove non-tariff barriers to trade[11] and forge the Community into a genuine Single Market. And it was Mrs Thatcher who accepted the introduction of majority voting in the Council of Ministers over Single Market measures. This important change, brought in by the Single European Act of 1986, was a clear dilution of sovereignty but justified to get the Single Market programme through smoothly by 1992.

Mrs Thatcher's success in her dogged efforts to obtain a further reduction in Britain's budget contribution at the Fontainebleau Summit in 1984 proved that tough negotiation as a committed and reliable partner in the Community worked. It was not until the energetic Commission president Jacques Delors took office in 1985 that more fundamental gaps began to open up between Mrs Thatcher and mainstream opinion in the Community over further steps of integration.

Though not such a big deal for the rest of the Community, the hard struggle Mrs Thatcher had had to get "our money back" from Brussels caused permanent damage to perceptions of Europe in the UK. The shadow of the dispute over the rebate, and the image of Mrs Thatcher's handbag-wielding defiance against unjustified demands for money, extended right into the 2016 referendum campaign. For one thing, it encouraged a one-sided assessment of the financial costs and benefits of membership of the EC and now the EU, which focussed on one narrow financial flow and ignored the indirect benefits from membership such as greater tariff-free trade. In the Leave campaign for the 2016 referendum this one-sided anti-economic way of thinking went so far as to ignore even parts of the direct financial flows themselves by citing the £350 million a week contribution figure without mentioning the automatic rebate Britain received or the flows back to the country in the form of direct payments for agriculture, regional development, research, and other purposes. Secondly, it entrenched the habit of British politicians and the media to portray relations with the EU as a battle against adversaries set on screwing as much money as possible out of Britain, and gaining advantages over it in other areas, rather than a relationship of partners.[12] A tradition grew up for British Prime ministers coming out of leaders' summits in Brussels to stress not the agreements reached with their colleagues to improve cooperation in particular areas in everyone's mutual interest, but the "victories" they had won in defence of specific British interests in the face of strong opposition. The "them and us" attitude to Britain's relations with Europe so prominent in the 2016 referendum campaign started in the Thatcher era. The image of a Europe favouring continental interests above British ones and of Britain being out of step with our European partners and an underdog in negotiations with them stuck. It proved impossible to reset to a more positive cooperative approach even for the pro-EU governments of the late 1990s and early 2000s.

The faster integration pushed by the Delors Commission, often against British opposition, confirmed the drift towards Britain's estrangement from the European "project." Proposals for a common currency were developed by a committee chaired by Mr Delors himself. He also proposed the transfer of new powers over the environment and transport to the European Community, expansion of the policy areas subject to majority voting, and the strengthening of its institutions such as the periodic summits of national leaders which would become a "European Council" with a permanent president—a "president of Europe." Such measures were too much, too soon, for Mrs Thatcher. Her negative reaction to the proposals was coloured by dislike of Delors and his high-flown oratory and haughty demeanour. The feeling was reciprocated. Mrs Thatcher's "No, No, No" rejection of Delors proposals to strengthen the powers of the European Commission, Council and Parliament in the House of Commons in 1990 and the less polite headline in *The Sun* "Up Yours Delors" represented a sharp worsening in UK-EC relations after a relatively amicable start and a period of constructive cooperation in the 1970s and most of the 1980s. By the time Mrs Thatcher had been replaced as leader of the government by John Major in 1990 attitudes towards the European Community in Britain were becoming increasingly polarized, with a faction of the Conservative party opposed to further integration and willing to contemplate departure from the bloc if these plans were realized.

2.3   The Battle of Maastricht, Normalization Under Labour, the Explosive Rise of Euroscepticism

With Euroscepticism growing in the country and the Conservative party, Mrs Thatcher's successor, John Major, negotiated British opt-outs from the Maastricht Treaty, signed in 1991, from the introduction of a common currency and the social chapter allowing social legislation to be approved by majority vote. He came back from the Maastricht summit claiming, in the triumphant way of British prime ministers returning from European meetings that has become traditional, to have "won game, set and match" in securing the opt-out from economic and monetary union from his partners.[13] But the battle with the Eurosceptics over ratifying the Maastricht Treaty was not over. There was pressure for a referendum to ratify the treaty. After first claiming he was amenable to the holding of a referendum, Major decided to seek ratification through Parliament instead and against strong opposition from the anti-European faction of his own backbenchers finally managed to scrape the vote through the Commons in August 1993.[14]

The rest of the period of Mr Major's government was comparatively tranquil, with the exception of the bovine spongiform encephalopathy (BSE) crisis. BSE, or "mad cow disease," was a new disease in cattle later found to be due to feeding them with bone meal containing material from cattle brains and spinal cords. Humans eating the beef of cattle infected with BSE could develop a fatal degenerative disease. BSE had first been observed in Britain but had not been detected in mainland Europe. The risks to human health prompted the EU in March 1996 to impose a ban on imports of British beef into mainland Europe and on exports of British beef outside the EU. Although measures were taken to make British beef safe again, including banning the feeding of bone meal to cattle and removing brain and spinal cord material from beef at slaughter, the ban on imports of British beef into Europe was maintained, in the opinion of the government and the newspapers, for longer than necessary after the risk had been eliminated. British beef imports were only allowed back into other EU countries in 1999, though France continued to ban such imports unilaterally until 2002, and the EU's worldwide ban on British beef exports was only lifted in 2006, with individual countries maintaining import bans for much longer still (Japan until 2019). Whatever the justification of the bans—and food safety is such a sensitive political issue that pressure to ban suspect imports often proves irresistible—the BSE crisis confirmed the widespread impression that the EU was unfair to Britain.

This was grist to the mill of a growing section of Eurosceptic public opinion which had been strengthened by the battle over Maastricht. This now included many leading newspapers, which were steadily moving towards adopting a default position of opposition to the EU and to supporting the calls for a referendum from fringe movements like Sir James Goldsmith's "Referendum Party" and later the "United Kingdom Independence Party" (UKIP). The growing Euroscepticism—or, more accurately, anti-European stance—of the newspapers that later supported Brexit in the 2016 referendum is clearly recognizable in this period, although it was not such a given of the newspapers' editorial policy as it later became, and dissenting pro-European voices were still to be heard in these papers.

Tony Blair began his term in office with a spurt of enthusiasm for Europe and a desire to move the country back towards the position of being "at the heart of Europe" it had lost in the later Thatcher years.

Other EU countries were pleasantly surprised by his positive, forward-looking attitude. It was the run-up to the introduction of the single currency, the euro, and, though on the advice of his chancellor of the exchequer, Gordon Brown, the government decided not to take the country into the euro immediately with the first batch of 11 countries in 1999, followed by the 12th, Greece, in 2001, Blair was prepared to do so later when, according to Brown's own criteria, "the time was right." Other than the euro, there were no major disagreements with Britain's EU partners. The Blair government, like that of John Major, supported the enlargement of the EU to central and eastern Europe, which was going to plan with the "Phare" investment and institution-building programme financed by the EU to prepare the countries for membership, and further huge investments by the London-based European Bank for Reconstruction and Development. Blair accepted on Britain's behalf the EU's powers to enact further measures in the social policy area, including the working hours directive. The Amsterdam and Nice Treaties of 1997 and 2000 approved relatively uncontroversial institutional changes like the voting weights of member states in the Council of Ministers under the majority voting procedure, the size of the European Commission, and extension of the powers of the European Parliament to decide legislation together with the Council of Ministers. The Blair government secured an opt-out for Britain in the Amsterdam Treaty from the "Schengen" passport-free travel area introduced in 1995, so this was not a cause of conflict with the EU either.

The period of amicable relations with Europe was shaken with Blair's decision to enter the Iraq war in 2003. This intervention was vehemently opposed by the French and Germans although they had been among the "coalition of the willing" against Al Qaeda in Afghanistan after 2001. The Iraq war caused bad blood between the British and other EU governments and relations were slow to recover. The European criticism of British action rankled among a large section of public opinion in Britain, including the newspapers which had virtually universally supported the intervention in the beginning, only to move over to a more critical position later on the grounds that they had been "misled" by the government's dossier containing rather shaky evidence of Saddam Hussein's possession of weapons of mass destruction.

The final stage in the 13-year series of Labour governments was the period of the financial crisis. Gordon Brown's management of the crisis was bold and decisive, just as was that of President Obama in the United States. Not being part of the euro gave Britain somewhat more flexibility in its response, but arguably not that much more, and euro membership involving a loss of control over the exchange rate did not lessen the ability of countries with strong economic fundamentals and without abnormally large exposure to property loans to manage the crisis by propping up the financial sector without overstretching their fiscal situation. Britain would probably have got through the crisis perfectly well even if it had been in the euro. The bail-outs and nationalizations of exposed banks was coordinated by the European Commission and Britain had no difficulty in complying with its rules, which were mainly to prevent the aid to failing banks unfairly damaging the competitive position of financially sound institutions.[15] Indeed, Gordon Brown was in the forefront of the bold bank bail-out policies pursued by European governments that proved an adequate response to the crisis in the "normal" countries with sound economic fundamentals.

The situation was different with the peripheral countries with weaker fundamentals, excessive borrowing, and banks with large bad loan portfolios, like Greece, Portugal, Ireland and Spain. The problems with these countries emerged in late 2009, just before the Conservatives won the May 2010 election and formed a coalition government with the Liberal Democrats.

In the counties with heavy government borrowing, membership of the euro was a handicap, associated as it was with the inability to devalue their own currency and the need to resort instead either to loans from the IMF and other Eurozone governments or "internal devaluation" through austerity measures, or both. The EU's tough response to the debt crisis in the southern European countries and Ireland, led by Germany, was heavily criticized in Britain and elsewhere as imposing unnecessary pain and suffering on these countries in the form of high unemployment and reductions in income. But the response to this unprecedented situation in a new single currency area was, while not perfect, at least adequate in that it over time forced their governments to carry out much-needed reforms that allowed them to return to the capital markets like before the crisis and to restore their financial sectors to relative health.

Regardless of whether or not the criticism was fair, the difficulties the EU had in managing the euro debt crisis worsened its image in Britain. The feeling was increased by the government's somewhat gloating satisfaction that it had managed to emerge from the recession induced by the financial crisis earlier than its European partners and that not having joined the euro it was spared the problems of handling the euro debt crisis.

The euro crisis illustrated the much more strained relations between the UK and the EU after 2010. Although its policies towards the EU were moderated by the presence in government of the pro-EU Liberal Democrats, the Conservative heart of the government around David Cameron and George Osborne was decidedly Eurosceptic in tone and approach, a considerable contrast to the basically pro-European Blair-Brown governments. In opposition between 1997 and 2010, the Conservative Party under Michael Howard, Iain Duncan Smith, William Hague and David Cameron had consistently adopted Eurosceptic positions on European issues both in elections and in parliament. The Eurosceptic wing of the party had grown in size and stridency. By the time Cameron assumed office, UKIP, a party with the sole aim of obtaining a referendum on EU membership and led by the charismatic and tireless campaigner Nigel Farage, had become a significant force in British politics and was taking votes off the Conservative Party. It had not won seats in the Westminster parliament but had gained the second largest number of seats in the European Parliament elections of 2009. The Cameron government constantly had an eye on UKIP and on trying to win back the support it had lost, and so tended to take Eurosceptic positions to impress the anti-EU base in its own ranks and among UKIP supporters.

The first Cameron government was basically a passive observer of the EU. It was a non-combatant in the euro crisis which was consuming all the EU's energies, much like Brexit has done in Britain. It watched this unfolding drama from the sidelines. From time to time, it would wake up from its previous seeming indifference to EU issues to make a stand on this or that issue of principle, like the size of the EU budget, which it claimed was wastefully spent and should be cut; the appointment of the "arch-federalist" Jean-Claude Juncker as president of the Commission; an increase in Britain's budget contribution which was correct according to the regulations but apparently had come as a surprise to Downing Street; and the fiscal compact of tighter budgetary rules which although not currently of concern to the UK as a non-euro member David Cameron vetoed. On these occasions, Cameron always took a stridently Eurosceptic line and, to an outside observer, seemed to be needlessly picking quarrels with the EU instead of negotiating in a spirit of compromise. The press conferences after summit meetings followed the pattern, since Thatcher, of the British Prime Minister announcing how he had fought Britain's corner with pragmatic, British common-sense arguments—not stubborn and ideologically driven like those of the rest—and had won against all the odds.

Little wonder that a few years later during the referendum campaign, David Cameron, and to a lesser extent George Osborne, were less than credible as supporters of staying in the EU.

Unlike the coalition government of 2010–15, the second Cameron administration from May 2015 was no longer mainly a passive observer of EU issues with sporadic interventions to protect Britain's interests as a non-Eurozone member state, but was consumed with its relationship with the EU as it prepared for the in-out referendum Cameron had promised in early 2013 and was forced to go ahead with, as the pro-European Lib-Dems were no longer in government and conveniently in a position to prevent it. The EU itself was preoccupied with the Syrian migrant crisis. As in the case of the euro debt crisis, Britain was not obliged to cooperate closely with the EU in this crisis; it could keep a low profile and hope the crisis would die down before the referendum campaign, in which immigration would be a sensitive issue. The bystander role Britain enjoyed was again thanks to opt-outs, the exemptions from the justice and home affairs provisions and the Schengen free travel area secured in the 1997 Amsterdam Treaty. Instead of working with the EU Commission and Germany to manage the flows of migrants already on EU soil, Britain could pursue its own preferred policies for addressing the crisis, such as helping to pay for the camps on the Syrian border, taking limited numbers of asylum seekers from these camps, and cooperating in the EU's policing of the Mediterranean to deter illegal crossings. The asylum policy opt-out exempted Britain from the compulsory re-allocation scheme of migrants from camps in Greece and Italy. In the discussion of the Commission's proposals to modernize the Dublin regulation, under which the country in which migrants first land is responsible for processing their asylum applications, the UK was content to join with the central and eastern Europeans in opposing change, although the Dublin rule is clearly unfair to "front line" countries like Greece and Italy. The migrant crisis is discussed in detail in Sect. 7.4.

The migrant crisis of 2015 was the second major event after the financial and euro and debt crisis that helped turn British public opinion further away from the EU. Between 2009 and 2015 Europe was in a constant state of crisis and the UK seemed well-off by comparison. It was easy for politicians and the media that were against the EU to portray it as a dysfunctional organization, anti-democratic in its treatment of Greece, and incapable of protecting its people from unmanageable immigration flows and the risks of terrorism. Large-scale terrorist acts in Belgium and France confirmed this image of Europe as out of control. While the claims of chronic dysfunctionality and decline were exaggerated, 2016 was certainly not an ideal time to hold a referendum on EU membership in an increasingly Eurosceptic Britain.

2.4   Referendums Versus Representative Democracy

Referendums on complex economic and political issues are a highly dubious form of democracy.[16] Such issues are surely better decided by the people's representatives in parliament. To leave such decisions to referendums, with all the disadvantages that attach to them, and without safeguards such as validity thresholds to ensure the vote is really representative of people's opinions on the question asked,[17] and that it is expressed on the basis of objective information, is arguably an abdication of responsibility by politicians.[18]

The combination of representative and plebiscitary democracy can obviously be made to work, because some countries like Switzerland have long traditions of holding referenda on particular issues alongside decision-making by elected representatives in government and parliament.

But even well-tried systems sometimes produce perverse outcomes. In 2013, the Swiss voted in a plebiscite to stop all immigration from EU countries. This would have led to the cancellation of virtually all cooperation with the EU, which the country had secured over years of negotiations and which was supported by all political parties as conducive to Switzerland's economic wellbeing and prosperity. In the end, the government and opposition parties collaborated in shifting public opinion to supporting measures that would incentivize employment of nationals without completely stopping immigration of EU workers, and were able to agree these measures with the EU so that the beneficial cooperation could continue.[19]

In California successive referendums on the state budget have forced through budget cuts which have led to schools being starved of public funds.[20]

Such examples demonstrate that on some subjects the outcome of referendums is virtually a foregone conclusion. Ask people about taxes and they will predictably vote "Yes" for reducing taxes and "No" for increasing them. The theoretical possibility for English and Welsh county councils to raise local property taxes on the strength of a referendum is useless.[21] The government might as well prohibit such rises and have done with it. The few councils that have tried have failed. But ask the people about improving public services and they will be in favour. Combine the two issues in a single referendum and a majority will vote to reduce taxes and improve services, like in California.

Referenda about immigration are similarly predictable, as the Swiss examples shows. However necessary immigration might be for the economy, for the health service, for farmers trying to harvest their crops, it is difficult if not impossible to convince a majority of people to vote for it.

A referendum on international cooperation or international trade is also highly likely to result in a "No" outcome. Take the Dutch referendum on the EU's proposed association agreement with the Ukraine or the series of referendums on changes to EU treaties.[22] The British EU referendum of 2016 was no different: in the prevailing economic and social conditions it was on a knife-edge right from the word Go.

This explains the reluctance of governments to hold referendums on taxation or international or trade matters: the highly likely negative referendum result will conflict with what the government and the majority of the elected representatives think is best for the country (as in the case of the British EU referendum), force them to make decisions they disagree with, or just generally make the job of government harder. In most cases, governments and parliaments will attempt to carry out the people's wishes and minimize the damage, as the Conservative government and Parliament have done since the 2016 referendum, and the Swiss did after the unworkable referendum decision on immigration. A possible option would be for a government that has campaigned against the referendum decision to resign and leave its implementation to the representatives of the winning side. But that would be tantamount to abandoning or undermining parliamentary democracy and opening the way to a dictatorship.[23]

At all events, referendums on such issues often come into conflict with the system of representative democracy. The likelihood of a vote against international cooperation or immigration is the reason why the political opponents of cooperation, generally the right wing, are so fervent supporters of referendums. They long campaigned for a referendum on the EU and criticized successive governments for resisting one. Having secured such a vote, Brexiteers fulminate against the two-thirds of MPs that voted Remain for trying to thwart the "will of the people" by softening the terms of Brexit in parliament. But there are many subjects on which they would resist a referendum just as fiercely as pro-Europeans did a referendum on the EU. How about testing the "will of the people" on the subject of private education? People are for referendums when they think they can win but against when they are sure they will lose.

Referendums are compatible with representative democracy when they complement and do not replace it. For example, referenda on social issues like abortion can settle such issues for a long time better than any parliamentary debates or court judgments could, and they relieve the pressure on parliament and the judiciary allowing them to get on with other work of government and of dispensing justice. Combining them with citizens' assemblies, as in the abortion debate in Ireland, increases their acceptability.

The drawbacks of referendums—and this applies particularly to those on broader subjects—are, firstly, the difficulty of ensuring a fair debate on the issue on the ballot paper and, secondly, the risk of extraneous issues such as grievances against the government or the Establishment being drawn into the vote.[24]

Media biased to one side of the argument or the other can swing a vote. This is easiest with government-controlled media. Dictators regularly use referendums to cement their power. They are "a device of dictators and demagogues."[25] Matteo Renzi, the former prime minister of Italy, would not have lost his referendum to change the constitution if there had not been a free press in Italy. Erdogan in Turkey and Orbán in Hungary have an easier time of it. But a free press is not a guarantee of a fair referendum campaign either. An overwhelmingly biased media, though ostensibly free, can sway the vote its way, too, as the majority of right-wing newspapers did in the British EU referendum.[26]

A fair debate presupposes not only a rough balance of opinion in the media as a whole, but also the absence of actual dis- or misinformation and lies purveyed by the main campaigners and the media outlets supporting them. Also, what if the misinformation and bias in a certain preponderant section of the media has persisted for many years before the referendum and has conditioned many voters to thinking their way about the issue?

In the British referendum, many lies were put about by the Leave campaign. It is claimed that Remain was also guilty of misinformation, so the two sides' misinformation cancelled one another out. This is not so. The degree of dishonesty practised by the two sides was not comparable. The Remain side was overly categorical about the likely immediate effects of a Leave vote; it circulated some overly precise figures about the loss to individual households in the event of a Brexit vote;[27] and it engaged in some stunts such as the austerity budget George Osborne said the government would bring in the day after such a vote. But these were more in the nature of dubious forecasts than the outright lies purveyed by Leave. The government and the Bank of England still stick by their overall forecasts of the medium-term damage to the economy and have confirmed them since.

The BBC provided a useful service to check the truth of information disseminated during the campaign which the other side contested, through the *BBC News* "Reality check" page, and similar highly professional services were provided by the charity *Full Fact* and the Remain-supporting *InFacts* organization. But there was no official body having the expertise or authority to censure campaigners for inaccurate or misleading claims. The Electoral Commission not only lacked the expert knowledge to detect lies but had no power to sanction them. Only the Office of Statistics challenged the Leave campaign on the misleading figures painted on the side of the "Leave" campaign bus about the UK's budget contribution being "£350 million a week." But such corrections of untruths as there were probably had little effect. Most voters quickly tired of the daily diet of claims and counterclaims on issues they often did not have the faintest idea about and reverted to their emotional "gut" feeling and default position. Among the newspaper-reading older voters, the default position was largely anti-EU, inspired by years of misinformation by the newspapers allied to the right-wing part of the Conservative party and latterly to UKIP.

The British referendum on the EU is a text book example of one of the risks to a fair referendum outcome, namely a biased media environment and active misinformation. It suffered equally from the other drawback of referenda, the entry into the vote of extraneous issues, such as grievances over a protracted austerity policy that had led to poverty, stagnant incomes, and public services and infrastructure starved of investment. As noted in the Introduction, for many voters, particularly in the predominantly Labour-supporting, old industrial areas of the Midlands and North of England and Wales, as well as in coastal towns and rural areas, the vote was an opportunity to give the government a "good kicking" for years of austerity and the associated stagnation in incomes and lack of investment; the EU was a scapegoat.

2.5   The Run-up to the Referendum

The anti-European right wing of the Conservative party started calling for referendums on the EU after the Maastricht Treaty was signed in 1991. Despite the opt-outs John Major had secured from the Social Chapter and the single currency, the Treaty's opponents still disliked the direction the

EU was taking towards ever-closer integration and ultimately, they feared, a "European super-state." Having failed to get the government to concede a referendum, they nearly defeated the government in a series of votes in parliament to ratify the new treaty. From 1994 to 1997 calls for a referendum were led by the Anglo-French financier and politician, James Goldsmith, who expressly for this purpose founded a new party, the "Referendum Party," which stood over 500 candidates in the 1997 general election. After Lord Goldsmith died in 1997, supporters of his party continued fighting for the cause from within other groups and parties including the United Kingdom Independence Party (UKIP), which was founded in 1991 but only became the most influential Eurosceptic party in 1997 after Nigel Farage assumed a leading role in the group.

During the early Blair years in the 1990s, there were calls for a referendum before Britain decided to join the euro, and Blair conceded that he would hold one before that eventuality. In the end, however, the government postponed euro membership and a referendum was not held. Pressure for a referendum on the Constitutional Treaty grew in 2005, which Blair again conceded but in the end was able to avoid because France and the Netherlands had had referendums first and had voted against the Treaty.

Meantime UKIP had managed to steadily increase its base of support and had begun to perform strongly in both national elections and those for the European Parliament. Though the "first-past-the-post" electoral system in the British parliament prevented them winning any seats in national elections, they were able to win seats in the European elections of 2009 thanks to a switch in the electoral system under which some of the seats were allocated by proportional representation. In the 2009 European Parliament elections, UKIP won 15 seats, of which 8 were won direct and seven awarded under the proportional representation system, against the Conservatives' 23, Labour's 26, and the Lib-Dems' 15. In the 2014 European elections, UKIP became the largest party among British MEPs with 26 seats, 16 won direct and 10 by proportional representation. The number of Conservative seats was down to 18, that of Labour to 17, and the Lib-Dems to 8.

UKIP's *raison d'être* was securing a referendum on Britain's membership of the EU and then campaigning to win the referendum and take Britain out of the bloc. UKIP did not really belong in the European Parliament. People who get elected to a parliament normally want to contribute to its work, but UKIP only did so in a negative sense of opposing any further moves towards European integration and Britain's involvement in it. Not being strong enough to prevent or seriously influence the passage of legislation, however, UKIP members tended to stay away from committee meetings where the bulk of legislative work was done and just attend the monthly plenary sessions. There Nigel Farage would make grandstanding speeches against the EU, which would be dutifully reported by the Brexit press back home, often to the exclusion of any other matters Parliament might have debated.

It is a moot point whether the presence of extreme anti-European parties like UKIP in the European Parliament serves any useful purpose for the Parliament itself. We will return to this question in Chap. 4 (Sect. 4.5.2). There is no doubt, however, that being in the European Parliament in such strength benefited UKIP and the cause of Brexit. The European Parliament gave UKIP a platform, relayed by an eager anti-EU press, from which to pressurize the government back home to concede a referendum, and it supplemented the funds it had available for campaigning in Britain, as in practice, albeit illegally, they could use the staff allowances they got ostensibly for European Parliament work for political activities back home instead.

The pressure on Prime Minister David Cameron from UKIP and his own ranks in the Conservative Party to hold a popular vote on EU membership was thus mounting from the time he assumed the premiership in 2010. In 2011, Cameron attempted to placate the proponents of a referendum on membership by getting parliament to pass a bill compelling the government to hold a referendum on any new transfer of power to the European Union, the Referendum (Transfer of Power) Act 2011. But for Brexiteers this was clearly a poor substitute for an in-out referendum on membership, as a vote against a new European treaty would not get Britain out of the EU. So the pressure did not abate and Cameron, in the end, gave way. In January 2013, reportedly against the advice of members of his cabinet including his closest ally the chancellor of the exchequer George Osborne, David Cameron announced that should a Conservative government be re-elected in 2015, it would hold an in-out referendum by the end of 2017.

Thus, Cameron finally conceded the referendum clamoured for by a vocal minority of MPs and a substantial section of the press for nearly 20 years. He calculated that postponing it until after the next election would both increase support for the Tories among potential UKIP voters, now that UKIP was not the only party committed to a referendum, and provide a chance of escaping from the commitment if the Conservatives did not win a majority and had to negotiate a coalition with the pro-EU Lib-Dems who would resist holding the promised referendum. In the event, the Lib-Dems part of the calculation underlying the 2013 announcement, assuming it was indeed a conscious part of it, fell away. The Conservatives surprisingly won a majority. So the referendum, to be held by the end of 2017 at the latest, was on.

In 2013 Cameron had announced his strategy for the referendum. He would first investigate the need for changes, including repatriating powers from the EU, in order to overcome the present stresses and strains in Britain's relationship with the bloc and put its future position on a more acceptable basis. He seemed to believe that fundamental reforms were possible and, rather unwisely, held out the firm prospect of such reforms. Having identified the requirements for changing the current relationship he would negotiate these changes with the EU. Should a satisfactory settlement be achieved, he would commend it to the British people in the referendum. Should the EU not agree to the British requests for changes in the relationship, he held out the prospect of campaigning in the referendum in favour of leaving the EU.

To identify the changes in Britain's relationship with the EU that were desirable, the government had the civil service conduct a root-and-branch review of all policy areas, from freedom of movement to food standards, to establish the current "balance of competences," or division of authority, between the UK and the EU in each area and make recommendations for changing the balance back in favour of the UK where it was considered necessary. The amount of power the EU and a member state have varies depending on the policy area. There are fields like trade policy in which the EU has more or less exclusive authority, areas like competition and regional development policy where authority is shared between the EU and the member states in varying proportions, with the EU being responsible for some matters and the member states for others, and areas where authority has more or less been entirely left with the member state. The latter comprise wide areas of government, including education, health, social security, defence, and the bulk of tax policy, despite popular misconceptions to the contrary fostered by the Brexit movement and the Leave campaign.

The "balance of competences" review was a thorough and highly professional exercise in which all relevant bodies and individual experts on the relevant subject matter were consulted both in writing and at special seminars and workshops. The results, conclusions and recommendations emerging from the consultation were then summarized in a set of reports. The 28 reports averaged 50–120 pages each but with hundreds of pages of appendices comprising the evidence in the form of the representations made to the relevant sponsoring department (Department of Transport, Department of Environment, Food and Rural Affairs (DEFRA), Home Office, etc.) by the various bodies, organizations and individuals that had answered the call to take part. The reports were published in batches between July 2013 and October 2014.

The House of Lords EU Committee issued its own report on the "balance of competences" exercise, in which it commended the thoroughness and high standard of the work and said it provided a good basis for the negotiations the government wanted to conduct with the EU. It urged the government to summarize the conclusions of the reports on the relationship of the UK with the EU in a single handy statement for use in any subsequent referendum debate.[28]

The government never took up this suggestion. If it had expected the "balance of competences" review to identify a ready-made list of candidates for repatriating powers from Brussels, it was disappointed. The overwhelming conclusion of the review was that in most policy areas the current division of powers between the country and the EU was fairly satisfactory and in many cases any reforms that seemed desirable concerned all the member states and not just Britain and so could be advanced by Britain applying pressure during the normal decision-making processes of the EU not in one-to-one negotiations.[29]

The reports were met with a torrent of criticism from the right wing of the Conservative party and their allies in the press that they were the product of a civil service that was clearly biased in favour of the EU, a "Whitehall whitewash."[30] As for the government, between 2013 and the end of the negotiations with the EU in early 2016 David Cameron was officially in "neutral" mode between the Leave and Remain wings of his party, having promised to recommend Leave if the renegotiation on the country's relationship with the EU did not reach a satisfactory conclusion. So he could not publicly endorse the conclusions of the reports because that would be taking the side of Remain. The reports were consequently quietly buried and never mentioned by the government again, even during the referendum campaign, where they would have provided much-needed, albeit not headline-grabbing, ammunition for Remain. The result was that one of the most comprehensive surveys not only of Britain's but of all the member states' relationships with the EU and of the balance of power between them and its adequacy in current circumstances was abandoned by its parent at birth, and in effect donated to other member states as a treasure trove of ideas for their own reforms of these policies after Britain has left, like the excellent reports of the House of Lords Committee on the EU itself.[31]

Private authors tried to resurrect the "balance of competences" review during the referendum. Even a few honest Leavers quoted from it as evidence of how closely Britain was enmeshed in the EU. But for the government, it was politically toxic. It undermined the first stage of the referendum strategy of delivering a list of points to renegotiate with a view to the repatriation of powers, which would be successfully renegotiated and presented as a "reformed EU" to popular acclaim and a positive referendum result. Unfortunately, the experts had not found enough wrong with the UK-EU relationship to be helpful to the strategy. Stage one of the strategy had thus failed. The civil service had fulfilled its role of speaking truth to power, but the truth was unwelcome.

Ever since the announcement of the referendum in January 2013 and the promise to renegotiate Britain's terms of membership, the government was practically on negotiation footing with its EU partners, even before Cameron had won the 2015 election and started considering what he was going to negotiate about apart from EU immigration, which was already so hot a political issue that it had to be included. So the official stance was to be tough with the EU and throw its weight around as much as possible. Though the government was passive in relation to most routine EU business, at the European Council summits it would leap into action, taking a hard line on the budget, sticking out against accepting the European Parliament's involvement in nominating the EU Commission President and the appointment to this role of Jean-Claude Juncker whom it considered too federalist, and presenting a picture of fury to the media at a justified but apparently unexpected request from the Commission to pay a higher budget contribution due to the UK's faster increase in Gross National Product (GNP) after coming out of recession more quickly than its partners.[32] Cameron also showed his strength by exercising the rarely used veto on the "Fiscal Compact" proposal to limit budget deficits, with the result that the member states except for Britain and the Czech Republic adopted it as an intergovernmental decision rather than a regulation applying to the whole EU. The government also challenged the EU directive limiting bankers' bonuses in the European Court of Justice, but later withdrew its action when it realized the measure was popular with the general public although not with bankers.

The combative Euroscepticism that had characterized the government's stance hitherto was abruptly changed overnight in February 2016. Cameron announced that on the basis of the changes he had secured in Britain's relationship, the government would be recommending staying in the EU in the referendum, which he set for 23 June the same year. The announcement was in accordance with stage 2 (renegotiation) and 3 (recommendation to vote Remain) in the playbook of the referendum strategy, but was hardly credible as the changes were more modest than he had expected to secure when he had devised the strategy. The claim that they amounted to a "reformed" EU was hard to sustain and was dismissed by critics on the right wing of the Conservative party and in the newspapers. The relative durations of the stances taken—consistently Eurosceptic for the nearly six years, and then pro-EU for the five months of the referendum campaign—also made the conversion hard to believe. Perhaps he should have waited. To please his backbenchers Cameron had overplayed his Euroscepticism and could not credibly return to a pro-EU position afterwards. However persuasive they may be—and Cameron certainly had the "gift of the gab"—politicians need to be consistent or they come across as manipulative. The inconsistency made the Remain campaign Cameron and Osborne later led less credible than if they had adopted a more positive, if still Eurosceptic, tone throughout the previous six years.

To win a referendum two years later, it should have been Cameron and not the Deputy Prime Minister Nick Clegg who debated against Nigel Farage in the two debates in April 2014 before the European Parliament elections. But Cameron had to maintain the appearance of neutrality at this stage in the preparation of the referendum. His government was committed to facing down the EU to extract a better relationship. Only then would it be able to swing wholeheartedly behind continued membership.

The modest reforms David Cameron secured from the EU were fourfold, but the most important, on immigration, fell far short of the original target. The government had originally wanted to reduce the attractiveness of the UK labour market to EU migrants by disqualifying them from receiving in-work benefits for the first five years of their stay. The other member states, in particular, Poland, rejected this as infringing the principle of free movement. The final agreement was only an "emergency brake" on further EU migrants that would be triggered after new arrivals had reached a certain threshold and the cuts in benefits would be degressive—that is, the cuts in benefits to migrants, in the beginning, would be gradually phased out until the migrants became eligible for the full rates. There was some ability to restrict housing benefit to EU nationals but no possibility of stopping the payment of child allowances to children living in their home country entirely, only to cap them to local levels.

The other changes were under the headings of "sovereignty"—clarifying that the UK would be an exception from the objective of pursuing "ever-closer union" and allowing member states' parliaments more time to come together to block draft EU legislation; "competitiveness"—further safeguards to prevent legislation being enacted that reduced the competitiveness of industry through unnecessary "red tape"; and "governance"—safeguarding the exceptional position of the UK and other non-Eurozone countries with regard to Eurozone legislation and the funding of possible bail-outs.

In the face of the ridicule of the pro-Brexit faction of the Conservative party and the right-wing newspapers, the Cameron government decided to tone down their defence of the new settlement with the EU in the referendum campaign. This was probably a mistake, for however imperfect the changes were, explaining them during the campaign would have taken up the challenge of the Leave camp's exaggerated claims on sovereignty and immigration and turned the debate back to facts of which Cameron's changes provided illustrations: for example, that EU legislation is not imposed by Commission bureaucrats but adopted by all the member states' ministers and their members of the European Parliament; or that EU migrants staff much of the National Health Service, pay taxes, and do not displace British workers.

Instead, the government avoided the immigration topic as too much of a hot potato, whereas confronting it might have allowed it to address the genuine concerns people had about immigration such as pressure on schools and housing and to promise measures to address such concerns—admittedly at the risk of conceding its own previous failings in this area.

As noted in the introduction, the franchise was not extended to 16- and 17-year olds[33] and legislation lifting the 15-year rule limiting the right to vote of British citizens abroad, though promised before the 2015 election, had not passed Parliament, so expatriates of over 15 years were excluded. This was disappointing since many expatriates of over 15 years standing often have relatives and friends in Britain and live in a virtual English-speaking bubble in Belgium, France, Cyprus or Spain, where they read British newspapers, watch and listen to the BBC, spend time in local British and Irish pubs, follow cricket, and so on, and are often pretty well informed about what is going on in Britain. Admittedly, they often do not pay British taxes.

During the passage of the EU Referendum Act the vote was stated by the government to be "advisory". There was no provision in the Act itself saying it would be binding, and the intention that it should not be binding was confirmed by the lack of specification of any threshold of the electorate, like the 40% threshold set in the legislation for the 1997 Scottish devolution referendum, beyond which it would be so. Only the 2011 referendum on proportional representation was expressed to be binding. Nevertheless, the government, in the leaflet it sent to all households, and the participants in the campaign promised to abide by the result. It is unusual for a referendum on a major constitutional change to be considered mandatory without passing a minimum threshold of the electorate or of those voting to have voted in favour of the change. Only 37% of the electorate voted Leave in the EU referendum.[34]

One organization on each side of the debate was designated as the lead campaign organization but other organizations could operate as well. For the Leave side, the "Vote Leave" organization led by Dominic Cummings and Matthew Elliott was designated as the lead campaigner, and "Leave. eu" led by Nigel Farage and Arron Banks and other smaller groupings campaigned also. Lead campaigners were limited to spending a maximum of £7 million during the campaign period of 15 April to 22 June. Registered campaign organizations other than the lead organization could spend £700,000. The government circumvented the spending limits for the Remain side by publishing a leaflet putting the case for "Remain" sent to all households on 15 March 2016. The Leave side and their newspapers severely criticized the government for using public money to spread "EU propaganda" in this way and—to make matters worse—having the leaflet printed by a foreign company. However, around the same time Peter Hargreaves, founder of a stockbrokers firm, also paid for a leaflet to be sent out to 15 million households in favour of Leave. Both Vote Leave and Leave.eu were fined by the Electoral Commission for exceeding spending limits. The latter was also fined by the Information Commissioner's Office (ICO) for using data from an insurance company owned by its main backer, Arron Banks, who provided £8.4 million in loans to the campaign.[35] The lead Remain campaign organization Britain Stronger in Europe was also fined for infringing the spending rules in some cases.[36]

On 14 February 2016 when David Cameron announced the referendum for 23 June he is said to have been confident of a Remain majority. This expectation was widely shared, based partly on the belief that as the vote approached undecided voters would plump for the status quo. In the course of the referendum campaign, the gap narrowed, for long periods the two sides were level-pegging, and towards the end the polls tended to show a majority for Leave. The inertia bounce for the status quo just before the vote did not materialize.

There were dissenting voices that the vote would be on a knife-edge. A thorough report in *The Economist* of 17 October 2015,[37] based on numerous interviews with experts, warned that a positive outcome for staying in the EU could not be guaranteed. The conditions were wholly different from 1975, one crucial difference being the overwhelming press support for staying in Europe in 1975 and the majority of anti-EU newspapers now.[38] Matthew Goodwin, professor of politics at Kent University, says that he contacted Downing Street shortly before the vote to warn against complacency about a Remain result, and that as the EU's *Eurobarometer* survey had long been showing a level of Euroscepticism in Britain far higher than in any other EU country, a No vote was on the cards right from the beginning.

2.6   THE REFERENDUM CAMPAIGN

A Belgian academic has claimed that the EU referendum campaign in Britain was a model of informed debate and an advertisement for the benefits of popular democracy.[39] I suspect this judgment was based on a partial observation of the process, such as the televised debates, panel discussions like *Question Time* and the detailed exploration of issues on programmes like *Newsnight*. There, it is true, the discourse was polite, civilized and restrained, the participants and interviewees were precisely balanced between the two sides, the chairpersons and interviewers were fair and non-partisan and managed the discussions well, and the audiences for debates and panel discussions were well-behaved, having been selected to maintain balance and avoid one side's applause or booing drowning out the other's. In the not so formal everyday rough-and-tumble of speeches at campaign meetings, impromptu statements to the press, radio and TV, and discussion on social media, however, the register of the discussion was much cruder and impassioned. Observers were often taken aback by the sheer bile, anger, indignation, and hostility to the EU displayed by audiences at meetings of the Leave campaign in small towns and rural areas of England. One glance at the "comments" after online articles on the BBC News website is enough: the "debate" on Europe had become polarized and a bad-tempered slanging match.[40]

The anger and bile had not arisen since the beginning of the campaign. It had been festering since the 1990s below the surface, fanned by the right-wing newspapers. The Cameron government had helped reignite the animosity with its periodic skirmishes with the EU over Juncker, the budget, its own superior national budgetary management and its critical, supercilious stance over the EU's struggles to manage the euro and refugee crises. Meanwhile, UKIP had continued to stoke the flames with its message of a bullying, vindictive, undemocratic EU screwing the British taxpayer and taking away British jobs with immigrants Britain could not control. The referendum campaign was thus not a calm, balanced debate but a heated confrontation in which the two sides were talking at cross purposes: Leave waging a populist anti-EU campaign which, broadly speaking, denied all benefits of EU membership and exaggerated the drawbacks like loss of national sovereignty, excessive budget contributions and uncontrolled immigration, and the Remain camp failing to engage the other side properly on the main criticisms of the EU and, more importantly, to present solid and principled counterarguments showing the political advantages of international cooperation in Europe. Instead, the thrust of the official Remain campaign was to issue warnings of the economic risks of leaving the biggest single market in the world which was the destination of nearly half of British trade. The Leave side dismissed such warnings as scaremongering, "Project Fear," a lack of patriotism and belief in Britain, "talking Britain down." The potential of the country, it claimed, would be huge once freed from the shackles of a dysfunctional, declining EU, and the warnings were also partly motivated by the self-interest of the Establishment in resisting change.[41]

Undecided voters complained of the lack of reliable information from the media during the campaign on which to base a considered judgment, because of the pattern of claims and counterclaims cancelling one another out. The question is, would a better campaign with both sides putting a broader case for or against membership with fewer populist slogans and oversimplification of specific issues have provided the basis for reasoned decisions by voters with little prior practical knowledge of the EU. It is doubtful whether it would have. That is the fundamental objection to referendums on complex political and economic issues like membership of a trading block, as opposed to single issues like abortion or whether to charge foreign lorry traffic a tax for passing through Switzerland.

In the absence—and perhaps given the practical impossibility—of balanced, reliable information on a highly complex issue such as this, most voters probably based their decision, like in any election, on (a) the personalities campaigning, (b) the advice given in their favoured news source, or (c) particular issues raised in the referendum (whether or not they had much to do with the EU) that they were interested in such as the common fisheries policy, the "tampon tax," compulsory parental leave, bananas, pints and litres, immigration, stagnant incomes, the NHS, or lack of investment in old industrial areas of the Midlands and North.

It has been claimed that the results of referendums are often more a vote on the politician holding the vote than on the question asked. If the leader calling the vote is popular, he will win; if he is not, he will lose. Whether this is true or not, one thing that is certain is that the popularity and effectiveness of the campaigners has a huge impact on the result and that this was the case in the British EU referendum of 2016.

Both leaders of the two Leave campaign organizations, Vote Leave and Leave.eu, Boris Johnson and Nigel Farage, are charismatic campaigners, persuasive, convincing, humorous and entertaining, but also ruthless advocates for their cause, hammering home well-rehearsed arguments relentlessly without ever conceding points to the opposition. It is probably true that Johnson's decision to campaign for Leave won them the referendum and they would not have won if he had been on the other side.[42] By comparison, the leader of the Remain campaign, the Prime Minister David Cameron, was less convincing. He was handicapped by his previous combatively Eurosceptic statements and actions in relation to the EU, and therefore constantly on the defensive about its imperfections, whereas Johnson and Farage gave the impression of being totally convinced of the justice of their case and brushed off challenges on incorrect facts, such the £350 million and 75 million Turks set to come to Britain, with aplomb. The Remain campaign was also handicapped by the lacklustre performance of the Labour leader Jeremy Corbyn, who failed to show, in support of the EU, any of the formidable campaigning conviction and passion he displayed in the general election of June 2017.[43] One of the lowest points in his campaign was giving the EU only seven out of ten when asked how he rated the organization, hardly a wholehearted endorsement, especially when set against the rousing and full-bodied aggression of Johnson's and Farage's speeches for Leave.[44]

There were other failures in the Remain campaign. Cameron decided the campaign strategy and was probably, with George Osborne, responsible for the negative tactic of warning against the risks of leaving rather than going on the offensive about the benefits the EU had brought for Britain and Europe, on which he was probably not well informed and would have been less convincing. Cameron certainly decided that the Remain campaign should steer clear of the immigration issue, although a tactic of talking about legal ways of giving greater priority to British workers in future might have paid off. Corbyn allegedly actively hindered campaigning by other Labour figures like Alan Johnson, Peter Mandelson and Tony Blair, who were much more passionate supporters of the EU.[45] Corbyn can be said to have put a damper on the Labour side of the Remain campaign. Both leaders' refusal to appear on platforms together also damaged the case for Remain. Overall, the tight grip on the Remain campaign maintained by Cameron and Corbyn took other lesser but more convincing figures like the Lib-Dem Nick Clegg and Caroline Lucas of the Greens out of the limelight. The reporting of the Remain campaign in the media was overwhelmingly concentrated on Cameron and Osborne. Many local events in which much more committed Remainers spoke were unreported.

For Remain campaigners, making a positive case for staying in the EU was more challenging than the task facing Leavers, especially with the majority of the press on their side. Remainers were defending a status quo based on international cooperation with people of different nationalities speaking different languages. European integration had brought economic benefits, but recent crises in the EU had thrown them into doubt. Leavers could exploit these doubts, while at the same time appealing to voters' emotions of national pride in past glories and distrust of Europeans kept alive by memories of the world wars that are cultivated in Britain more than anywhere else in Europe. Without doubt, the Remain campaign should have been bolder and more assertive in making the positive case for staying: for example, the EU's prioritization of cooperation over conflict; its historical contribution to peace in Europe; the practical advantages of collective rule-making instead of insisting on national sovereignty in many areas—it saves time and money and the outcome is usually the same; the joys and convenience of barrier-free life in modern Europe which could not have come about without the EU; even the positive contribution EU migrants are making to Britain, in working in the NHS, for example. Instead, the Remain campaign focussed on negative arguments for staying, namely the economic damage leaving would cause, and prefaced any positive arguments with "The EU isn't perfect, but...." [46] The Leave side was more aggressive, dismissing warnings of economic damage flatly as "scaremongering" or "Project Fear" and hammering home their own populist messages about Europe ripping Britain off, imposing needless bureaucracy, or flooding the country with immigrants.

As well as Johnson and Farage, Michael Gove and Daniel Hannan were also prominent for Leave. The Leave campaign also benefited from politically astute backroom organizations led by Matthew Elliott, who had written a sourcebook of anti-EU slogans on which most Leave campaigners drew—and still draw—heavily, and Dominic Cummings, a brilliant and fearless strategist for whom winning at any cost and by whatever means was paramount. Elliott had earned his spurs leading the successful campaign in the referendum on whether to introduce proportional representation in the British electoral system. Leave also had the more effective social media operation, especially towards the end of the campaign when it allegedly managed to persuade many people who had never voted before to go out and vote this time; it did it partly through skilful targeted advertising using data obtained from social media.

Another advantage Leave had was that the two support organizations, Vote Leave and Leave.eu, complemented one another, with the latter campaigning aggressively on immigration and generally behaving with less inhibitions, and the former publicly disapproving of Leave.eu's tactics but privately knowing that the campaign as a whole gained from the brash approach of the self-styled "bad boys of Brexit" among working-class UKIP-leaning voters.[47] On the other hand, the Britain Stronger In Europe Conservative party operation led by Cameron entirely dominated the separate Labour operation and inhibited it from developing a more visible and possibly more effective strategy of its own. This, as well as Jeremy Corbyn's lacklustre and ambivalent leadership, limited Labour's contribution to the campaign.

It should be remembered that Leave had the support of the majority of the newspapers. The *Telegraph*, *Mail*, *Express* and *Sun* had helped lay the foundations for the Leave victory through partisan reporting about the EU over the previous 20 years and they were determined not to let the "prize" of Brexit slip from their grasp. Only occasional token gestures to the Remain side were made on their pages during the referendum. For example, Barack Obama's appeal to British voters was printed in the

Telegraph. Nor have they relaxed their determination to see Brexit through since the referendum. Brexit is still the No 1 story on the news, editorial and comment pages of these newspapers. After important developments in Brexit such as Boris Johnson's resignation, all of them will devote a large proportion of their space to keeping Britain on the straight and narrow path out of the EU. To claim any degree of objective reporting on this issue, as the *Telegraph* did in its "reality check" of the Cameron "EU propaganda" leaflet of March 2016, is highly questionable. With regard to Britain's relations with the EU, these newspapers are wholly partisan. A partisan press is not necessarily a bad thing provided that over the whole newspaper landscape a balance of opinions is presented that broadly reflects public opinion and that the newspapers maintain acceptable standards of factual accuracy and do not stoop to populism. The problem is that the British press scene fails both these tests and this had a deleterious effect on the fairness of the referendum.

On 16 June 2016, one week before the referendum, the MP Jo Cox was murdered on a street in her Yorkshire constituency by an English white supremacist. The Leave campaign cannot be blamed for this act of terrorism any more than law-abiding British Muslims can be blamed for the suicide bombing at the Manchester Arena by an Islamist extremist.[48] What the incident shows, however, is that immigration should be handled sensitively by politicians in a way that does not stir up racial hatred. The number of hate crimes against immigrants rose after the referendum. Some Leave campaigners and their cheerleader newspapers did overstep the boundaries of sensitive treatment of immigration, for example, in raising the spectre of columns of refugees and of millions of Turks heading for Britain where neither was even remotely in prospect.

The referendum did not help to heal the divisions in British society, or even only in the Tory party, but has exacerbated them. It may even lead to the break-up of the United Kingdom. It raised unrealistic expectations among those taken in by the mendacious promises and populist rhetoric of Leave campaigners and their newspaper backers. It has not moved Britain any closer to addressing the "burning injustices" in society which Mrs May wanted to tackle when she entered Downing Street; on the contrary, by monopolizing the government's attention for three years it has proved a distraction to tackling these problems or those of the scandalous inequalities in regional development, health and education that are a blight on Britain.

2.7   Aftermath

A taste of the chaos to come was David Cameron's resignation the day after the referendum and a month later the election of Mrs May as prime minister by Conservative MPs after other candidates including the star of the Leave campaign Boris Johnson had dropped out of the race.[49] The motives for Boris Johnson's withdrawal from the leadership contest, which would give the winner the responsibility for leading the country into Brexit, the goal he had so vigorously campaigned for, are puzzling. Was it the shock at the "stab in the back" by his closest ally in the Brexit campaign Michael Gove, who was reneging on a promise not to stand himself but to back Johnson's leadership bid? Or did he suddenly doubt his capacity to master the challenge of disentangling Britain from 40 years of integration into Europe? An article Johnson wrote in the *Daily Telegraph* two days after the vote implying that little need to change in Britain's relations with the EU and that negotiating Brexit would be a stroll in the park was hardly a sign of panic at the magnitude of the task ahead, but rather of complacency. Michael Gove indeed cited the article as evidence of his former ally's insufficient intellectual maturity to lead the country through Brexit and as the reason he decided to stand himself.

Part of the reason for Johnson's failure to stand for the leadership is probably the calculation that his level of support among Conservative MPs at that stage, with the wounds of the campaign still fresh, was insufficient to get him through the two rounds of voting by MPs into the final choice of two to be put to the Conservative Party rank and file. He was, therefore, biding his time for another leadership bid later under more propitious conditions. This version has been borne out by his subsequent behaviour.

Nigel Farage also resigned as leader of UKIP immediately after the referendum vote. Thus, the situation in July 2016 was that both the leading lights of the Brexit campaign, Johnson and Farage, had disappeared from the scene and the referendum decision they had fought for was to be carried out by others. One cannot say they both deliberately made themselves scarce once the war had been won, leaving others to sort out its aftermath and fulfil the Leave side's promises of milk and honey and "sunny uplands" post-Brexit. They did not have much alternative. The parliamentary arithmetic was stacked against Johnson's becoming prime minister at that time and Farage was an outsider without a track record of public office and in the British system had no chance of being given a responsible position in government. Farage's lifelong goal was realized and he could continue cajoling and agitating for delivery of a true-blue Brexit from his base as a member of the European Parliament—until Britain left. Johnson also continued his fight for Brexit from the cabinet after Theresa May unexpectedly appointed him foreign secretary. Indeed, he became the champion, alongside Jacob Rees-Mogg, of the hard, "clean-break" version of Brexit advocated by the caucus of die-hard Tory backbench Brexiteers in the European Reform Group.

Theresa May in July 2016 took up a harder job in negotiating Britain's way out of the EU than Edward Heath ever had in negotiating its entry in 1973.

- Parliament was not going to give the government an easy ride, because half of the Conservatives and most of Labour were pro-Remain and set on limiting the damage through a soft Brexit, a noisy caucus of Conservative Brexit extremists demanded a hard Brexit, and a few in the Commons and many of the Lords did not want Brexit it all. So it was always likely that some form of soft Brexit would emerge as a compromise, but that this would then raise the question what the point of it all was and why not have another referendum and a chance of ditching the whole idea.
- In the beginning, Mrs May wanted to shut Parliament out of the negotiations as far as possible. Giving a "running commentary," she said, would weaken the government's negotiating hand. Following a legal challenge, she quickly found that parliament could not be sidelined. Labour and pro-Remain Conservatives cleverly exploited this contradiction between the avowed purpose of Brexit of defending British parliamentary sovereignty and a government wanting to shut parliament out of the biggest realignment of the country's geopolitical relations since the war. So they secured a "meaningful vote" by Parliament on the exit package negotiated by the government—just how a parliamentary democracy ought to operate.
- The government found that negotiating Brexit was not the stroll in the park Brexiteers had promised. Britain was not in a stronger negotiating position than the EU. The slogan, "They need us more than we need them," and the assumption that the EU would soon realize the folly of holding out against British demands to cherry-pick the bits of the EU it liked—while discarding the other bits and the tedious obligations of membership—quickly proved to be a chimera.

Britain did not have a stronger hand than the EU because the Germans exported more cars and the Italians and French more wine and cheese to Britain than vice versa. The EU would not, as soon as it knew which side its bread was buttered on, see reason and let Britain "have its cake and eat it" (so many food metaphors!). That, as noted earlier, is based on a fundamental misconception. The EU is being perfectly rational in wishing to keep the benefits of membership for members and not let them leach out to non-members, for this would be a recipe for the break-up of the EU, an EU which the other 27 countries support for reasons of political stability as well as commercial advantage. This is not blind ideology on the EU's part but a rational political calculation, which trumps short-term commercial considerations. Brexiteers are the last people to criticize the EU for prioritizing political ideology.

- After triggering Article 50 and imposing a time constraint on itself, it became clear that the British government was actually in a weak position. It had to accept the timing decided by the EU, of first negotiating the divorce and only then turning to the future trading and other relationships. It had to accept an exit bill of around £39 billion despite having long argued, on the basis of a dubious legal opinion untypically endorsed by the House of Lords, that it had no legal obligations to the EU and could leave without paying a penny (though admittedly with the practical problem that the EU might then be less inclined to give the UK an advantageous post-Brexit deal—or any deal at all). It had to agree to a temporary special status for Northern Ireland in order keep an open border between Northern Ireland and the Republic of Ireland when this becomes in effect an external EU border. It had to accept relaxations of traditional Home Office practices to simplify the procedures for registering EU citizens and their dependents as entitled to stay in the UK and to allow an element of supervision over these procedures by the European Court of Justice, and it had to agree to EU citizens who come to the UK during the transition period, after Brexit, acquiring the same right to settled status as those resident on "Brexit day." So the government negotiations, following multiple resignations of ministers and civil servants, have been a history of repeated climb-downs from untenable positions.

- This pattern is set to continue, if Brexit happens, in the negotiations on the final relationship between Britain and the EU.

Mrs May had a hard job and showed remarkable resilience, surviving a disastrous general election, upsets at party conferences, no-confidence motions, constant mockery, and picking herself up off the canvas time after time to take even more punishment.

Arguably, it has not been a happy three years, for her or Britain more broadly. Let's hope the future will be brighter for all concerned. The next chapter will go into the social and media environment that helps explain why we are where we are.

NOTES

1. *BBC Radio 4.* 2018–2019. Brexit: A Love Story? Podcast, starting from 29 March 2018, presented by Mark Mardell.
2. *BBC Radio 4.* 2018. Why I changed my mind. 25 July. Interview with Gisela Stuart.
3. El-Agraa, Ali M. (ed.). 2007. *The European Union: Economics and Politics*, (8th ed.), 23 *et seq.* Cambridge: Cambridge University Press; McCormick, John. 2015. *European Union Politics*, (2nd ed.), 57 *et seq.* London: Palgrave Macmillan.
4. Churchill, Winston, 1946. Speech at University of Zürich. 19 September. *International Churchill Society.* McCormick, op. cit., 68.
5. Peel, Quentin. 2016. Historic misunderstanding underlies UK-EU relationship on Churchill anniversary. *Financial Times.* 19 September.
6. Dinan, Desmond. 2005. *Ever-Closer Union. An Introduction to European Integration*, (3rd ed.), 11–35. Basingstoke: Palgrave Macmillan; El-Agraa, op. cit., 23–31; McCormick, op. cit., 68–85.
7. See George, Stephen. 1994. *An Awkward Partner: Britain in the European Community* (2nd ed.). Oxford: Oxford University Press.
8. Greenslade, Roy. 2016. Did national papers' pro-European bias in 1975 affect referendum? *The Guardian.* 4 February.
9. George, op. cit., 96–106.
10. George, op. cit., 174–177.
11. Such as national standards for beer, which allowed countries like Germany with its Beer Purity law to prevent imports of foreign beer produced to other standards.
12. British journalists and British members of the European Commission who supported a more cooperative, less adversarial approach to the EU were said to have "gone native." Lord Cockfield who was nominated a commissioner by Margaret Thatcher in 1984 earned this criticism for throwing himself too enthusiastically into planning the programme for completing the Single Market by 1992 and he was not proposed for a second term.

Lord Hill, appointed a commissioner in 2014, was also criticized in this way, probably because he did not demonstrate his previous Eurosceptic credentials while a commissioner: Samuel, Juliet. 2017. Juliet Samuel Notebook. *Daily Telegraph.* 27 April.

13. Comparing Major and Cameron: *The Economist.* 2011. Game, set and mismatch: What do you get when you mix political differences and inept diplomacy? Britain's bust-up with the rest of the EU. 17 December.

14. See Dinan, op. cit., 118–128; George, op. cit., 241–248.

15. See Chap. 5, Sect. 5.5.2.

16. Grayling, A. C. 2017. *Democracy and Its Crisis*, 189–197. London: Oneworld.

17. Ibid., 190.

18. *BBC Radio 4.* 2018. Why I changed my mind. 25 July. Interview with Gisela Stuart. See also Kuper, Simon. 2017. Opening shot: Brexit Britain's gift to the world. *Financial Times.* 29 September, on the massive pitfalls of referendums that the EU vote demonstrated, such as "wedge issues," real-time election regulators, transition costs and complexity.

19. MacShane, Denis. 2017. *Brexit, No Exit: Why (In the End) Britain Won't Leave Europe.* London: I.B. Tauris.

20. *The Economist.* 2011. The perils of extreme democracy: California enters warning to voters all over the world. 20 April.

21. Since 2012, increases in Council Tax above a 5% cap (for local authorities financing social care) have required a referendum: *The Guardian.* 2017. Surrey council abandons plan to raise council tax by 15%. 7 February.

22. *Reuters.* 2016. EU agrees to Dutch demands on Ukraine deal to avoid "present for Russia." 15 December. On a turnout of only 32%, 65% voted against the Ukraine association agreement. After the government had gained assurances from the EU that the agreement did not make Ukraine a candidate for membership, did not involve financial aid or military assistance, and did not lead to freedom of movement for Ukrainian workers in the EU, the Dutch Parliament ratified the agreement by a two-thirds majority. See *DutchNews.nl.* 2016. 18 November: the main motives of voters had been corruption in Ukraine and the possibility of Ukraine becoming a member of the EU; only 7.5% said they had been voting against the EU.

23. Bogdanor, Vernon. 2019. Post-Brexit Britain may need a constitution—or face disintegration: The EU is the glue that holds the UK together. *The Guardian.* 18 January. Bogdanor, Vernon. 2019. *Beyond Brexit: Towards a British Constitution.* London: I.B. Tauris.

24. Curtice, John. 2017. Why Leave won the UK's referendum. *Journal of Common Market Studies 55 Annual Review*, 19–37.

25. Clement Attlee's dictum that referendums "have all too often been the instrument of Nazism and fascism" was repeated with approval by Margaret Thatcher in 1975 when she termed them "a device of dictators

and demagogues." Saunders, Robert. 2019. How Britain embraced referendums, the instrument of dictators and demagogues. *The Economist: Open Future.* 17 January.

26. Greenslade. Roy. 2016. Did national papers' pro-European bias in 1975 affect the referendum? *The Guardian.* 4 February.

27. HM Treasury Analysis: The Long-term Economic Impact of EU Membership and the Alternatives, HM Gov, 2016. Cm 9250: "Every person £4300 worse off by 2030."

28. House of Lords, EU Select Committee. 2015. Review of the Balance of Competences between the UK and the EU. 23 March.

29. Emerson, Michael (ed.). 2016. *Britain's Future in Europe. The Known Plan A to Remain and the Unknown Plan B to Leave.* London: Rowman and Littlefield International.

30. Institute of International and European Affairs. 2016. The curious incident of the UK competences review. 1 March; Shipman, Tim. 2013. 'Whitehall whitewash' that claims EU is GOOD for Britain: Tory MPs' dismay at Brussels power. *Mail Online.* 23 July.

31. See also Kuper, op. cit.

32. *The Guardian.* 2014. David Cameron refuses to pay £1.7bn EU bill by 1 December. 24 October.

33. A House of Lords amendment was rejected.

34. Grayling, op. cit.

35. *Financial Times.* 2018. Brexiters face fresh scrutiny over EU referendum spending. 19 September; *Reuters.* 2018. Brexit group Leave-EU fined for breaking referendum spending rules. 11 May; *BBC News.* 2018. Brexit: Vote Leave broke electoral law, says Electoral Commission. 17 July; *Guardian.* 2019 Leave.EU and Arron Banks' insurance firm fined £120,000 for data breaches. 1 February.

36. *BBC News.* 2018. Remain EU referendum spending claims rejected. 2 August.

37. *The Economist.* 2015. Special Report Britain and Europe: The reluctant European. 17 October.

38. MacShane, Denis. 2015. *How Britain Left Europe.* London I.B.Tauris.

39. Bourgaux, Anne-Emmanuelle. 2016. En démocratie, on ne doit pas craindre le peuple. *Le Soir.* 14 July.

40. *The Economist.* 2016. Charlemagne—Commented out. 25 June.

41. Buckledee, Steve. 2018. *The Language of Brexit. How Britain Talked Its Way Out of the European Union.* London: Bloomsbury.

42. Clarke, Harold D., Matthew Goodwin and Paul Whitely. 2017. *Brexit: Why Britain Voted to Leave the European Union,* 170–172. Cambridge: Cambridge University Press.

43. *The Economist.* 2016. Jeremy Corbyn, saboteur. 11 June.

44. There have been long-standing misunderstandings about EU policies in the "Lexit" wing of Labour party since Tony Benn, such as that the EU does not allow state aid or nationalization.

45. Shipman, Tim. 2017. *All Out War: The Full Story of Brexit*. London: William Collins. Oliver, Craig. 2016. *Unleashing Demons: The Inside Story of Brexit*. London: Hodder and Stoughton.

46. Buckledee, Steve. 2018. *The Language of Brexit: How Britain Talked its Way Out of the European Union*, 1–17. London: Bloomsbury.

47. Banks, Arron. 2017. *The Bad Boys of Brexit: Tales of Mischief, Mayhem and Guerilla Warfare in the EU Referendum Campaign*. London: Biteback.

48. UKIP's occasional descents into anti-immigrant, anti-Muslim extremism only supplemented traditional Conservative attitudes, which actually won the referendum, according to Sebastian Payne, *Financial Times*. 2017. 20 September.

49. Shipman, Tim. 2017. *Fall Out: A Year of Political Mayhem*. London: William Collins.

CHAPTER 3

National Identity, the British Media, and Press Propaganda

3.1 British Identity and Attitudes—a Complex Amalgam of History, Geography and Much Else, with Nostalgia and Nationalism Thrown into the Mix

Some things one can say about the attitudes of British people towards the outside world are uncontroversial. It is safe to say most people are proud of their country because of its history as a great power. The past has left an enviable heritage of traditions and institutions that are still cherished: the monarchy with its pomp and ceremony but also its symbolism of national identity, democracy and parliament, country houses, pubs, national parks, horse racing, monuments to the industrial revolution, its armed forces, the BBC, and fish and chips, to name but a few, and not in any order of importance. It has produced world-famous artists, musicians, writers, philosophers and scientists, political leaders, actors, and film-makers. It overachieves internationally at many sports, some of which it invented, including cricket, and runs one of the world's best football leagues. For all these reasons, if not for its weather, it is a popular tourist destination. People love to come to Britain for its historical sights, its olde-worldeness, its theatre, and to experience one of world's most vibrant multicultural cities, London. It boasts world-class universities like Oxford and Cambridge, world-leading research facilities, an enviable tally of scientific achievements and Nobel prizes, and a phenomenally successful creative

© The Author(s) 2019
F. Rawlinson, *How Press Propaganda Paved the Way to Brexit*,
https://doi.org/10.1007/978-3-030-27765-9_3

media sector whose output is seen and heard the world over. So, we Brits (I still use the "we" despite having lived abroad for over 40 years) have much to be proud of.

There is a downside to this national pride, however: a tendency to nostalgia for a supposedly more glorious past of empire and influence that is no more or much reduced, resentment at the usurpation of our previous status by others and at the loss of prestige, admiration and gratitude we feel the world owes us for our achievements, and insecurity about what Britain's future role should be as only a middle-ranking world power. These feelings sometimes come across as arrogance and as nationalism rather than justified national pride.

Has the status of English as the world's lingua franca made the world Britain's oyster or, on the contrary, made its understanding of non-English-speaking countries, even its European neighbours, more difficult and Britain more isolated? A shared English language does not guarantee the absence of cultural barriers, even within the "Anglosphere," as is clear from the US after Trump.[1]

Foreign language learning has long been in steady decline in Britain. That is a pity because languages are not only a communication tool, but build bridges, create empathy, fun, and a sense of solidarity. Relying only on English reduces the pleasure of cultural interaction; but not only that, it also leads to misunderstandings and eventually mistrust. It seems to me that mistrust is one of the dominant feelings many British people now have towards Europe: the perception that Europe is out to do Britain down, that Europeans do not appreciate or even like us, that they are our deadly rivals, arch-enemies even, and can never be our partners. It cannot only be the traumatic experience of the two world wars that is responsible for Britain's estrangement from Europe, for they are long past. Germans no longer hate us, quite the reverse; they all now speak our language. There are many factors, but languages—or lack of them—are one of the reasons why, to many Europeans, Britain appears to be turning its back on their continent. Language barriers have not disappeared for us with English becoming a world language; by denying ourselves the joys and benefits of language learning, we have allowed barriers to grow.

The feeling of alienation is reinforced—and here I do become controversial—by unreconstructed memories of the two world wars, which are fresher in Britain than on the continent. Germany rightfully confronted the aberration of Nazism and came to terms with it. Germans are now educated about the holocaust and warned of the dangers of extremism.

Germany and France have been thoroughly reconciled. Their relations with one another and with other EU countries they fought with in the two world wars are closer than ever. In Britain, however, little re-examination— let alone criticism—of its role in the wars has entered the public consciousness. Efforts at reconciliation in recognition of the catastrophic loss of life on both sides were common 20 or 30 years ago—like those between Coventry and Dresden, two cities destroyed by the other country's bombing—but they are no longer as vigorous as before. This is not because as time has passed memories of the wars have receded in Britain. Quite the reverse. They are remembered more than ever. But the remembrance is different, more nationalistic, recalling only the suffering, sacrifice and heroism of the British side and not those of the other, and, in the case of World War I, to some extent rewriting its history as a British sacrifice for freedom and democracy on the Continent, rather than an accidental conflict that had more to do with nationalism, armaments, alliances and finance.[2]

Films and documentaries about Britain's wartime achievements, the "Dunkirk spirit," and the heroism of its soldiers are still staples of the British media. It seems as if the nation needs to keep reminding itself of its past glories and the sacrifices its people made for Europe and the gratitude they are owed, but do not always receive, from those they saved from tyranny. Since the Brexit vote, the remembrance of the battles of World War I, culminating in the ceremonies marking 100 years since the Armistice of 1918, has intensified and assumed quasi-nationalistic traits, with jingoistic newspapers like the *Express* leading the fray and the May government, eager to burnish its Brexit credentials among the right wing of the Conservative party, not far behind. While it is clearly right to honour our own war dead, the celebrations should be inclusive and aware of the circumstances that led to the war and the mistakes made not only in the slaughter itself but in its aftermath. Otherwise, remembrance of old wars becomes politicized and sows discord, as it did and still does in Northern Ireland.

Fintan O'Toole sees the casting of the EU in the role of an oppressor as a part of a pattern of peculiarly English feelings of victimhood.[3] The constant and uncritical dwelling on wartime exploits and sacrifice may be good for Britain's self-esteem, but it helps maintain attitudes of distrust towards its European allies that are not conducive to cooperation in Europe.

Geography, clearly, also plays a role in Britain's attitudes to Europe. It separates Britain physically from the Continent and has shaped its history as a global seafaring power and a fortress able to resist invasion. These, in turn, are a subject of national pride and foster a belief that Britain, the world's fifth biggest economic power, can go it alone again. It doesn't need Europe to make its way in the world. It can again stride the world stage as a respected and sought-after trading partner. This, too, was a powerful patriotic message in the Leave campaign.

The fortress idea helped make control of immigration such a powerful message for Brexit. With only sea borders except on the island of Ireland, people could easily be persuaded that, but for EU freedom of movement, it would be easy to reduce immigration. The camps of migrants in Calais, prevented from getting to Britain by the barrier of the Channel, were a symbol of Britain under siege, which was precisely the image the Leave campaign wanted to keep in voters' minds as a compelling reason for getting out of Europe. They reinforced it with the imaginary spectre of millions more waiting to invade Britain when Turkey joined.

There are marked social and regional inequalities in Britain. Social mobility in Britain used to be increasing, but in the last decade it has stagnated and even gone into reverse.[4] For example, in terms of disposable income, the top 10% of households are almost nine times better off than the bottom 10%.[5] Company directors and top bankers frequently earn multiples of a 100 or more of what their employees take home.[6] Over 4 million working people are earning less than the poverty line. Some 4.1 million children, an increase of 500,000 in five years, live in poverty.[7] Many are in old industrial areas that have suffered from the closure of factories in the course of the globalization of the economy but have not managed to attract alternative activities paying similar levels of wages and are therefore in decline. This is compounded by a lack of investment in infrastructure, schools and hospitals in such areas as a result of cuts in budgets during the long period of austerity after the financial crisis. On socioeconomic measures such as educational attainment of the population, numbers living in poverty and of children receiving free school meals, in terms of life expectancy, and on purely economic measures such as the quality of public transport, such areas in England and Wales are severely disadvantaged compared with London and the South East.[8]

Differences in educational opportunities persist and reinforce the class system which, while attenuated compared with 50 years ago, still lives on in a large private fee-paying school sector. Private education remains popular, indeed *de rigueur*, for parents with inherited wealth, and "nouveaux riches," as a passport to top universities and success in many professions.

Half of undergraduate places at Oxford and Cambridge still go to the 7% of pupils educated at "public" (i.e. private as opposed to state) schools and, by geographical origin, to people from London and the South East. Over two-thirds of senior judges in Britain have this public school and Oxbridge background, as do a high proportion of Conservative MPs and leading journalists.[9] The system of private education that exists in Britain and helps maintain social privilege and a still vibrant class system is unique in Europe. Even educational reformers such as Sir Peter Lampl concede that the system is too entrenched to be challenged except by organic improvement of the state system to the point where it becomes as good or better.[10] This is confirmed by the fact that the role of private education in bolstering social inequality seems nowadays to have become a taboo subject. In a recent debate about the difficulty of access to Oxbridge by pupils from outside the South East or ethnic minorities, the focus was only on geography and ethnicity; private education was the elephant in the room which was not mentioned.

Given this social and regional inequality, those in lower income strata due to lesser educational qualifications and social disadvantage, including many typical white working class voters living in "left behind" industrial areas and in coastal towns that have suffered from the decline in the fishing industry and traditional holiday patterns, feel, quite understandably and justifiably in many cases, resentment against the better off and privileged, the "cosmopolitan elite," "fat cat" bankers and company directors, or just the "posh," the "toffs," the upper classes (and, who knows, maybe even eurocrats!).[11]

In the EU referendum, dissatisfaction about social and regional inequalities probably played a role in two ways. First, the underprivileged on low incomes or benefits, and living in disadvantaged areas starved of investment compared with the more privileged South East, wanted to give the Establishment "a good kicking" to get them to tackle those inequalities. Secondly, whether the inequality and injustice had anything to do with the EU or not, the EU was blamed for them by association, as a perceived part of the Establishment. In this view they were encouraged by the press and books like "The Great European Rip-Off" by David Craig and Matthew Elliott with their stories of the excessive pay of EU commissioners, Members of the European Parliament (MEPs), and EU officials, their generous expenses, the bloated bureaucracy, and the monthly "gravy train" of the European Parliament from its base in Brussels to Strasbourg for its plenary meetings.

Among older voters, the old beliefs of Labour party left-wingers like Tony Benn, that the EU was part of a capitalist world order exploiting the working classes, fed into this narrative. It was bolstered by the portrayal of the treatment of Greece in the euro crisis as the action of a bullying German-led EU designed to rescue the big banks on the backs of the workers. But it was a distorted picture. In fact, the EU has a strong record of legislation to protect workers' rights and promote equality, and it devotes a large part of its regional and cohesion policy budget to schemes for retraining the unemployed and stimulating entrepreneurship. The British trade union movement was firmly on the side of Remain in the referendum, as were nearly all Labour MPs, but many Labour voters ignored them and believed the Leave campaign instead. The EU became a scapegoat for inequalities and injustices in British society which should have been laid at the door of its government.

3.2   The British Media Landscape

Media, in which I include the publishing and the film industry as well as broadcasters, newspapers and magazines, and, nowadays, social media platforms, inform, educate, and entertain but also often seek to persuade people of a particular point of view. In the latter type of activity, they may utilize pre-existing social attitudes, ways of thinking and prejudices towards the outside world to reinforce their message. Passing populist or nationalist messages by appealing to social attitudes is easier than persuading people that actually international cooperation and understanding are more in their interest. Social attitudes tend to relate to feelings of national identity, pride, and difference from others rather than common humanity and universal values.

3.2.1   Books

How have books, first of all, helped shape British public opinion about Europe? Books about the EU fall into two main categories, those for academic or professional users and those for general readers. Very many British universities have departments and courses in European studies or European law, and there are numerous textbooks for the use of students on such courses. Similarly, a large number of law firms in Britain specialize in European law and the lawyers practising this branch of the law—often for clients on the European mainland—use a wide range of rigorously accurate, comprehensive, and frequently updated compilations of the law as a daily tool in their work. Among the many dependable standard works of this kind are *Wyatt and Dashwood's European Union Law*[12] for general EU law and *Bellamy & Child*[13] for competition law, which are designed both for advanced students and practitioners. There are other, shorter books intended as textbooks or for both academic and general audiences like El-Agraa,[14] Dimon,[15] Cini[16] and Corner,[17] all descriptive and basically positive towards the EU. Specialist academic periodicals like the *Common Market Law Review* complete this picture of a vigorous academic and professional scene in the field of EU law and economics in Britain, with a reputation just as high as in Germany. Such books and periodicals sometimes take a critical stance on certain aspects of Court of Justice judgments or Commission decisions in a particular case, but would rarely call into question the rationale of an EU policy or the EU as a whole.

Books about the EU for general readers also used to be based on a political consensus in favour of European integration. Right up to the mid-1990s, former European commissioners like Christopher Tugendhat[18] and Leon Brittan[19] could write memoirs about their time working in the European Community institutions and be largely positive, though perhaps critical of the direction the EU was taking in certain areas, without being condemned as having "gone native," that is, forgotten their British roots and sold out to the "enemy." Since the mid-1990s, however, the tenor of most general books about the EU published in Britain has changed to mildly or strongly Eurosceptic, and a number have been written specifically to canvas support for a referendum to get Britain out of the EU. In the latter category are books like Booker and North's *The Great Deception*[20], Craig and Elliott's *The Great European Rip-Off*,[21] and Roger Bootle's *The Trouble with Europe*.[22]

Matthew Elliott was a co-founder and long-term chief executive of the right-wing pressure group the Taxpayers' Alliance and led the successful referendum against proportional representation in 2011 before becoming the chief executive of the main Leave campaign organization, Vote Leave. The title of his book with David Craig makes its purpose crystal clear and the contents do not disappoint. It is a hatchet job: the EU has no good side and not even good intentions; it is corrupt and wasteful, costing every man, woman and child in Europe £2000 a year; it is a bloated bureaucracy which is as inefficient as it is out of touch. The book is based on selective, tendentiously interpreted facts, half-truths and exaggerations. Booker and North's book is a weightier tome but likewise one-sidedly polemical and distortive of its facts. The basic tenet of the book is that the EU has turned into a monster under the noses of the unsuspecting people of Europe, and the British most of all. Bootle argues on the basis of its recent problems, especially the euro crisis, that the EU is close to disintegrating and only major reforms towards more liberal trade policies and away from centralizing projects like the euro—policies long advocated by British Conservatives—could save it, but reform being unlikely Britain's better course will be to leave a fundamentally flawed organization. A similar message is conveyed by the Conservative Member of the European Parliament Daniel Hannan in his book *A Doomed Marriage: Britain and Europe.*[23]

The euro crisis was ending just as Britain was moving towards the EU referendum. It prompted a cluster of new books, most of which were highly critical of the EU's management of the crisis and its treatment of Greece, some from a left-wing perspective such as that by the *Guardian* writer Larry Elliott *Europe Isn't Working,*[24] who also criticized the EU for its control of state aid, one of the main critiques of the anti-EU Labour movement, and Yanis Varoufakis' first-hand account of the crisis as Greek finance minister,[25] while others like the former BBC Europe Editor Gavin Hewitt's *The Lost Continent: Europe's Darkest Hour Since World War Two*[26] took a critical but more constructive line.

A surge of books setting out the case for staying in or leaving the EU appeared in the run-up to the referendum. Many of them supported Brexit, such as new editions of Bootle, Booker and North and Elliot and Atkinson's books already mentioned, while some were pro-EU such as the books by the passionate Europhile and EU expert Denis MacShane, who predicted a Leave vote because of the strength of the anti-EU Establishment, including most of the press, and the complacency of much of the pro-EU camp, including business which was inclined to stay neutral.[27] Other pro-EU books came from Michel Emerson of the Centre for European Policy Studies[28] and the former Prime Minister Gordon Brown.[29] Some non-partisan guides to Brexit were laudable attempts to present a balanced picture of the arguments for and against, but were probably less effective at explaining points of contention than fact-checking sites like BBC News "*Reality Check.*" For example, the Connell Guide intended for schools by Jane Lewis, *Stay or Go,*[30] so balanced the two sides of the argument that it might as well have enclosed a coin in a pouch at the back of the book for readers to toss in case of doubt.

After the Brexit vote, there was a flood of new books: books documenting the referendum campaign like those of Tim Shipman, Craig Oliver, and Arron Banks, seen in the previous chapter; books and articles explaining Brexit in political science terms like Clarke/Goodwin/Whiteley and Curtice, from a historical and sociological perspective like Fintan O'Toole (referred to above), or in terms of language such as Buckledee (see above); books rejoicing in the opportunities presented by Brexit and usually advocating a particular form of it like Halligan/Lyons,[31] Bootle's Brexit edition of *The Trouble With Europe*,[32] and the similarly revised edition of Elliott and Atkinson's *Europe Doesn't Work*, now called *Europe Didn't Work*[33]; books lamenting Brexit, wondering why it happened and worrying about the future, such as Ian Dunt,[34] Kenneth A. Armstrong[35] and Robert Peston[36]; those explaining particular problems of Brexit like Charter,[37] Connelly (the problems for Ireland),[38] and very expertly on the reinventing-the-wheel intricacies of Brexit, MacShane[39]; calls for a second referendum like Nick Clegg's[40] and, implicitly, MacShane; and finally, on the mistakes made in the negotiations, Ivan Rogers.[41]

The Brexit bookshelf be a-burstin'.

3.2.2   Film

After books, what about films? Films about the two world wars are still extraordinarily popular in Britain and they continue to be made in large numbers both in Britain and America. The world wars clearly hold a strong fascination in the British psyche. Why is this? Obviously, people enjoy stories about wars in which their ancestors ended up as victors rather than the opposite, and as liberators rather than oppressors who committed war crimes like the holocaust. For that reason, the genre could never be as popular in Germany. One must not forget also that films about the two world wars in Europe are action movies with identifiable heroes and villains. The action is exciting and fairly realistic, though not so much as to present modern warfare in all its gruesome horror, which would put the audience off. Films like *All Quiet on the Western Front* are rare. Normal war films do not set out primarily to confront historical questions about whether the war was justified or whether or not the wartime leaders and generals made mistakes. They seek to inspire and entertain with stories of loyalty, courage, stoicism, compassion and romance. These are laudable emotions.

Whilst they cannot be said to glorify war as such or to foment hatred, films about the world wars do reinforce stereotypes about our former enemies on the Continent as less humane, intelligent and trustworthy than us British, and about ourselves as a pragmatic, plucky, ingenious and resilient race who won through against heavy odds to overcome the enemy and liberate the occupied lands across the Channel which though our allies had been too weak to defend themselves. The sheer number of such films and television series that over the years have perpetuated these stereotypes are bound to have influenced British people's attitudes towards Europe. The influence is likely to be stronger among older people. The intense cultivation of remembrance of the First World War in Britain, on the basis of an oversimplified and discredited view of its history, reflects and fosters the same spirit—a spirit that continues to separate us from Europe rather than bringing us together, a feeling of "Them and Us."

However, newspapers have probably played a more active part in cultivating such attitudes than film because they are in daily contact with a large part of the population whereas films impact on us only occasionally.

3.2.3   *Newspapers*

The British press is highly partisan in its opinions of Europe and European integration. Table 3.1 shows the main English daily national newspapers, their print circulations in 2016, their political orientation and affiliation to party (if any), and their stance in the EU referendum. These newspapers are the ones mainly read in England and Wales. Scotland and Northern Ireland have their own influential local newspapers which are more widely read than English-based ones. The list is in order of print circulation. Online usage widens the readership considerably. *Metro* and the *London Evening Standard* are distributed free.

The Independent, which now has a small circulation only on line, supported Remain.

Many of the daily newspapers have Sunday editions with a similar circulation. The biggest are the *Sun on Sunday*, the *Mail on Sunday*, the *Sunday Times* and the *Sunday Mirror*. The *Sun on Sunday* and the *Sunday Times* supported Leave, as did the *Sunday Telegraph*, the *Sunday Express* and the *Star on Sunday*. The *Mail on Sunday*, though belonging to the same group as the *Daily Mail*, has a different editorial policy and supported Remain. The opposite is true of the *Sunday Times*, which backed Leave, like its stable companions the daily and Sunday *Sun* titles, but unlike its other fellow Murdoch-owned paper the daily *Times*. This shows that the support for Leave or Remain was a matter of choice of editorial policy rather than principle for many British newspaper groups, and most had adopted

Table 3.1 UK newspapers by print circulation, political orientation/party affiliation, and stance in EU referendum

Newspaper	Print circulation (millions of copies/day)	Right/left orientation and party affiliation (if any)	Stance in EU referendum
The Sun	1.7	Centre right/Conservative	Leave
Daily Mail	1.5	Centre right/Conservative	Leave
Metro	1.3	Centre	Neutral
London Evening Standard	0.9	Centre right	Remain
Daily Mirror	0.8	Centre left/Labour	Remain
Daily Telegraph	0.5	Centre right/Conservative	Leave
Daily Star	0.4	Centre right/no longer party-political affiliation	Leave
Daily Express	0.4	Centre-far right/Conservative/ UKIP	Leave
The Times	0.4	Centre	Remain
The 'i'	0.3	Centre left/Labour/ Liberal-Democrat	Remain
The Financial Times	0.2	Centre	Remain
The Guardian	0.2	Centre left/Labour/ Liberal-Democrat	Remain

Source: *Earth Newspapers.com.* 2016. UK newspaper circulation figures. 3 August; *HuffPost.* 2016. Which newspapers support Brexit in the EU referendum? 21 June

anti-EU positions years before and so continued to follow them in the referendum. The *Sunday Mirror*, like its sister daily, was for Remain, as was the *Observer*, the companion paper of *The Guardian*. The weekly magazines were more pro-Remain, with the liberal *The Economist* and *New Statesman* both canvassing to stay in the EU, but *The Spectator*, continuing its long-standing position against European integration which it had taken even in the first referendum of 1975, and advocating Leave.

The salient fact which emerges from this snapshot of the British press in 2016 is that, by circulation, the newspapers were around 60%–40% for Leave. On other measures, such as articles published, the imbalance was more even more skewed. The Oxford Reuters Institute of Journalism found from a sample of over 900 articles on Brexit that nearly twice as many articles supported Leave as Remain (45% against 27% with 22% undecided),[42] while a University of Loughborough study found the disproportion as high as 82%–18%.[43] This suggests that as well as being at a numerical disadvantage with regard to the size of the footprint of the pro-EU press, the Remain side lost the battle in terms of the intensity of their engagement with the public through "their" newspapers. Whether this was through a lack of effort, or the complacency and passivity of a part of the Remain camp such as business, is unclear.[44] But the apparently less dynamic press campaign of the Remain side compared with Leave follows the pattern in the field, where at least according to the news bulletins in the media it often seemed to come off second best.

While the newspapers' print circulations are rapidly declining (from over 9 million in 2010 to just over 6 million in 2016), their online readership is steadily increasing and magnifies the overall impact on public opinion of the major press groups like the *Mail, Sun* and *Telegraph*. In total, 68% of the audience consuming news online said they accessed *MailOnline/Daily Mail*, and 64% *Sun Online*; *BBC* sites were accessed by 86%.[45] The relative weights of the newspaper groups in terms of their combined print and digital readership are roughly in proportion to their print circulations, though the *Guardian/Observer* group stands out with a disproportionately large online presence.[46]

Consumers now obtain a large proportion of their news from television, radio, and a wide variety of online sources including, besides newspaper sites and apps, broadcaster websites/apps, social media sites, and search engines. In 2016, only 29% of people said they consumed news through printed newspapers, and online consumption of newspapers through websites and apps, while it has increased enormously, is only about 15% of the total.[47] Nevertheless, this more varied picture of news consumption does not necessarily equate with a steep decline in the influence wielded by newspapers on public opinion, because newspapers still largely set the news agenda, on television and radio and on the internet. This is clearly on view in the BBC current affairs programmes like *Today* and the *Andrew Marr Show*, where press reviews in which presenters read out bulletins of the main newspaper headlines and stories without comment or panels of other journalists discuss them are a staple part of their content.[48] I return to the issue of social media below.

The influence of anti-EU newspapers on the referendum raises the chicken-and-egg question: did the newspapers foment or stimulate their readers' negative views about the EU or rather were they just reflecting them? The newspapers obviously prefer the latter interpretation. Two considerations help in answering this question: the nature of the information being disseminated and the reactions it was calculated to produce, and the duration of the exposure of readers to anti-EU stories by these newspapers. With regard to the first, while the newspapers took their cue from readers at an emotional level by appealing to the feelings of national pride, independence, and distrust of outsiders described earlier—so propaganda had fertile ground to fall on—the information they reported about the EU did not come from their readers; it was the newspapers that reported the information and in so doing could interpret and distort it as they wished without much fear of contradiction from their readers, who were mostly "on the same page" as far as Europe was concerned. The reporting of the Eurosceptic press was at best only biased, at its worst it was deliberate misinformation.

As for the time scale, the argument that the newspapers only reflected the opinions of their readers and did not help form those opinions might hold water if they only adopted a stance on Britain's membership of the EU in the run-up to the referendum, and before that had reported about the EU in an objective and balanced manner. But the fact is that the same newspapers had proselytized against the EU—in the words of Germaine Greer, "couldn't run a single good story about the EU"[49]—for the previous 20 years before the referendum. It is pretty improbable that that the press did not help to form British public opinion against Europe but only reflected it. The discussion of the press is continued in Sect. 3.3 below.

3.2.4   Broadcasting

Broadcasters in the UK are bound to observe due impartiality and due accuracy in their news and political programming.[50] Overall, they broadly succeeded in doing so in relation to the EU referendum, which was fought out at a hectic pace and in a febrile and increasingly acrimonious atmosphere. The main TV channels in the UK are BBC, ITV and Sky, and BBC radio channels dominate the radio market along with a number of influential private stations like *LBC*. They provided extensive coverage of the debate and managed to observe a broad balance between the two sides of the argument. In this respect, TV and radio were in stark contrast to the more partisan newspapers.

A valid criticism of the BBC's output was that it paid insufficient attention to the precept of *due* impartiality, in that it tended to allot equal amounts of time to the two sides on every issue, regardless of the strength of their arguments. *Ofcom*'s guidance suggests that rigorous division of airtime and ensuring every statement is met by a counterclaim is not necessary to maintain an appropriate balance.[51] But this appeared to be BBC's policy during the referendum, no doubt in order to answer the habitual charges of pro-EU bias from the Brexit-supporting right wing of the Conservative party, at a time when the then Culture Secretary John Whittingdale was threatening restrictions on its future freedom of action.[52] Discussions on BBC Radio 4's flagship *Today* programme, for example, tended to end up leaving no one any the wiser after a succession of tit-for-tat statements and rejoinders had cancelled one another out.[53] Patently false statements went unchallenged, whether to avoid the presenters having to depart from their scripted list of questions, because they were unsure of their ground, or in order once again to maintain an unassailable defence of impartiality.

TV and radio current affairs programmes also feature regular recitals of the headlines and main news items from the newspapers and news websites. On BBC's *Today*, they are read out in a reverent tone without the slightest hint of criticism, somewhat defeating the object of balance as the newspapers are predominantly anti-EU. Although the newspapers have no inhibitions about attacking the BBC, all hell would break loose if the BBC dared to directly criticize a Conservative newspaper. There would be a dangerous backlash, not only from the target of the criticism but from MPs in Parliament, potentially leading to restrictions on the BBC's independence. The BBC is treading a tightrope in its relations with the press.

The *BBC News* website, and especially its excellent "Reality Check" series, made up for some of the imperfections of its broadcasting output during the referendum campaign due to the constraints of impartiality. Yet that did not stop members of the public feeling hopelessly confused at the torrent of claims and counterclaims and the absence of answers to fairly simple questions. The excellent TV debates put on by all the TV channels and panel discussions like BBC 1's *Question Time* were enthralling to watch, but with their carefully selected audiences and panellists were hardly likely to lift the fog surrounding the EU question for the average undecided voter.

Nevertheless, I agree with Timothy Garton Ash that the BBC is one of the finest news organizations in the world.[54] The BBC and the other broadcasters are a bulwark of democracy, hold the government to account through their investigative journalism and consumer programmes, and act as powerful educators, roles unfortunately not achieved to the same extent by a major segment of the press because of its tendency to pursue political objectives instead of journalistic objectivity.

Part of the reason for the BBC's success must be the breadth of talent it attracts, many of course from the same somewhat privileged backgrounds as the journalists of right-wing newspapers, but often of different political persuasions, and many also from humbler backgrounds. I wonder whether the British right-wing press might have become so partisan and conservative if it had varied its recruitment beyond people of the same background and political persuasions as their editors, and had encouraged dissent and not conformity.

3.2.5   Social Media

In 2016, 20% of British adults who went online for their news used social media and nearly half of these mostly got their news this way. The second most popular news source after the BBC website or app was Facebook.[55] In the referendum campaign, Leave had the more effective social media operation, especially towards the end of the campaign when it allegedly managed to persuade many people who had never bothered to vote before to go the polls through skilfully targeted advertising using data obtained from social media. The main Leave campaign organization Vote Leave paid the digital advertising company Aggregate IQ £2.7 million for online advertising, much of it on Facebook.

Since the referendum and the findings of breaches of spending limits during it, some of them apparently involving use of social media, there have been calls for changes in the law to ensure greater transparency of online political campaigning. The House of Commons Digital, Culture, Media and Sport Committee reported on the matter in February 2019. Its Chairman, Damian Collins, said when presenting the report:

> Democracy is at risk from the malicious and relentless targeting of citizens with disinformation and personalized 'dark adverts' from unidentifiable sources, delivered through the major social media platforms we use every day. Much of this is directed from agencies working in foreign countries, including Russia.

The report concluded that "current electoral law is not fit for purpose. It has failed to reflect a move away from billboards and leaflets to online micro-targeted campaigning." It called for "absolute transparency of political campaigning, with clear banners on all paid-for political advertisements and videos, identifying the source and the advertiser. It would be backed by a legal definition of digital campaigning and online political advertising."

There also needs to be an acknowledgement of the role and power of unpaid campaigns and Facebook Groups that influence elections and referendums (both inside and outside the designated period).[56]

On *Today* of 28 July 2018, Tom Baldwin, the author of *Ctrl Alt Delete. How Politics and the Media Crashed our Democracy,* argued that in the light of the House of Commons report, adverts that target fake news and highly partisan political opinions at subjects identified as susceptible to such messages should be banned as they are impossible to regulate effectively.

It is difficult to evaluate the impact of social media and automated and targeted political advertising from social media platforms during the referendum. What is clear, however, is that abuses of these media occurred in the referendum campaign and that many of the targeted advertisements sent were found to contain misinformation and lies. As newspaper readership declines, the potential for using digital media to subvert democracy through hidden political advertising that skews elections is a dangerous development. A recent example was fake news about the Lisbon Treaty which went viral and seemed to be part of an orchestrated campaign to keep less educated Brexit voters on message.[57]

3.3   THE EUROSCEPTIC BRITISH PRESS—SOCIOPOLITICAL BACKGROUND

The strength of anti-EU sentiment in Britain prior to the referendum was surprising to many European observers when they compared it with attitudes towards the EU in their own country. The London correspondent of one the main Finnish newspapers, *Helsingin Sanomat*, Annamari Sipilä, wrote in late 2015 that people in Britain had an emotional reaction to the EU. She quoted John Curtice of Strathclyde University and Simon Hix of the London School of Economics who said there was a "them and us" attitude towards the EU: the EU was the villain—especially after the BSE crisis, when the Europeans had banned British beef imports—and the UK was the victim. British people knew little about the EU and were not interested in finding out. Successive governments, even Tony Blair's, had shied away from trying to enlighten public opinion about it because any such efforts would provoke a backlash. The predominantly anti-EU newspapers had fomented Eurosceptic attitudes.[58] The previous year Ms Sipilä had already thought Britain could be a lost cause as far as the EU was concerned, given the hostile climate.[59] The newspapers' level of hostility to the EU was even greater than that among the general public as seen in the periodical *Eurobarometer* surveys, where the level of Euroscepticism in Britain was always an outlier anyway.[60]

The degree of anti-EU sentiment being propagated by Eurosceptic newspapers would also probably come as a surprise to many British readers of the more pro-EU papers. Their only contact with the Eurosceptic papers will be press reviews on television and radio and occasional glances at other websites. The rest of the time they will stick to their familiar *Financial Times, Times,* or *Guardian.* It would be an eye-opener for them to swap their usual paper for the *Daily Telegraph* or *Mail,* or even the *Sun* or *Express,* for a time.

Why are the biggest UK newspapers Eurosceptic? The answer lies in the backgrounds of their proprietors, editors and leading journalists. While the proprietors of the *Telegraph,* the billionaire Barclay Brothers, are the only one of the four owners to impose an anti-EU editorial policy on their papers, and the owners of the other three main Eurosceptic papers leave the editorial policy to their editors, the proprietors' backgrounds as owners of large media interests will make them gravitate closer to the right of the political spectrum, which in the UK equates with being against European integration. Lord Rothermere, the *Mail* proprietor, allowed the editors of the *Daily Mail* and *Mail on Sunday* to take different sides on Brexit. With Rupert Murdoch, the owner of the *Times* and *Sun* titles, the picture was more complicated with only the *Times* daily paper supporting Remain but the *Sunday Times* along with *The Sun* and the *Sun on Sunday* being for Leave. Murdoch's other media interests like *Fox News* in the US show the predominantly rightwards slant of his media offerings. The *Express* titles have been right-wing nationalist, anti-German and anti-EU in outlook since time immemorial through numerous changes of proprietor, latterly Richard Desmond who owned the paper from 2000 to 2018.

As for the editors and leading journalists, even those writing for the mass-market *Mail, Sun* and *Express* can certainly not be considered to come from, or represent, the working class. Most are as much part of the British Establishment as MPs on the right wing of the Conservative Party, most, though not all, have been to the same schools, move in the same circles, and live in the same areas of the country, London and the South East.[61] The *Sun* and *Mail* nevertheless like to be seen to be opposing the Establishment and siding with the "outsiders," the "people," their readers.[62] Many flit seamlessly between journalism and public office such as Andy Coulson, who after editing the Murdoch paper *News of the World* became David Cameron's Communications Director.

Alistair Campbell was interviewed by Julia Hartley-Brewer on talkRADIO on 24 October 2017 and she objected to him repeatedly referring to Brexit campaigners as "your kind of people," as if they were part of an identifiable social group and not "from the people."[63] But actually he was quite right. They are as similar to one another and different from the man or woman on the street of Britain who voted Leave as Charles Moore of the *Telegraph* and Boris Johnson are.

The *Telegraph* and *Mail* were not always Eurosceptic. They gradually became so from the early 1990s in the middle of the dispute in the Conservative party about the rapid steps towards further European integration being planned in the Maastricht Treaty. In the early 1990s, the *Daily Telegraph*'s Brussels correspondents were still reporting news neutrally and its editorials were moderate in their criticism of EU developments. The end of the 1980s was when Boris Johnson became the paper's Brussels correspondent and began writing a weekly satirical column, making playful fun of happenings on the EU scene, its eccentric personages and the floods of rather crazy regulations emerging from it, the latter recounted with a certain amount of poetic licence as to the facts. Johnson's satire undoubtedly helped turn any more open-minded readers off the EU.

From the middle of the 1990s onwards, the *Telegraph*'s coverage of the EU became predominantly negative. This coincided with the purchase of the newspaper by the Canadian businessman Conrad Black in 1996. While the *Telegraph* positions itself close to the mainstream Conservative Party on many issues, on the EU it has aligned itself firmly with the right wing of the party. It threw itself wholeheartedly into the referendum campaign on the side of Brexit. So attached is it to this cause that even reports of economic developments are slanted towards Brexit, as is the selection of readers' letters. The economic policy of the paper is right-wing Conservative, supporting free trade and opposing regulation and "red tape", for example on health and safety and renewable energy. Its reporting of European political developments shows a strong anti-EU bias.[64] Its stance on social issues inclines to the libertarian, advocating restrictions on social benefits, strong law and order policies, and policies favouring the upper middle class, which are of course its readership. The sheer quantity of the paper's Brexit coverage, which is of high quality and 90% pro-Leave, is overpowering.

The *Daily Mail* has maintained a consistently critical stance on Britain's involvement in the EU ever since Paul Dacre became editor of the paper in 1992. He started off his editorship by opposing the plans to take Britain into the Exchange Rate Mechanism (ERM). The ERM pegged European Community member country currencies to maximum spreads as a prelude to introduction of the euro. Britain's membership of the ERM was short-lived as speculation against sterling forced it to drop out of the system six months after joining in November 1992. With his forceful reporting and opinion pieces which tended towards extremely conservative and often sensationalized positions on issues like immigration, and by employing star columnists whom he succeeded in attracting to the paper, Dacre built the *Mail* into the biggest selling daily with a circulation of 2.4 million at its height in 2004. Together with the *Sun*, the *Mail* exerted considerable political influence. Dennis MacShane, Europe Minister in the Blair government, writes that he once tried to encourage Tony Blair to be more vocal in his support for the EU, but Blair said he could not afford to as it would antagonize the *Daily Mail*.[65] Blair was not the only prime minister to be afraid of the *Mail*. In February 2016, David Cameron, desperate to get the *Mail* to tone down its opposition to the UK's remaining in the EU, reportedly met Dacre to try to persuade him. When Dacre refused, Cameron reportedly tried to get the paper's owner Lord Rothermere to sack him.[66] On BBC Radio 4's *PM* programme of 7 June 2018, the former editor of the *Sun* between 1998 and 2003, David Yelland, said he was convinced that without Dacre there would not have been Brexit. The paper pushed voters over the edge on Brexit. Dacre would say it was the people, but in reality it was the *Mail*.

The *Mail* has been widely criticized for its brash and aggressive treatment of issues the editor feels strongly about, its vicious persecution of opponents or critics, and its frequent disregard for facts. Dacre always claimed the *Mail* was the defender of the man in the street against the Establishment, but while it is true that the *Mail* has never been in the thrall of any government, the editor's own and his staff's backgrounds and links to conservative circles especially on the right of the Conservative party show that, in fact, it is a mouthpiece of a significant right-wing part of the conservative Establishment, just as the *Telegraph* is.

The *Daily Express*, though it supported staying in the European Community in the 1975 referendum, has maintained its opposition to Britain's involvement in Europe ever since. There have been no periods in its history when, unlike the *Mail* or the *Sun*, it has been even mildly supportive of European cooperation. It did, however, once, in the 2001 election, come out in support of Labour, at the same time calling for a referendum on the euro. In 2011 it started a "Campaign for Freedom" to get Britain out of the EU with a petition that collected 800,000 signatures, and in 2013 started a "crusade" against Romanian and Bulgarian migrants coming to Britain, which was widely criticized as xenophobic. In the run-up to the 2016 referendum, the campaign against the EU was also called a "crusade" with a logo suggesting the Christian crusades to the Holy Lands and portraying withdrawal from the EU as a divine mission of salvation.

The *Express* has long been closely aligned with the right wing of the Conservative Party. In the 2015 election it endorsed UKIP, before reverting to the Tories in 2017. The paper, including its Sunday edition the *Sunday Express*, has frequently attracted criticism for its sensational reporting of royalty, its support for conspiracy theories about the death of Princess Diana, and far-fetched allegations about unsolved crimes such as the disappearance of the little girl Madeleine McCann in Portugal in 2007. These have caused it to incur substantial libel damages. In 2000, the *Express* group was acquired by Richard Desmond who was also a publisher of soft porn magazines, leading some of its best-known journalists like Peter Hitchens to leave for other newspapers.

The *Sun* was acquired by Rupert Murdoch in 1969 and reached the peak of its popularity in the late 1980s, but its circulation suffered from the repeated controversies in which it was embroiled, notably its unfair blaming of Liverpool football supporters for the Hillsborough disaster, which led to its being boycotted by newsagents and readers in the city. The paper has switched support between the Conservative and Labour parties at general elections and at the height of its influence even claimed to have swung an election in Labour's favour. However, it has always been against the EU, citing needless regulation, excessive concern for human rights, or decisions going against Britain in the European Court of Justice or Council of Ministers. Its support for Brexit in the 2016 referendum was the culmination of almost 40 years of anti-EU agitation. In its endorsement of Leave, the paper wrote that it had "campaigned relentlessly against the ever-expanding superstate."[67] In the 1980s and 1990s, there was an anti-French and anti-German element in its headlines and articles. Roy Greenslade, a former assistant editor of *The Sun* and now of *The Guardian*, thinks that *Sun* readers did not need much encouragement to be against the EU. Its various anti-EU campaigns were received enthusiastically by the readership.

Where the *Sun* excels is in its pithy and terse style. In this, it is similar to the best traditions of popular journalism on the continent, as in the German *Bild-Zeitung*. It is also a champion of punchy headlines, often built around puns and stretching the bounds of good taste. Among the most famous were the scandalous "Gotcha!," about the sinking of the Argentinian battleship General Belgrano with heavy loss of life in the Falklands War, or the rather rude "Up Yours Delors," telling the Commission President what the paper thought of his plans for the euro in 1990. The same headline was reprised in 2017, when there were rumours that the Spanish might question the sovereignty of Gibraltar post Brexit, as "Up Yours Senors."

It is a pity the *Sun* with its maverick and independent spirit could not have shown a more positive approach to Europe like its stable companion *The Times*, also owned by News Corporation, or the *Daily Mirror*, which serves a similar readership to the *Sun*. It can only be assumed this was more for tactical (e.g. circulation) than ideological reasons as with the *Telegraph*, *Mail* and *Express*. Especially with the latter two papers, Euroscepticism seems to be in the DNA of their editors and journalists, rooted in a deep conservativism if not nationalism.

The Brexit-supporting newspapers have maintained their anti-EU stance since the referendum. Indeed, the negotiations have given them an opportunity to step up their attacks on the EU, now that it is unambiguously on the other side and defending its own interests, whereas during the referendum campaign EU leaders tried to stay out of the argument to avoid being accused of interference. Talk of plots and intransigence on the part of the EU and personal insults directed at EU leaders have escalated.[68]

3.4   Is the British Press Really More Eurosceptic Than That of Continental Countries?

Even a cursory glance at the newspapers of other EU countries shows the answer to the above question to be a decided "Yes." With a few exceptions such as Hungary where the press is controlled by the government, no European country has a press that is so overwhelmingly critical of if not hostile to the European Union as Britain—or, more precisely, England, as this applies to the London-based national press, not to the local papers in Scotland and Northern Ireland, which are more balanced.

In no other country is the majority of the press (by circulation) consistently and solidly Eurosceptic. In other countries, the overwhelming majority of the press supports the EU, though all newspapers will occasionally criticize it and there may be individual newspapers that regularly take an anti-EU line, albeit rarely so virulently as their British counterparts.

Could not the reason for the difference be that the British press is freer and better? Does the Eurosceptic British press tell the truth about the EU whereas that of Continental countries is cowed by political or business interests to toe a pro-EU line?

I do not think that this either can be seriously argued in relation to the press of any country in western Europe. They all have a press that is at least as free from interference or pressure as Britain's. This is as true of the smaller countries like Finland or Belgium as it is of the big ones like Germany and Italy.

Continental European journalists, who follow the British newspapers closely of course, are conscious of the anti-EU stance of the majority of their counterparts in Britain and not a little puzzled by it. Paavo Rautio of *Helsingin Sanomat* is aghast at the fall in journalistic standards that condones caricature, distortion and exaggeration as acceptable reporting where the EU is concerned and traces the practice back to Boris Johnson's missives as the *Telegraph*'s Brussels correspondent.[69] During the referendum campaign, Annamari Sipilä, the paper's London correspondent, mentioned earlier, noted how biased against the EU the British press was and that this was not a recent phenomenon but the British newspapers had been gloating over the troubles of the EU and ignoring its benefits for years.[70] The Belgian press, especially that of the Dutch-language community, which feels very close to the British, is so used to the British habit of never missing an opportunity of turning a story, even a football match, against the EU they just laugh it off with a patient shrug of the shoulders at the incorrigible quirkiness of their British brethren.[71] The German newspapers, too, have reached the stage of accepting the depth of Euroscepticism among their British counterparts as an inexplicable but inalterable fact. On the *Today* programme of 26 November 2018, the London correspondent of *Die Welt*, Stephanie Bolzen, said her paper had run a feature on Brexit called "Madhouse on the Thames" in which she had tried to explain to German readers why on earth Britain was risking the immediate future of the country, "*just to leave the EU.*"

The EU Commission President Jean-Claude Juncker has often said it is obvious that a steady diet of anti-EU propaganda, by the press and politicians, is bound to have consequences at the ballot box when people vote on European issues. In the same *Today* programme of 26 November 2018, asked by Katja Adler if he did not think the EU was partly to blame for the difficulties of negotiating Brexit, he said: "If you are telling people year after year, month after month, day after day, that membership of the European Union is a bad thing for British citizens, then I don't think the European Union is guilty for (*sic*) the result. It's the responsibility of Britain, only of Britain, of nobody else."[72] To Continental Europeans like Juncker, this is obvious because they are used to relatively balanced reporting of EU matters. To many British whose only experience is of an anti-EU press which to them is normal, Juncker's claim is itself incomprehensible.[73]

If political interference in Continental countries is not the explanation why there is much less Euroscepticism in their press, what is? I think the main reason is that the British Eurosceptic newspapers, the *Telegraph*, *Mail*, *Express* and *Sun*, have remained, through all the vicissitudes of changes of government, ownership and editors, conservative and nationalist in their outlook, and have retained a close affiliation to the right wing of the Conservative Party which has long been opposed to the close involvement of Britain in the European Union. These newspapers have recruited journalists with the same conservative values. Unlike broadcasters, particularly the BBC, they have not spread their net to recruit from a wider background of opinion and political persuasion, leading to a strict, consistent but unbalanced conservative editorial policy that, on Europe, is predominantly negative and adversarial.

I would also maintain that despite the high educational standards and journalistic capacity of many of the staff of the Eurosceptic press, ignorance about the EU is a factor. If editors set no store by accuracy in reporting about EU affairs because of the basic line that any bad news about Europe is good news, why should journalists bother to be accurate, let alone fair? It is obvious that many of the Brexit-press journalists stopped learning about Europe in the 1990s. They trot out daily the hoary myths of unelected bureaucrats, Brussels "diktats," financial mismanagement, "gravy trains," corruption, and undemocratic systems, as they have been doing for 20 years. As there is no one to hold them to account, there is no need for fact-checking or research, and in time, the journalists anyway come to believe their own propaganda and cease to be real, open-minded journalists where the EU is concerned.

The language barrier isolates the British Eurosceptic press as well. Without being on the spot in Europe, without access to newspapers and media from Europe because they do not understand the language, much of what is going on in Europe will escape the notice of journalists supposed to be reporting on the EU, just as it does British politicians and the general public. The opposite is true for continental media, journalists and politicians: they are intimately aware of events and opinion in Britain. There is no language barrier because they can all read English.

If the situation were different and British people could still read European newspapers, they would be surprised at the high standards of journalism still to be found there, in which reporting facts is kept separate from expressing political opinion and national newspapers do not see their main purpose as the pursuit of ideological campaigns to which journalistic standards of truth and fairness must be sacrificed. A few examples of how the press of continental countries report on EU affairs might open a few eyes.

A final thought before we take a look at the European press scene: if it was just the truth the British newspapers were after with their visceral anti-EU coverage, why does that "truth" suddenly appear much less threatening when the paper's editor changes? Consider the slight moderation in tone towards the EU in the *Daily Mail* since Paul Dacre retired and Geordie Greig, a comparative Europhile, took his place. The truth is that the "truth" for Brexit papers is what the editor says it is.[74]

3.4.1   Germany

The doyen of the vibrant newspaper landscape in Germany is the *Frankfurter Allgemeine Zeitung*, or simply the *Frankfurter Allgemeine* or "*FAZ*" ("Frankfurt General [Newspaper]"). It is a serious newspaper similar in style and status consciousness to how the British *Times* used to be before changing to tabloid format. It is a true old-fashioned "heavyweight," a newspaper that prides itself on the quality of its reporting and opinion columns, which are highly influential. It is stolidly centrist in its editorial policy and a staunch supporter of the EU and European integration.

In that respect, the "FAZ" is no different from the other main national dailies in Germany, the *Süddeutsche Zeitung* ("South-German Newspaper") based in Munich, the Hamburg-based *Die Welt* ("The World"), and the tabloid *Bild-Zeitung* (or simply *Bild*—"Picture [Newspaper]"). All German papers share a basically pro-EU stance and they report EU affairs in depth and accurately, though sometimes critically, but then also constructively without the wholesale denigration of all things EU that is typical of the British Eurosceptic press.

None of the newspapers, even *Bild*, has moved much to the right to reflect the rise of the anti-immigration Alternative für Deutschland (AfD) party. On 9 April 2019, for example, *Die Welt* reported on the meeting of fellow populist parties convened by the leader of the Italian "League" party, Matteo Salvini, which was notable for the absence of representatives of the populist parties in France, Hungary and Austria and showed they were having difficulty finding common cause in fighting the European Parliament elections.[75] The paper also featured interviews with a political historian on populist movements and with Frans Timmermans, the Dutch Vice-President of the European Commission who was the socialist candidate for President after Juncker. *Bild* is notable for its extremely pithy style of reporting—comparable in that respect to the English *Sun*—and its small number of pages, bucking the trend to ever greater length.

3.4.2   France

France's "FAZ" is *Le Monde*, which occupies the centre-left ground of a press representing a wider spectrum of political opinion, particularly on the hard left, than in Germany. Extended articles in *Le Monde* of 5 September 2018 about poverty in France and carbon taxation were typical of the thoroughly researched journalism of this French broadsheet. *Le Figaro* and *Libération* represent the right and left wings in the press landscape. *Le Figaro* is a serious and responsible source of news and opinion which gives space to more right-wing views on immigration, for instance, but does not hold entrenched positions on such issues. In the edition of 8 September 2018, it reported at length, but neutrally, on immigration in Sweden on the eve of the elections at which the anti-immigration Swedish Democrats party were expected to do well, and published an opinion piece by a French academic on immigration and rising crime figures. The newspaper also contained neutral reports on the aspirations of Mme Le Pen's *Rassemblement national* ("National Rally," formerly "National Front") party, and the left-wing populists led by Jean-Luc Mélenchon, for the

European Parliament election in May 2019. Mme Le Pen was aiming to make the RN the biggest French party, just as UKIP was in the 2014 European Parliament election in Britain. *Le Figaro* also reported in a similar neutral and factual vein on the meeting between President Macron and Angela Merkel in Marseilles to prepare the discussion of migration at an informal EU summit in Salzburg.

All French newspapers are basically supportive of the EU and European cooperation, though on individual issues they can be more critical than the German press, even to be the point of blaming "Bruxelles" or "la Commission de Bruxelles" for wrongs or rigidities in the French economy.[76] The newspapers were taking a somewhat harsher line on immigration with the increased strength of Mme Le Pen's RN party, but were not endorsing her stance against the euro or against the EU as such, nor the similar anti-EU policies of Jean-Luc Mélenchon's far-left LFI ("La France Insoumise"—"France Unbowed") party.

3.4.3   Italy

Italy has a relatively small press sector compared with Britain and the other countries mentioned in this survey. Instead, television news is highly influential, though there has been a significant shift towards social media for news consumption over the last few years, as is the case in other countries. There are a huge number of televised political debates in Italy. It is a country that is obsessed with politics.

Newspaper sales have collapsed in Italy like everywhere else. While the big regional dailies like *Corriere della Sera, La Repubblica*, and *La Stampa* have tended to draw a readership from among the educated elite, local dailies like *Il Messaggero* in Rome or *Il Mattino* in Naples used to be read by everyone. There is also a niche market for newspapers that are close to political parties or public figures, such as *Il Fatto Quotidiano, Il Secolo d'Italia*, and *Il Giornale*.

The most widely read newspaper is now *Corriere della Sera*, published in Milan, followed by *La Repubblica*, printed in Rome, *La Stampa*, published in Turin, and *Il Sole 24 Ore*, a mainly business paper, the Italian equivalent of the *Financial Times*, published in Milan by the Italian *Confindustria* employers' confederation. The bigger papers are all privately and locally owned, with links to major industrial groups. They are densely printed with scarcely any advertising. *Corriere della Sera* traditionally takes a centrist political position, while *La Repubblica* is more left wing.

The political situation of Italy with a government composed of a coalition of parties without previous experience and with differing political programmes made good journalism difficult for two newspapers traditionally occupying the political centre ground. Nevertheless, they appeared in early 2019 to be coping with this unusual situation well and reporting on the tumultuous Trump-like developments with professional *aplomb* and calm, remaining factual and non-partisan. The *Corriere* of 30 March and 9 April 2019 reported on the arrival of a migrant boat in the port of Lampedusa after another stand-off with the *Lega* party leader (and Interior Minister) Matteo Salvini, and went on to detail Mr Salvini's defence before Parliament against charges of "hostage-taking" in the same context. It also had articles on the closure of orphanages in Bulgaria under an EU-funded programme, on a memorandum Italy was to sign with the Chinese premier on the "Belt and Road" Initiative, in which Italy was going to be the first European country to commit itself to participating, and on the discussions of flat-rate tax proposals made by the coalition government. Opinion pieces and comment were kept separate from news items. One opinion column advocated a more liberal policy on immigration than the xenophobic, "keep-them-out" approach of the government, another that the Fidesz party of Prime Minister Orbán of Hungary, who is pursuing a policy of "illiberal democracy," be excluded from the European People's Party grouping in the European Parliament.

La Repubblica of 27 February 2019 led on an ultimatum issued by Matteo Salvini to hold a referendum on the Turin-Lyon high-speed railway line (which involves a 57-km tunnel under the Alps) in 2020, should the tendering still be held up, and on the heated negotiations on this project between the government and the treasury. It also had a neutral report about the latest developments in Mrs May's struggle to get the British Parliament to approve her withdrawal agreement with the EU.

The Italian newspapers convey an aura of studied calm and measured deliberation on the basis of facts, logic and experience, quite the reverse of the stereotype of emotional confrontation that would occur to most British people when thinking about Italian politics. Though political debate is very heated in Italy, which contributes to the stereotype, newspapers stay above the fray and avoid fomenting hysteria and spreading borderline fake news, as is unfortunately the case in the UK.

It was clear from the reports that the EU is part of the furniture in Italy, not an unwelcome intruder. Would this were the case in Britain! Italians are pragmatic and resilient and though there is some anti-EU sentiment, even the Italian hard-right (which, on paper, is much more extreme than Britain's) is not as ideologically opposed to the EU as the right of the Conservative party. There is resentment over the euro and some anti-Brussels rhetoric, but it pretty much ends there.

3.4.4   Belgium

Le Soir, *La Libre Belgique*, and *La Dernière Heure* are the three biggest-selling French-language papers in Belgium. They all take a centrist line on national politics and are solidly pro-EU. This is not only because of the benefits they receive from the presence of the main European institutions in Brussels; it stems from a long-standing attachment to European coop-eration as an antidote to the chaos experienced on their soil during the world wars. As a founder member of the European Community, Belgium like Germany is steadfastly committed to European integration. Both poli-tics and newspapers take European cooperation for granted and are per-plexed by the different climate of opinion in Britain and its wish to cut itself off from its Continental neighbours.

Belgium's small size, multilingual status with three official languages (French, Dutch and German), and its close links to and interdependence with its European neighbours lead newspapers to cover Continental European affairs more closely than British newspapers with the exception of the *Financial Times*. For example, the 5 September 2018 edition of *Le Soir* carried stories about France and Germany as well as local politics. In France it reported on a government reshuffle by President Macron follow-ing resignations and his decision to press ahead with a reform of income tax collection (a move to withholding tax principles) from the beginning of 2019. It also published a profile of the leader of the extreme left party *Die Linke* in the German Parliament, Sahra Wagenknecht, and her founda-tion of a new popular left-wing movement *Aufstehen* (Rise Up) to counter the far-right anti-immigration party *Alternative für Deutschland* (Alternative for Germany). The reports—by the newspaper's foreign correspondents in Paris and Berlin—were factual and neutral, without the typical intermingling of fact and (invariably negative) comment found in British newspapers reporting European affairs.

The same day's *Le Soir* contained a feature on inflation since the intro-duction of the euro and whether the single currency had caused inflation to be higher than would otherwise have been the case. According to Eurostat figures, inflation in Belgium between 2000 and 2017 had amounted to 38.8%, which was less than other Eurozone countries for some categories of goods and more for others. Relying on the opinion of Belgian economists, the article concluded that based on inflation trends in the preceding period, the introduction of the euro had probably not affected the level of inflation and that claims to the contrary on social media were not borne out by the facts. Only the *Financial Times* among British newspapers reported the Eurostat inflation figures. Brexit papers would no doubt have seized the opportunity to criticize the euro and press home their usual message of what a lucky escape Britain has had in not joining the single currency if the British inflation figures had been lower than the Belgian ones over the period since introduction of the euro. But this was not so: in fact, the British figures had been considerably higher!

In a similar vein, *La Libre Belgique* of 3 September 2018 contained a solid piece on the 2008–09 financial crisis and the progress made since then in the EU and nationally to make banks safer from collapse and to improve the protection of their customers. For this story the paper based itself on an interview with the president of the Belgian banking and insurance supervisory authority at the time. The paper also showed its more liberal colours with an article about the town of Farciennes, a depressed former coalmining area that used to be a byword for high unemployment, drug abuse and anti-social behaviour but is gradually pulling itself up by its bootstraps with investment, education and cultural initiatives pushed by a dynamic young socialist mayor who is also a member of the European Parliament. *La Libre* showed itself sympathetic to the town in its battle against being a butt of jokes and notes that the town, 19 of the 21 seats on whose council are occupied by Socialist Party members, has taken a quite different route to the French town of Beaucaire with which it has a twinning arrangement. Beaucaire is one of the towns in depressed old industrial areas of France that has elected a National Front mayor. Farciennes has for the time being frozen its twinning arrangements with Beaucaire, the paper said.

The neutral stance taken by Belgian newspapers in their reporting of the EU is exemplified in a story in the third main French-language paper *La Dernière Heure* of 3 September 2018. The Irish band U2 was using a concert tour to push a strong pro-immigrant and pro-EU message. In Berlin a huge EU flag had been projected above the stage, the introduction had featured speech at the end of the Charlie Chaplin film *The Dictator*, and videos of migrant boats were shown during some songs. The paper reported that in a Germany divided on the issue of immigration, as shown by recent demonstrations in Chemnitz, the message was not appreciated by all the audience. The appearance of the flag was greeted with catcalls and whistles and the pro-immigrant line Bono had taken in press interviews had been criticized on social media. As the tour continued, the paper expected a similar controversy at other German venues, not to speak of those in Italy and "Brexit Britain." The report remained factual and non-polemical, leaving readers to make up their own minds, save to remark that U2 had certainly not made its tour easier by nailing its colours to the EU mast.

The three main Dutch-language newspapers are *Het Laatste Nieuws* ("The Latest News"), *De Standard*, and *De Morgen* ("Morning"). The edition of *Het Laatste Nieuws* on 3 September 2018 had a report on the visit of the Dutch anti-immigrant party leader Geert Wilders to Antwerp to support Filip Dewinter of his sister right-wing Vlaams Belang ("Flemish Interest") party in the forthcoming local elections. Vlaams Belang was fighting to retain control of the city and even had a Dutch national as a candidate, to attract the many Dutch people living in Antwerp who can vote in the elections. The paper quoted parts of Wilders' speech criticizing Islam as tyrannical and intolerant and European leaders as never putting their own people first, but favouring elites and opportunists. It then reported Dewinter speaking in a similar incendiary vein with the slogan "Antwerp needs to be the southernmost town of the Netherlands, not the most northerly outpost of Islam."

On 28 June 2018, the day of the final first-round match in the 2018 World Cup between England and Belgium, *De Morgen* featured a light-hearted piece about the match by their sports columnist Hans Vandeweghe entitled "Brexit Game." The article pokes fun at British fans, but for them it was more in the nature of a gentle ribbing; the main criticism was directed at their Brexit-obsessed newspapers, which the European press thinks have been one of the main drivers in Britain's estrangement from Europe.

The column starts with quotes from the book by the *Financial Times* journalist Simon Kuper, "Soccernomics." Kuper traces in the book the typical cycle observable in England World Cup attempts, from initial boundless optimism to final humiliation and despair. The second stage in this cycle is anxiety, when England comes up against an old wartime enemy. And as a former world power, Vandeweghe wryly notes, Britain has many old enemies!

The match that evening was a dead rubber—both teams had already qualified—and although the Belgians and the British were actually on the same side in two world wars and Belgians were eternally grateful to the British for liberating them at the cost of many British lives, the British press had managed to conjure up the usual image of their Belgian opponents being an ex-enemy. How did they work that out? Well, they had linked the game to Brexit. The match was a crucial "Brexit game." Exactly what Belgium had to do with Brexit was not so clear; perhaps, the reasoning was that the EU was in Brussels and Brussels was the capital of the EU as well as the capital of Belgium, so Belgium was on the other side from Britain in Brexit.

But not all English stupidity is attributable to the tabloids, Vandeweghe said: the high-brow but Brexit-supporting *Daily Telegraph* had also stirred the pot. The *Telegraph* had asked FIFA whether it would object to England fans chanting Brexit slogans, a topical question because FIFA had just fined Albanian Kosovar players for hand gestures meant as a political protest against Serbia. FIFA replied to the British paper that, Yes, political actions by spectators or on the pitch could be sanctioned. The *Telegraph* duly came out with an exclusive FIFA story: the association would punish Brexit chanting. The tabloids immediately took up the story and the Twittersphere exploded: disgusting how the long arm of Europe could stretch out even to FIFA in Russia! Foreign Minister Boris Johnson was "outraged" at this interference—but apparently not about English fans engaging in racist chants and Hitler salutes in a Russian bar earlier in the week, Vandeweghe noted. The writer concluded: "English football supporters are known to be pro Brexit. Two years ago in France they chanted 'F... off Europe, we're all voting out.' Half way through the European Championship, on 23 June 2016, between the group stage and the last 16, England voted for Brexit and at the next match the fans chanted triumphantly 'F... off Europe, we all voted out.'—only to get a drubbing from tiny Iceland!"

The news pages of the same day's *De Morgen* had stories about the Brussels borough of Anderlecht, allegedly on health grounds, expelling gypsies from empty land they were on with the owner's permission; about new warnings from major European companies like Airbus and BMW that a hard Brexit would lead them to reconsider their investments in Britain and the differing reactions of ministers to these warnings, either dismissing them as "Project Fear Mark II" (Jeremy Hunt) or with an obscenity (Boris Johnson), or urging the government to take them seriously (Greg

Clark); and about the coming weekend's EU meeting on the migration crisis between Mrs Merkel and several other EU leaders including the new Italian government and those of the Visegrad countries that were resisting taking any migrants. Together with the latter story, the paper carried an interview with the Canadian migration minister, himself an immigrant from Somalia, about the country's open door policy to immigrants under the motto that the country was strong because, not in spite, of diversity. All the articles were written factually without any obvious attempt to persuade the readers of the paper's point of view, its liberal and EU-neutral stance still clearly showing through but letting the facts speak for themselves—*Financial Times* standard.

3.4.5   *Finland*

The biggest newspaper by circulation in Finland is the *Helsingin Sanomat* ("Helsinki News"). Despite the country's small size, there are several other national and regional newspapers. All appear to aim for high standards of factual accuracy and even regional papers contain quite wide coverage of international matters, including the EU. This also applies to the twin red-top tabloids, *Ilta-Sanomat* ("Evening News") and *Ilta-Lehti* ("Evening Paper"), which alongside gossip about celebrities run serious discussions of domestic and international issues. The Finnish press is like the Finns, serious, honest, reliable and accurate. It even publishes interviews with young scientists about their just completed PhD theses, an indication of how much store the Finns set by education.

Here are just a few of the reports, editorials and extended readers' letters about international and EU matters published in the *Helsingin Sanomat* over ten days in April 2018:

- Editorial about Facebook's Mark Zuckerberg's testimony before the US Congress, welcoming the recognition that the EU's General Data Protection Regulation could become an international standard for data protection in social media (14 April).
- A detailed article about the EU's €2.1 billion venture capital "fund of funds" and the need to adapt Finnish tax law to draw maximum benefits from the fund (14 April).
- A feature about the need to amend Finnish immigration law to widen the right of migrants arriving in Finland before the age of maturity to be allowed to be rejoined by their families, following a preliminary

ruling handed down by the European Court of Justice at the request of a Dutch court. The article quotes a ministry spokesman as saying that Finland is going to amend its law urgently (17 April).

- An article about the impact of Brexit on Northern Ireland, particularly the threat to the open border and unimpeded border crossing by local people, and the revival of calls for a referendum on the unification of North and South (18 April).
- A piece about President Macron's address to the European Parliament on 17 April, in which he spoke of a "civil war" between the traditional liberal and democratic values of the EU and the illiberal forces now challenging them, and reporting the mainly positive comments by MEPs (18 April).
- A short piece about a judgment by the European Court of Justice on a case brought by the European Commission against Poland for tree felling in a protected primeval forest. The Court found the felling was in breach of Poland's obligations. Poland said it would comply (18 April).
- A report on the decision by a French court to quash the interior ministry's decision to deport an Afghan asylum seeker back to Finland, the country in which she first registered for asylum (under the "Dublin regulation" the country of first arrival of an asylum seeker in the EU is supposed to deal with his application). The court found that sending the refugee back to Finland would be tantamount to returning her to Afghanistan as Finland had already rejected her application and, unlike Finland and Sweden, France regarded Afghanistan as a country in which she would not be safe from death or persecution (19 April).
- A report on the European Parliament's debate and critical statement about the appointment of Martin Selmayr, the former head of Jean-Claude Juncker's private office, to be the Commission's new Secretary General. The report included a comment by the Finnish member of the Commission, former Finnish Prime Minister Jyrki Katainen, that Parliament was making a big fuss about an appointment that was perfectly within the rights of the Commission to make (19 April).
- An editorial about possible trade-offs between France and Germany on reforms to the governance of the euro and their impact on the Nord Stream II gas pipeline project which Finland and Germany support (20 April).

- A detailed, well-argued reader's letter about the Organization for Economic Cooperation and Development's (OECD) recommendation to Finland to change its social benefit system to the UK's "Universal Credit" model, pointing out the many teething troubles being experienced with the new British system (20 April).
- An article by the newspaper's long-standing London correspondent Annamari Sipilä[77] about the scandal of the treatment of West Indian immigrants who came to the UK between the 1950s and the 1970s and some of whom, because of not having the documentation needed to prove their legal right to be in the UK, have lost their jobs and been threatened with deportation. The correspondent showed her knowledge of the British scene by noting that even the *Daily Mail*, not known for its defence of immigration and refugees, was criticizing the government for its heartless treatment of these immigrants. She referred to the doubt this has created about the capacity of the British authorities to deal with the registration of three million EU nationals after Brexit and to a case where a Finnish student had been deported back to Finland in 2017 (21 April).
- A comment column supporting the maintenance of a strong EU regional policy after 2020, claiming that the investments resulting from EU regional policy have benefitted millions of EU citizens (23 April).
- An article on a proposed EU directive to protect whistle-blowers. The writer was in favour of the directive as without a law to protect whistle-blowers abuses often went undiscovered. It said seven EU countries including Finland did not currently have legislation protecting whistle-blowers (24 April).

Just a week's selection. No references to unelected bureaucrats, unsigned-off accounts, straight or bendy bananas, Brussels bans on coffee and cognac after dinner (a Finnish custom), or being swamped by immigrants. Just factual reporting you can trust. The quality of the *Helsingin Sanomat* in terms of the accuracy and the reliability of its content is of *Financial Times* or *Corriere della Sera* standard.

The anti-EU British newspapers, on the other hand, even the *Telegraph* which aims for a similar readership as *Helsingin Sanomat*, cannot aspire to be as comprehensive and as objective in their coverage of the EU as this little known newspaper from a far-flung corner of Europe. This is because their editorial policy and journalistic standards have long been subordinated to the paramount goal of putting the EU in the worst possible light in order to "deliver" Brexit.

3.5   PROPAGANDA

Relentless, long-term biased reporting, or misinformation, about something, someone or somewhere by media is propaganda. Few of those exposed to the daily drip-drip of negative news and criticism of the EU in their most trusted media outlet, which for most older people is their daily newspaper, could fail to adopt the same views, or fail to see their own anti-EU opinions as confirmed.

Leave campaigners painted the pro-European views expressed in the media and by the government during the campaign—and, in particular, the government leaflet delivered to all British households supporting the case for remaining in the EU[78]—as EU "propaganda." But, the boot had long been on the other foot. The pro-EU views expressed in newspapers and other media outlets in the years running up to the referendum had always been moderate and pragmatic, with a fair amount of criticism of the EU included, even in generally pro-European papers like the *Guardian*. But, it is hard to find a word other than "propaganda" to describe the one-sidedly negative coverage of the EU disseminated over decades by the Eurosceptic majority of London-based newspapers.

Free speech or the expression of partisan or Eurosceptic opinions is not under question. Propaganda is. Propaganda is unfair, a virtue sometimes proudly claimed to be a particularly British trait, but sadly not always in evidence. In purveying propaganda instead of objective reporting, even if tending to the critical, journalists fail in their duty to present a balanced account of the news so as to educate their readers. Instead, they are using their readers as a means of advancing the ideologies and usually right-wing causes of their editors and proprietors.

A longstanding goal of the Eurosceptic press since the 1990s has been to get Britain out of the EU. Through propaganda, the editors and proprietors of the Brexit press have primed their readers to vote against Europe in a referendum. The Eurosceptic press pandered to the nationalist prejudices of many of their readers and channelled them against the EU, with a constant diet of biased content. The British public has been used as mere voting fodder.[79]

The characteristics of propaganda are the deliberate and sustained use of misinformation, lies, fabrications and selective reporting about a subject, in order to persuade the public of a particular agenda. Mere exercise of free speech should, at a minimum, be free of deliberate and sustained misinformation.

Propagandists report facts selectively and distort facts when it suits the narrative. Thus, achievements of the EU like reduced mobile roaming charges, better data protection, successful regional projects, or easier internet banking will not be reported, or, if reported, the credit will not be given to the EU but it will be implied that it was due to national efforts. And problems will regularly be blamed unfairly on the EU when the UK government has been fully involved in making the decision with its EU partners and is at least equally to blame, such as when in the summer of 2017 there were long queues for British holidaymakers at foreign airports due to the introduction of stricter passport checks for non-Schengen country nationals, and Spanish or other countries' border control authorities had not recruited enough additional personnel.

Propaganda cultivates a "narrative" about the target, a stock of false or distorted claims and slogans that the user constantly repeats when reporting news or expressing opinions about the target, in order to drive their message home and turn public opinion in the desired direction.

The false Eurosceptic narrative about the EU has grown up over the past 25 years. It did not start yesterday.[80] Initially, only the view of a minority of right-wing politicians, authors and journalists, the right-wing newspapers that form a majority of the print media in Britain have turned it into a mainstream view in British public opinion by disseminating propaganda containing its messages.

Here are the main myths that are the elements of this propaganda narrative, followed by the corresponding facts. The myths and the facts will be compared and contrasted in detail in Chaps. 4–7. The summary below gives a flavour of how starkly the myths contrast with reality, which explains why they are so persistent.

3.5.1   The Anti-EU Narrative and Its Demolition

Myth 1
The European Union is an organization run by "unelected bureaucrats" who lay down laws and regulations and take decisions which they impose on the member countries with little or no consultation (Chap. 4).

Fact 1
The EU Commission, the EU's administration, has a board, whose members are appointed for a fixed term, and career civil servants working under

them, but the Commission only proposes legislation and performs other administrative tasks. Legislation is passed by two directly or indirectly democratically elected bodies, the Council of the European Union, or "Council of Ministers," (national government ministers from the 28 member countries), and the European Parliament; the members of the latter two bodies are not "unelected bureaucrats," but—except for a few national minsters— elected politicians. The top decision-making body of the EU, which determines its strategic direction and other important matters, is the European Council, which is made up of the 28 heads of state and government, that is, the national prime ministers or presidents. They are not "unelected bureaucrats" either. Though some minor legislation (equivalent to British statutory instruments) is passed by the Commission under delegated powers, the normal procedure for primary legislation is that the proposals made by the Commission are discussed in detail by advisory or management committees composed of member states' civil servants and representatives of industry, the scientific community and other interests, before being adopted, often after amendment, by national ministers in the Council of Ministers and by the European Parliament. Member states' parliaments have opportunities to influence draft EU legislation by questioning their governments, debating the draft legislation in their own national parliament and lobbying their MEPs. Britain is notable for to a large extent failing to take such opportunities, which is its own fault. An EU law, or some provision of it, can only be said to be "imposed" on a member state when it is subject to majority voting in the Council of Ministers and the member state is outvoted, and if the vote on the same law or provision also goes against it in the European Parliament. Such cases are rare.

Myth 2
Many EU laws and regulations are needless "red tape" that imposes unnecessary burdens on member states and their businesses. By quitting the EU, Britain could make its own laws more suited to UK interests (Chap. 5).

Fact 2
While, on occasion, EU laws may be considered overly prescriptive, this criticism is not exclusive to EU laws but is also levelled at national British laws. Most EU laws concern agriculture, standards for food, industrial products, services, professional qualifications, employment rights, and environmental rules. They may sometimes be burdensome for businesses

but are nevertheless necessary for the common good in an advanced country. They are only "needless red tape" for people on the libertarian, anti-government, right wing of politics.[81] Britain would have similar rules if it were outside the EU. It is a telling fact that the Withdrawal Act imports all these ("needless") EU rules into British law pending review sometime in the future. It does not scrap them.

Myth 3

As a member of the EU, the UK has transferred its sovereignty, law-making ability and independence, wholesale, to a supranational organization. To become a self-respecting fully sovereign and independent country again, it needs to take back control by leaving the EU (Chap. 5).

Fact 3

The UK has pooled its sovereignty in certain areas of policy with other member states. Pooling sovereignty involves making laws jointly and cooperating with one's partners in these areas. Pooling sovereignty does not mean losing it completely. It remains substantially intact and in addition the country gains influence on the policies of its partners. There are vast areas of policy—social security, education, health, defence, and the bulk of taxation—where the UK like other member states retains full sovereignty, as the EU has little or no power to act in these areas. To claim the country has lost its independence or "control" over its destiny is an exaggeration. No country in the modern world is completely independent. All are connected by trade, trade agreements, treaties and conventions, making them economically and politically interdependent. The pooling of certain fields of sovereignty to supranational organizations like the EU or under trade and other international agreements brings benefits in the form of extra trade, prosperity, freedom of movement, cultural exchanges, and security. These benefits outweigh the loss of a degree of self-determination in areas of modern life where international cooperation is often essential.

Myth 4

The EU exacts high membership contributions from its member countries for a budget which is opaque, mismanaged and largely wasted. The organization is not audited and, therefore, open to corruption. According to the Leave side during the referendum campaign, the UK pays the EU £350 million a week. If Britain left it would be able to spend this money on public services like the NHS (Chap. 6).

Fact 4

The membership fee varies depending on the prosperity of the member state. The poorer countries pay less into the EU budget and receive more back from EU spending programmes than the richer countries like the UK which pay more in and receive less back. The budget, thus, redistributes resources towards the economically weaker member states. The average gross budgetary payment per country (before payments back to the country under EU spending programmes) is 1% of Gross Domestic Product (GDP), which compared with national public spending of between 35% and 50% of GDP is quite small. The UK's net contribution to the EU budget (after the automatic rebate negotiated by Margaret Thatcher and receipts of agricultural, regional development, science and other payments from the EU budget) is under half the amount claimed by the Leave side in the referendum campaign. The EU budget, which the Commission manages, is audited every year by the independent European Court of Auditors (ECA). The ECA has in recent years always approved the accounts subject to qualifications concerning money spent in member states, mainly on regional development programmes. The ECA's qualifications of the accounts for this reason have decreased over time as the EU Commission has tightened up its monitoring of how member states spend this money. The ECA finds that little money is lost to fraud. This is confirmed by the Commission's own internal fraud prevention agency Olaf. However, some corruption involving misuse of EU funds is found, particularly in some of the central and eastern European countries like Hungary, Bulgaria and Romania. The EU is trying to stamp out corruption with EU funds in these member states. Money is occasionally wasted on projects that fail. Another potential source of waste is the European Parliament's monthly travel from Brussels to Strasbourg for its plenary session, but there are historical and political reasons for this situation which is hard to change. An old problem of abuse of the European Parliament's expenses regimes for the travel and staff costs of MEPs has been solved. The Commission has its own internal audit service whose task is to increase efficiency and prevent waste. The problems of waste in the EU are certainly no greater than in the UK administration.

Myth 5

The EU is out of touch with ordinary people. It exercises a stranglehold on economic progress. In recent years it has become dysfunctional due to its pursuit of unrealistic projects like the euro and a common policy of immigration. The EU is in decline and now at a serious risk of disintegration. Staying in endangers Britain's future prosperity (Chaps. 4 and 5).

Fact 5
National governments and political parties, including in the UK, are also accused of being out of touch with ordinary people. The EU keeps in touch with people through, inter alia, the members of the European Parliament, the European Economic and Social Committee and the Committee of the Regions, its around 45 specialist agencies, the 300 or so local and regional representative offices from member states in Brussels, and the many lobbying organizations ranging from the European Trade Union Confederation to the European Automobile Manufacturers Association (see also Sect. 4.6.1 below). The EU is not dysfunctional. It works efficiently in areas of policy in which it has long experience. It sometimes struggles with unprecedented situations, but no more than would a national government. The euro crisis of 2010–15 and the migrant crisis of 2015–16 taxed the EU's resilience and resourcefulness to the utmost and has not resulted in perfect solutions to the problems, but it at least dealt with the crises with a measure of success: the euro is still viable and has brought enormous benefits; a common policy on immigration is still work in progress but is feasible in the medium term. The Single Market and the rules it necessitates are not a stranglehold on British industry, any more than they have been on successful economies like Germany's. The EU is not a corpse. Until 2018, it was growing faster than the UK. With programmes like the energy and capital markets union and the digital Common Market, it is developing its cooperation further in ways that will benefit the economies of its member states. It is leading the world on the environment, data protection, human rights, competition policy and the taxation of multinationals like Apple.

Myth 6
Nevertheless, the EU still harbours ambitions of becoming a federation, a "United States of Europe" (Chap. 5).

Fact 6
The EU is already a federal state in the policy areas where member states have agreed to pool sovereignty, such as customs, trade policy, the Single Market, competition policy, agriculture, regional policy, the euro, and the environment. It is gradually advancing to a federal set-up in other areas like energy, telecommunications, transport, immigration, security and defence, but these advances could still take many years to materialize. The EU can only exercise powers in a policy area if the member states have agreed in the treaty to delegate such powers to it. Whether and to what

extent they will agree to transfer powers in other areas like social security, taxation, health, education, and criminal and civil law, and whether indeed there is any need for the EU to have powers in these areas, and if so which, is a matter for debate and in most of these areas further transfers are not in prospect in the medium or even longer term. In the US, which has a settled federal system, the states retain extensive powers in many areas, because it is more efficient to leave these matters to state level. The same principle of limiting the transfer of powers to the EU to areas where it is necessary and leaving power in other areas to the member states is also followed by the EU and is called "subsidiarity."

Myth 7
The UK needs to free itself from the behemoth of a would-be European "superstate" in order to seize the vast opportunities that present themselves in a fast-growing world outside the declining and protectionist Europe. As a nimbler, "global Britain," it would be able to strike free trade deals with the rest of the world (Chap. 5).

Fact 7
The EU allows flexibility for unwilling member states to move more slowly towards more federal power-sharing, as is the case with the UK's exemptions from the euro, Schengen and much of the justice and home affairs cooperation provisions, including asylum policy. The degree of federalism already realized and now planned is nothing to be afraid of because the clear benefits outweigh the disadvantage of no longer having total control over the nitty-gritty of policy and legislation in these restricted areas. An "independent" UK would end up deciding similar rules to the EU anyway. Why reinvent the wheel? In an interdependent world where more and more matters require government intervention, deciding rules on matters of common interest together, albeit at the cost of occasionally not getting 100% of what you originally wanted, saves resources and makes sense. It allows a national government to concentrate on other matters essential for domestic public welfare. It remains to be seen whether the UK will gain, or lose, influence in the world by leaving the EU and whether it will gain or lose trade volume when it gives up part of its market access in Europe and negotiates entirely new trade agreements outside the EU on its own. It is likely that new trade agreements will not be enough to make up for the trade the UK loses through Brexit within the EU single market and with the around 50 countries with which the EU has free trade agree-

ments. The EU is not exceptionally protectionist. It has pursued a relatively liberal trade policy on a par with that of other advanced industrialized countries like the US and Japan. It has been a strong supporter of multilateral trade liberalization through General Agreement on Tariffs and Trade (GATT) and now the World Trade Organization (WTO)—two former EU commissioners have become heads of the WTO—and the EU has been active in concluding bilateral free trade agreements with many countries, including preferential trading arrangements with developing countries in Africa and elsewhere. The EU is not a behemoth, but a well-organized, efficient and relatively lean organization based on a clearly defined allocation of tasks between the central institutions and the member states. The UK's problems with and distrust of the EU have stemmed from its lack of commitment to this relationship and its unwillingness, during a large part of the time it has been a member, to sacrifice the tiniest bit of national interest to the common good of Europe, unlike Germany and France. Europe's relative economic weight in the world is declining but so is Britain's and membership of the bloc does not restrict its ability to develop links to faster growing parts of the world.

Myth 8
EU citizens who are free to come and settle in Britain under the free movement rules are abusing the welfare system and placing a strain on services like the NHS, education and housing. They are a net drain on public finances, depress pay levels for British workers and take their jobs. Even larger inflows of migrants from Turkey (potentially 75 million) and southeastern Europe are imminent given the impending accession of these countries to the EU, which Britain cannot prevent. The EU is also a conduit for illegal migrants and terrorists from the Middle East and Africa. There is no way Britain can reduce the numbers of EU nationals and illegal immigrants coming into the country except by leaving the EU. Britain must take back control of its borders (Chap. 7).

Fact 8
There is little evidence that EU migrants abuse the welfare system. The evidence also shows that EU migrants, who are mostly young and economically active, make a net contribution to Britain's finances. While EU migrants may depress wages to some extent in certain sectors like the construction industry, often through abuse of EU rules allowing organized recruitment of workers paid home country rates of pay (rules that

are now being tightened up to close the loopholes), the evidence is that in most sectors like agriculture, food processing, road haulage, the hotel and catering industry, as well as in the health and care services, EU migrants are not displacing British workers but doing work for which no British people are available or willing to undertake the work. In the NHS, far from EU migrants placing a strain on its resources, native British people are more often likely to be treated by EU doctors and nurses than to meet EU people waiting in the same queue. Migration from outside the EU has been running in recent years at a similar level to EU migration. Non-EU migration is controlled through a work permit system and a system for admitting family members of existing residents. The fact that despite these controls non-EU migrants are admitted to work in Britain shows that there is a demand for them from the British economy. Since the Brexit vote, the number of new EU migrants entering Britain has already fallen and the number of those leaving has increased. Whether the number of EU migrants will continue to fall as a result of introducing a work permit system is uncertain. However, the demand from certain sectors of the British economy is unlikely to decline and failing to admit enough migrants to meet this demand may lead to labour shortages.

There are ways Britain could have limited the numbers of EU citizens coming to work in the country while in the EU. It could have made advertising of vacancies directed at prospective British workers compulsory before entertaining offers from EU citizens or restricted admission to EU citizens with a firm job offer. Other countries routinely do this. It could also have increased provision for training British workers. The failure to take such measures is entirely the UK's own fault and has more to do with its historical desire to give precedence to a favourable environment for business with easy access to labour over reducing immigration.

The accession of Turkey and further Balkan states is a long way off, in Turkey's case at least 20 years. Each member state including the UK has to approve any new accession. In other words, Britain has a veto. After a new country joins the EU, existing countries can restrict the freedom of nationals of the acceding country to enter its labour market for a certain period. Turkish or other new EU migrants are, therefore, unlikely to be free to come to Britain until far in the future.

Britain has never joined the EU Schengen system abolishing passport checks on internal EU borders and was allowed to opt out of treaty provisions requiring acceptance of quotas of asylum seekers and refugees. So for non-EU citizens it retains full control of its borders and can refuse them entry. It is true that non-EU migrants who obtain the citizenship of another EU country—such as the around a million migrants who came to Germany during the 2015 migrant crisis and, if accepted as refugees, will eventually have the chance of getting German passports—would then be free to come to live and work in Britain, but to apply for citizenship after acquiring refugee status they have to have lived in Germany for six to eight years.[82] Leaving the EU will also not make Britain any less exposed to terrorists approaching through the EU. If they can get through Britain's defences now with its current border controls, they will be able to do so in the future too. In fact, Britain's anti-terrorist defences could be weakened should it fail to replicate the intensive security cooperation with European agencies and individual EU countries that it currently enjoys as an EU member.

There never was any obligation on Britain to change its passport colour from blue to maroon. It did so entirely voluntarily.

3.5.2   Slogans, Mantras, Alarm Buttons and Dog Whistles—The Stock in Trade of Propaganda

The propaganda character of the misinformation about the EU spread by the right-wing British press is confirmed by the fact that these myths have been repeated so often that often a single-word slogan or a short phrase suffices to drive the message home without any further substantiation of the claim. Virtually any of the articles quoted in Chaps. 4–7 from the anti-EU newspapers will be found to contain such slogans and stock phrases. They are a part of the Brexit newspaper journalist's and sub-editor's toolbox.

Thus, references to the EU can be prefaced gratuitously with epithets like "undemocratic," "anti-democratic," "corrupt," "bloated," "dysfunctional" or "wasteful"; the members of the Commission, who supposedly impose laws dreamt up in their ivory tower on unsuspecting member states can be termed "unelected bureaucrats" and abused in any way the newspaper pleases; the EU laws and policies they supposedly dream up and impose on us can be called "diktats," "bureaucratic," "red tape," or "hated"; and the UK's budget contribution to the EU can be called "vast" and disappearing into a "black hole," all with impunity or the need for further justification.

So conditioned are the public to these stimuluses and anger or anxiety buttons that the newspaper or politician actioning them can count on their inducing an angry reaction from readers and listeners, and on that angry reaction making the readers or listeners more receptive to the anti-

Table 3.2   Stock anti-EU propaganda cues, slogans and dog whistles

Concept	Slogan, "dog whistle," cue
European Union	Undemocratic, anti-democratic, corrupt, bloated, sprawling, dysfunctional, wasteful, protectionist, failing, tottering, sclerotic, European superstate, corpse, bankrupt, the European project, EU.
European Commission	Unelected bureaucrats, Brussels, arrogant, autocratic, unaccountable, irremovable, out of touch, aggressive, bullying, intransigent, hard-drinking, foreign bureaucracy, mean-spirited, gloating, self-serving, mocking[a].
EU laws and policies	Diktats, stifling bureaucracy, red tape, hated, straitjacket, shackles, burden, tied to Brussels.
UK's budget contribution	Vast sums, disappearing into a black hole, unsupervised, unaudited, mismanaged.
Remainer	Remoaner, eurofanatic, arch-federalist, "You lost, get over it," true believer, the Establishment, elites, besotted, obsessive, sanctimonious, fawning, die-hard.
Brexit Britain	Sovereign, independent, global, freedom.

[a]The boot was on the other foot. It was mainly Britain, its Eurosceptic politicians and newspapers that were doing the mocking of the EU during the negotiations. The EU side like Council President Tusk just indulged in a little ribbing and sarcasm from time to time. The Labour party were right in saying that the Brexit negotiations were not helped by the unpleasant atmosphere created by the constant abuse of the EU by ministers and in the press during the negotiations. "Mocking the other side in public—as Greece's Yanis Varoufakis did, and as British politicians now do regularly—is therefore a losing tactic"[83]

EU sentiment being expressed. For some people, the mere mention of "Brussels" or "the EU" actions the angry reaction—one-word cues are enough to "get them going." Such slogans, mantras and cues are "dog whistles," like Trump's "Make America great again" or "America first," and Hitler's "Wollt ihr den totalen Krieg?" ("Do you want total war?"). They are the stock in trade of demagogues.

Responsible journalism and campaigning rely on balanced argument to persuade the public of their point of view. When campaigners and newspapers rely more on propaganda effects than argument, they are showing they think the end justifies the means, that facts and truth are secondary, that the audience is "voting fodder" who can be manipulated to do the speaker's will (Table 3.2).

3.5.3   Brexiteer Anger and How to Tackle It

The propaganda fed to the British people on a daily basis by the newspapers has succeeded. During the referendum campaign, the anger against the EU and "Brussels" among the audiences at public meetings was palpable and frightening. You can still sense it among BBC "Question Time" audiences and even more in the comments posted on BBC News websites. The reasons audience members and social media users give for voting Brexit are almost always identical to the ones the Brexit newspapers propagated. The myths are so deep seated that it can be exasperating trying to disabuse people of them. James O'Brien on his *LBC* phone-in programme sets a good example of directly challenging such myths. More pro-EU politicians and commentators should do the same in debates and not let Brexit clichés go unchallenged. It is not disrespectful, arrogant or condescending to do so; it is trying to help someone overcome prejudice or unjustified anger; sometimes, the conversation can benefit both sides and enlighten the challenger as well.[84] We need "global philosophers"[85] more than we need a "global Britain."

3.6   Introduction to Part II

Part II of this book will attempt to correct the propaganda narrative of the Brexit press and Leave campaigners about the European Union in detail, in the three key areas of sovereignty, money and immigration, encapsulated by the slogan "taking back control of our laws, our money and our borders." There are four chapters. The sovereignty question is divided between Chaps. 4 and 5, the first one dealing with the institutions of the EU and their part in the legislative process and the issue of whether this is democratic, the second covering the extent of the pooling of sovereignty with the EU, the rationality and advantages of such delegation, "red tape," and the bogeyman that is the European Court of Justice. Chapter 6 is about the money—how much is our budget contribution, how it is audited and with what results, waste and corruption, and how much Brexit will cost. The final main chapter is about immigration, which was the subject of some justifiable concern but also not a few myths and considerable manipulation.

Notes

1. Sopel, Jon. 2017. *If Only They Didn't Speak English: Notes from Trump's America.* London: BBC Books.
2. Clark, Christopher. 2013. *Sleepwalkers: How Europe Went to War in 1914,* xxvii. London: Penguin. Ham, Paul. 2018. 1918 was a victory, but we won nothing. *Daily Telegraph.* 21 February.

3. O'Toole, Fintan. 2018. *Heroic Failure: Brexit and the Politics of Pain.* London: Head of Zeus. The role of Britain's rather deficient history teaching in explaining its feeling of nationalist exceptionalism which was an important factor in the Brexit vote is also highlighted in Dorling, Danny, and Sally Tomlinson. 2019. *Rule Britannia: Brexit and the End of Empire.* London: Biteback Publishing.

4. *The Guardian.* 2018. Britain's equality efforts overshadowed by 'backwards steps', EHRC warns. 25 October.

5. The Equality Trust. 2017. The Level of Economic Inequality in the UK.

6. *BBC News.* 2018. UK firms will have to justify pay gap between workers and bosses. 10 June.

7. Joseph Rowntree Trust. 2018. UK Poverty 2018. 4 December. *The Guardian.* 2018. Poverty causes 'misery' in UK, and ministers are in denial, says UN official. 25 October.

8. *BBC News.* 2016. Britain's Inequality map—stark and growing. 2 December.

9. Kirby, Philip. 2016. *Leading People UK. The educational backgrounds of the UK professional elites.* February 2016. Sutton Trust.

10. *BBC Radio 4. Desert Island Disks,* 18 May 2018; Green, Francis, and David Kynaston. 2019. *Engines of Privilege: Britain's Private School Problem.* London: Bloomsbury.

11. Payne, Sebastian. 2018. Millions voted to leave the EU in good faith, fed up with politics as usual and yearning for a better life. *Financial Times.* 20 September.

12. Dashwood, Alan, et al. 2011. *Wyatt and Dashwood's European Union Law,* 6th ed. London: Hart Publishing.

13. Bailey, David (ed.), and Laura Elizabeth John (ed.). 2018. *Bellamy & Child. European Union Law of Competition,* 8th ed. Oxford: Oxford University Press.

14. El-Agraa, Ali. M. 2011. *The European Union: Economics and Politics,* 9th ed. Cambridge: Cambridge University Press.

15. Dinan, Desmond. 2005. *Ever-Closer Union. An Introduction to European Integration,* 3rd ed. Basingstoke: Palgrave Macmillan.

16. Cini, Michelle, and Pérez-Solórzano Borragán. 2010. *European Union Politics,* 3rd ed. Oxford: Oxford University Press.

17. Corner, Mark. 2014. *The European Union: An Introduction.* London: I. B. Tauris.

18. Tugendhat, Christopher, 1986. *Making Sense of Europe.* London: Viking Penguin.

19. Brittan, Leon. 1994. *Europe: The Europe We Need.* London: Hamish Hamilton Penguin.

20. Booker, Christopher, and Richard North. 2005. *The Great Deception: The Secret History of the European Union.* London: Bloomsbury, republished as

a referendum edition in 2016: *The Great Deception: Can the European Union Survive.* London: Bloomsbury.

21. Craig, David, and Matthew Elliott. 2009. *The Great European Rip-Off: How the Corrupt, Wasteful EU is Taking Control of Our Lives.* London: Random House.

22. Bootle, Roger. 2016. *The Trouble with Europe*, 3rd ed. London: Nicholas Brealey Publishing, and 4th, Brexit edition 2017. *The Trouble with Europe: Making a Success of Brexit and Reforming the EU.*

23. Hannan, Daniel. 2011. *A Doomed Marriage: Britain and Europe.* London: Notting Hill Editions.

24. Elliott, Larry, and Dan Atkinson. 2016. *Europe Isn't Working.* New Haven and London: Yale University Press.

25. Varoufakis, Yanis. 2016. *And the Weak Suffer What They Must? Europe, Austerity and the Threat to Global Stability.* London: Bodley Head.

26. Hewitt, Gavin. 2013. *The Lost Continent: Europe's Darkest Hour Since World War Two.* London: Hodder and Stoughton.

27. MacShane, Denis. 2015. *Brexit: How Britain Will Leave Europe.* London: I. B. Tauris; 2016. *Let's Stay Together: Why Yes to Europe.* London: I. B. Tauris.

28. Emerson, Michael (ed.). 2016. *Britain's Future in Europe: The Known Plan A to Remain or the Unknown Plan B to Leave.* Brussels: Centre for European Policy Studies.

29. Brown, Gordon. 2016. *Britain: Leading, not Leaving: The Patriotic Case for Remaining in Europe.* Selkirk: Deerpark Press.

30. Lewis, Jane. 2016. *The Connell Guide to the EU Referendum. Stay or Go?* London: Connell Guides Publishing. This guide also contained some important errors. Like Bootle, it got the EU's legislative process completely wrong, claiming that the European Commission passes laws, probably because, like Bootle, it did not appreciate that the "Council" has a dual role with a completely different composition in each role: the European Council is the top EU body and is made up of the member states' leaders and takes major strategic decisions; the Council of Ministers (or, officially, the "Council of the European Union") is the day-to-day legislative body composed of national ministers which passes laws proposed by the European Commission as part of a two-chamber legislative system with the European Parliament. The guide also made the common mistake of taking the European Court of Human Rights for an EU body. See below Sect. 3.5.1 and Chap. 4, Sect. 4.2.

31. Halligan, Liam, and Gerard Lyons. 2018. *Clean Brexit: Why Leaving the EU Still Makes Sense—Building a Post-Brexit Economy for All.* London: Biteback.

32. Bootle, Roger. 2017. *Making a Success of Brexit and Reforming the EU.* London: Nicholas Brealey Publishing.

33. Elliott, Larry, and Dan Atkinson. 2017. *Europe Didn't Work: Why We Left and How to Get the Best from Brexit*. New Haven and London: Yale University Press.

34. Dunt, Ian. 2016. *Brexit: What the Hell Happens Now?* Kingston upon Thames: Cadbury Press.

35. Armstrong, Kenneth A. 2017. *Brexit Time: Leaving the EU—Why, How and When*. Cambridge: Cambridge University Press.

36. Peston, Robert. 2017. *WTF: What have we done? Why Did it Happen? How Do We Take Back Control?* London: Hodder and Stoughton.

37. Charter, David. 2017. *What has the EU ever done for us? How the European Union changed Britain: What to keep and what to scrap*. London: Biteback.

38. Connelly, Tony. 2017. *Brexit and Ireland. The Dangers, the Opportunities, and the Inside Story of the Irish Response*. London: Penguin Random House.

39. MacShane, Denis. 2017. *Brexit, No Exit: Why (In the End) Britain Won't Leave Europe*. London: I.B. Tauris.

40. Clegg, Nick. 2017. *How to Stop Brexit (and Make Britain Great Again)*. London: Bodley Head.

41. Rogers, Ivan. 2019. *9 Lessons of Brexit*. London: Shirt Books.

42. Piras, Annalisa. 2016. Read all about it? Brexit press coverage skewed!. *InFacts*. 23 May.

43. *HuffPost*. 2016. Which newspapers support Brexit in the EU referendum? 21 June. See also Martinson, Jane. 2016. Did the Mail and Sun help swing the UK towards Brexit? *The Guardian*. 24 June.

44. Denis MacShane complains of an apparent desire to keep a low profile on the part of business. MacShane, Denis. 2016. *Let's stay together: Why Yes to Europe*, 3. London: I.B. Tauris.

45. *Ofcom*. 2017. News consumption in the UK 2016. 29 June.

46. Ibid., Table 4.3 Combined print and digital monthly readership of newspapers, 2015–2016.

47. *Ofcom*, Ibid.

48. See also Martinson, Jane. 2016. Did the Mail and Sun help swing the UK towards Brexit? *The Guardian*. 24 June, quoting David Deacon, Professor of Communication and Media Analysis at Loughborough University.

49. BBC Radio 4's *Question Time*, 3 August 2017: "We have this extraordinary tabloid press that couldn't run a single good story about the EU. We were told rubbish about straight bananas and all sorts of nonsense." See also *Daily Telegraph*. 2017. Let's not jeopardise this important task. 19 June: "For those who struggled for decades to reverse the decision to join the EU, and by so doing reclaim the sovereignty this nation lost with membership, it is an incredible moment."

50. See *Ofcom*. 2017. Sect. 5: Due impartiality and due accuracy. 3 April.

51. *Ofcom*, Ibid.

52. Garton Ash, Timothy. 2016. The BBC is too timid. Being impartial on the EU is not enough. *The Guardian*. 1 April.

53. Cushion, Stephen, and Justin Lewis. 2017. Impartiality, statistical tit-for-tats and the construction of balance: UK television news reporting of the 2016 EU referendum campaign. *European Journal of Communications,* 32, 208–223.
54. Op. cit.
55. *Ofcom.* 2017. News consumption in the UK 2016. 29 June.
56. Parliament UK. 2019. House of Commons Select Committee on Digital, Culture, Media and Sport. 18 February. The Committee also noted an unclear relationship with the insurance company Eldon Insurance owned by Leave.eu's main backer Arron Banks which held a large quantity of personal data on its British clients, and considered there was evidence that the data analysis company Aggregate IQ collected, stored, and shared data belonging to UK citizens in the context of its work for the main Leave campaigning organization Vote Leave.
57. *FullFacts.* 2019. There's a lot wrong with this viral list about the Lisbon Treaty. 11 March. Toynbee, Polly. 2019. The anti-EU lies are back to exploit Britain's weak spot again. *The Guardian.* 4 March.
58. Sipilä, Annamari. 2015. EU on Britanniassa tunteen asia ("In Britain the EU is a matter of feeling"). *Helsingin Sanomat.* 10 September. For a similar analysis of the behaviour of the Eurosceptic press during the referendum campaign by a press insider, see Rusbridger, Alan. 2018. *Breaking News: The Remaking of Journalism and Why It Matters Now,* 361–365. Edinburgh: Canongate Books.
59. Sipilä, Annamari. 2014. Britannia voi olla EU:lle jo menetetty tapaus ("Britain could already be a lost cause for the EU"). *Helsingin Sanomat.* 30 August.
60. See, for example, European Commission. 2016. *Standard Eurobarometer 85 Spring 2016: Public opinion in the European Union.* July 2016.
61. Hardman, Isabel. 2018. *Why We Get the Wrong Politicians,* 198–199. London: Atlantic Books.
62. Greenslade, Roy. 2016. The Sun's Brexit call is unsurprising but it has a symbolic significance. *The Guardian.* 14 June.
63. talkRADIO. 4 October 2017. Julia Hartley-Brewer and Alistair Campbell. YouTube.
64. See, for example, Lynn, Matthew. 2017. Ignore the hype, this 'Merkron' axis is likely to leave Europe worse off. *Daily Telegraph.* 27 June, exaggerating the protectionist or socialist nature of proposals on takeovers, public procurement and social measures that President Macron had made to Mrs Merkel in a relaunch of the Franco-German axis after his election.
65. MacShane. Denis. 2015. *How Britain Will Leave Europe.* London. I. B. Tauris.
66. *The Guardian.* 2017. David Cameron asked Daily Mail owner to sack Paul Dacre over Brexit. 1 February.

67. Greenslade. Roy. 2016. The Sun's Brexit call is unsurprising but it has a symbolic significance. *The Guardian*. 14 June.

68. For example, the EU Commission President's remarks that negotiating the issue of citizens' rights would take longer than a few weeks after Mrs May had said she hoped for a deal by the end of June was called a "plot": *Daily Telegraph*. 2017. EU plots to block May's deal on expats. 2 May. Pro-Brexit propaganda has also continued unabated on social media.

69. Rautio, Paavo. 2016. *Helsingin Sanomat*. Vinoista paloista syntyy vino kuva ("Crooked pieces make a distorted picture"). 27 July. More on the noble sport of Eurobashing in Chap. 5, Sect. 5.4.1.

70. Sipilä. Annamari. 2016. *Helsingin Sanomat*. Äänestäjiä pitää osata pelotella ajoissa ("You have to be able frighten voters early enough.") 24 May. See also Sect. 3.4.5 below.

71. See Sect. 3.4.4 below, article in *De Morgen* by Hans Vandeweghe.

72. BBC Radio 4. 2018. *Today*. 26 November. See also comments in a similar vein by Juncker to the German TV network ARD, reported on *BBC News* on 25 May 2019.

73. Juncker's statement was met with silence. But British journalists who know Europe believe Juncker is right. Simon Kuper of the *Financial Times*, for example, wrote that the only major purveyors of fake news in Europe are the UK's tabloids: *Financial Times*. 2017. Why there will never be a Trump in western Europe. 1 July.

74. Barnett, Steven. 2018. Daily Mail: new editor, new 'enemies of the people'. *The Conversation*. 19 November. Nevertheless, the paper is still staunchly Eurosceptic and pro-Leave.

75. *Die Welt*. 2019. Kleinlaute Populisten ("Subdued populists"). 9 April.

76. The book of the *Libération* journalist Jean Quatremer. 2017. Les Salauds de l'Europe: Guide à l'usage des eurosceptiques. Paris: Calmann Levy, debunks the myths of Euroscepticism while not denying the EU's imperfections.

77. Who predicted a Leave win in the 2016 referendum almost two years beforehand, in view of the prevailing Eurosceptic mood among the population and the country's largely anti-EU press: *Helsingin Sanomat*. 2014. Britannia voi olla EU:lle jo menetetty tapaus. ("Britain could already be a lost cause for the EU"). 30 August.

78. *HM Gov*. 2016. Why the Government believes that voting to remain in the European Union is the best decision for the UK. 7 April.

79. What Kelvin MacKenzie thought of his *Sun* readers is documented in Chippendale, Peter and Chris Horrie. 1991. *Stick it Up Your Punter: The Rise and Fall of the Sun*. London, William Heinemann. See also Rusbridger, Alan. 2018. *Breaking News: The Remaking of Journalism and Why It Matters Now*, 49. Edinburgh: Canongate Books. See also Müller, Reinhard. 2017. Das Volk ist kein Stimmvieh. ("People are not voting fodder.") *Frankfurter Allgemeine*. 28 April.

80. See Anderson, Peter J., and Tony Weymouth. 1999. *Insulting the Public? The British Press and the European Union.* London and New York: Longman. Also, Morgan, David. 1995. "British Media and European Union News: The Brussels News Beat and its Problems." *European Journal of Communication*, 321–343. See also the complaints about euromyths and the EU's attempts to counter them in the 1990s referred to in Chap. 5.

81. See O'Brien, James. 2018. *How to be right … in a world gone wrong.* London: W. H. Allen, Chap. 6: Nanny States and classical liberals.

82. *BBC News.* 2016. Reality Check: How many refugees in Germany will become EU citizens? The number of refugees claimed likely to come to Europe has turned out to be much exaggerated. 29 April.

83. Kuper, Simon. 2017. Brexit: Britain's gift to the world. *Financial Times.* 29 September.

84. O'Brien, James. 2018. *How to be right … in a world gone wrong.* London: W. H. Allen.

85. An appreciative reference to BBC Radio 4's "Global Philosopher" with Michael Sandel.

PART II

Busting Myths

CHAPTER 4

"Taking Back Control of Our Laws": I. Democracy

4.1 INTRODUCTION: DEMOCRACY AND SOVEREIGNTY

"Taking back control" became the key slogan of the Leave campaign in the EU referendum. It was arguably as simplistic and as misleading as "Make America Great Again" in Trump's campaign to become US president.

The narrative was that Britain had ceded control over its laws, its money and its borders to the EU and it could only regain that control and become a "fully sovereign and independent country" again by leaving the EU. Looking first at the question of sovereignty (the ability to decide laws), there were several things wrong with this claim.

It exaggerated the extent of the powers ceded to the EU, implying that all sovereignty has been lost, whereas in fact the ceding of sovereignty only concerned particular policy areas.

It ignored the benefits received in return for ceding sovereignty in these areas. In any international agreement involving common decision-making there must be benefits or otherwise countries would not agree to cede sovereignty. The British Eurosceptic narrative misled the public by denying any benefits of the joint action and stressing only its disadvantages in the form of "red tape" or restrictive rules.

It wrongly portrayed sovereignty as absolute, as all or nothing, as either kept or lost 100%, thus discounting the possibility of power-sharing with partners in which each partner sacrifices a degree of his own sovereignty but thereby gains influence over the sovereignty of his partners, which can have major advantages.

© The Author(s) 2019
F. Rawlinson, *How Press Propaganda Paved the Way to Brexit*,
https://doi.org/10.1007/978-3-030-27765-9_4

It ignored the practical impossibility in the modern world of keeping 100% of one's sovereignty. All international cooperation and agreements impinge on sovereignty and constrain one's freedom of action. Even the few countries that shun international cooperation like North Korea find their freedom of action curtailed by outside pressure. The world is inextricably interdependent.

A more serious problem than these misleading implications about the extent of Britain's ceding of sovereignty to the EU, the lack of any benefits in return, and the possibility of maintaining absolute sovereignty in the modern world, were the lies told about the EU's exercise of the sovereignty ceded to it.

The EU, so the narrative goes, is undemocratic in the way it takes decisions and makes laws. EU laws, the story goes, are essentially enacted by the Commission. The Commission is appointed, not elected; it is an unelected bureaucracy. It cannot be removed from office by the voters in EU countries like a government can. It is unaccountable to the public.

This distorts the truth about the legislative process in the EU. Laws are passed by the Council of Ministers and the European Parliament, both of which institutions are at least indirectly elected. These institutions are ignored in the narrative of an unelected, unaccountable Commission passing laws.

Ignoring the democratic institutions that actually pass EU laws allowed the propagandists to further claim that EU laws are imposed, practically without consultation, on the unwitting member countries and their long-suffering public. To anyone even only vaguely familiar with EU processes this claim is laughable, but like all the false claims it was believed because the public did not know any better and the Brexit newspapers made sure they remained ignorant.

Furthermore, the narrative continued with the claim that many, if not most, of these EU regulations were unnecessary "red tape," and an "independent" Britain could jettison these restrictive and suffocating rules and become a nimbler, more flexible, more innovative country.

As well as being undemocratic, the EU bureaucracy is also, according to the Brexit narrative, bloated, inefficient, incompetent, dysfunctional, not to mention arrogant, overpaid and corrupt.

If they were true, these charges levelled against the EU would be damning to any fair-minded person brought up to believe in democracy. Obviously, the quicker Britain got out of this club and took back control the better. On sovereignty grounds alone the case for Brexit was compelling. The vast membership fee we paid, which—according to this narrative—could be saved and spent on public services back home made it more so.

But the narrative was not true. The case for leaving on these grounds does not hold water because:

a. The EU is not run and its legislative process controlled by an unelected Commission unaccountable to the people. The Commission manages the EU, but on legislation it only proposes; a two-chamber legislature disposes, the two chambers consisting of the Council of Ministers (member states' governments) and the European Parliament. The European Council of national leaders conducts the whole orchestra and decides its future programme. As well as legislating, Parliament supervises the Commission's management and has an increasing role in setting the budget and hence the EU's future direction, together with national leaders. The claims of a lack of democratic legitimacy—the so-called democratic deficit—are nowadays largely unjustified. The system is basically democratic, though differently compared to national systems, and admittedly perfectible as it is still relatively new;

b. EU legislation is limited in scope and volume, it is not all "red tape," and the European Court of Justice's enforcement of EU law is necessary and proportionate;

c. pooling of sovereignty in these areas makes sense, as the government's own exhaustive survey of the balance between EU and domestic law before the referendum made clear;

d. and finally, the EU is well run, fit for purpose, and worth the money, albeit like any system of government there is room for improvement.

These four headings are a convenient starting point from which to rebut the case for Brexit on sovereignty grounds. The rest of this chapter will deal with point (a) about the institutions, which centres on the question of democracy: whether the EU legislative process is democratic, who runs the show, how EU laws are made, and the so-called democratic deficit. It is a long chapter because in Britain few understand the political machinery of the EU, and myths and "alternative facts" can be repeated with impunity and without fear of contradiction, so no one is ever the wiser.

Points (b) to (d) will be covered in Chap. 5. They take us to the heart of the matter, the nature of sovereignty itself, which in the referendum was presented in simplistic terms as all or nothing, subjugation or independence. The chapter explains that, on the contrary, sovereignty is always shared in one form or another and that it makes clear political and economic sense to do so. It also assails the powerful myths of the all-enveloping reach of EU law, which has usurped national sovereignty and is leading inexorably to a European "super-state"; of federalism being a step change rather than a matter of degree; of EU laws being red tape; and of the alleged dysfunctionality of the EU. And it asks whether British-made laws will necessarily be better, or is it once again more a question of the common British preoccupation of form over substance; and why people get so worked up about the European Court of Justice.

To understand how the EU works, a beginner should start by reading some good books, of the kind referred to in the first paragraph of Sect. 3.2.1, such as El-Agraa.[1] There is a wide selection: so read widely. By all means then read books written by Eurosceptics, like Bootle, and Halligan and Lyons, to get another perspective. The main thing is to keep learning and not to develop a closed mind. Correct and verifiable information is available from many sources, not least from the many official European Union websites.

And choose your newspaper carefully.

4.2   Democracy: The EU Legislative Process—Is It Undemocratic?

Here are a few of the myths, distortions, slogans, misunderstandings and "alternative facts" disseminated about the EU's legislative process.

> The British people are profoundly democratic and do not accept to be governed by bureaucrats who are not accountable for their mistakes. [...] Always these laws handed down from on high would be laws coming from them in which we had no say. [...] The Commission is not elected and its legislation is neither publicly introduced nor openly discussed. [...] The referendum gave these people a voice and what they have told us is that this country, its laws and its sovereignty are more important to them than the edicts of anonymous bureaucrats striving to rule them from nowhere.[2]
> (Roger Scruton on BBC Radio 4)

[T] he [European] Council does not pass laws, but it is responsible for appointing the members of the European Commission which does.[3] (Jane Lewis, *Stay or Go?*)

Parliamentary sovereignty [has been] eroded by faceless bureaucrats in Brussels.[4] (Edward Heathcoat Amory in *Daily Mail*)

[The European Commission] is the powerful civil service of the EU. It is where EU laws are born. It is political. The European Parliament has become a serious player, voting on almost all the laws proposed by the European Commission. [The Council of Ministers] is where the member states have their say.[5] (BBC News)

[The EU is] a profoundly anti-democratic organization. [...] Many of us, having had this utterly anti-democratic rule from Brussels, no longer wish to be part of it. [...] Every year that goes past, we are asked to swallow more and more things for which we have never voted and upon which we have never been consulted.[6] (Simon Heffer, speech in Peterborough 2016)

[T]here are massive levels of opposition in almost all its member states to the anti-democratic way [the EU] works.[7] (*Sunday Telegraph*)

[W]ithout any control by parliament, our Government is forced to enact any law from Brussels.[8] (*The Sun*)

There is also the Council of Ministers where national leaders meet with one another face to face. In practice, many key decisions are taken in bilateral meetings between Prime Ministers and Presidents.[9] (Roger Bootle, *The Trouble with Europe*)

The statements quoted above misrepresent the EU legislative process: laws are decided by the unelected (and "faceless") bureaucrats of the Commission; the laws are not publicly presented or discussed: admittedly, according to the BBC, the member states in the Council of Ministers do "have their say"; national governments are forced to enact any law from Brussels; the Council of Ministers is a meeting of national leaders (prime ministers and presidents?), who take some key decisions but their role, if any, in legislation is unclear; at all events, the way the EU works is "anti-democratic."

What is the real situation with the passage of EU legislation? The normal procedure is shown in Fig. 4.1.

As is shown in the figure, the Commission drafts a legislative proposal, in English legal parlance a "bill." It consults widely both internally and outside the Commission before finalizing a proposal. There are mandatory mechanisms for consulting committees of member states' officials on proposals and requiring that the committee must give a favourable opinion

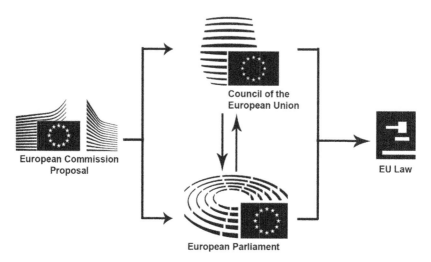

Fig. 4.1 EU legislative process

on the draft legislation. The final proposal is sent to the two legislative institutions of the EU, the Council of Ministers (officially the "Council of the European Union") and the European Parliament. Each of these institutions discusses the proposal individually. On the basis of their deliberations they may change the draft, often in major respects, and finally they consult and together approve a final version, which becomes an EU law.

The proposals the Commission brings forward for deliberation by the legislators are not entirely its own initiative. They are requested by the EU's supreme decision-making body, the European Council, which brings together the 28 EU leaders (prime ministers or, in a few cases, like France, presidents.)

Thus, EU laws are not normally passed by the European Commission, but by the Council of Ministers and the European Parliament. Presently, we will look at the composition of the two legislative bodies, at whether or not they are democratically elected, and at the extent to which national parliaments and other national bodies are involved in the process of EU legislation. But let's try first to debunk the myths about the Commission. I say "try" because this peculiarly British picture of what the Commission does and the powers it has have become an alternative reality in this country, a perception which while like fake news patently false is almost impossible to disabuse people of.

4.3   THE EUROPEAN (EU) COMMISSION

The "European Commission" or "EU Commission" is an institution with a board or executive committee and a staff that carries out the board's instructions. The board, called the "college," consists of 28 members or "commissioners," one from each member state. They are nominated by their respective governments. Although nominated by their member state, they represent the interests of the European Union, not their own country. While they will clearly retain close links with their government, they commit themselves to act independently and not to follow instructions.

There is currently a different procedure for the appointment of the president of the Commission than for the other 27 members. The nominee for president is chosen by the EU's supreme decision-making body, the European Council (28 prime ministers or presidents). For the period 2014–19, the European Council tried a new procedure for appointing the Commission president to make it more democratic. They agreed to appoint as Commission president the candidate of the political grouping in the European Parliament elections of May 2014 that won the most seats. Before the elections, the Parliament organized televised debates between the rival candidates. The winning group was the centre-right "European People's Party" and their candidate Jean-Claude Juncker from Luxembourg was duly appointed as Commission president and then endorsed by a vote of the European Parliament.

The other 27 prospective members of the Commission nominated by their governments and proposed by the Commission president are screened by the European Parliament, in a procedure similar to that for the approval of nominees for public offices by the US Congress. The Parliament can reject a nominee it finds unsatisfactory and sometimes does so. Most members of the Commission are former national ministers and some indeed former prime ministers. After their stint in the Commission, many commissioners go on to hold other national or international public offices. They are rarely political lightweights.

The term of office of the Commission and all its members is five years, renewable once.

4.3.1   Unelected Bureaucrats, Unaccountable and Irremovable

It is true then that the members of the Commission are not elected, though for the president an attempt was made in 2014 to obtain greater democratic legitimacy for the appointment. But it is perfectly normal for them not to be elected, considering the tasks the Commission performs.

First, what does the Commission not do? Answer: it does not pass laws, except delegated secondary legislation.

What does it do? Answer: its tasks are typical of a civil service, but specific to the civil service of a supranational organization, viz:

- legislative drafting and developing policies, and in this context carrying out the necessary prior consultations with member states, professional organizations and NGOs. Before drafting primary legislation for adoption by the legislative bodies, the Council of Ministers and the Parliament, the Commission seeks the approval of the European Council, the supreme decision-making body of the EU, for its plans. Thus, it does not act in complete independence from the member countries of the EU, its political masters, or indeed autocratically;
- disseminating information;
- implementing established policies through decisions in individual cases, and supervising specialized agencies that administer such policies;
- checking whether member states are observing EU law and launching infringement proceedings in the European Court of Justice when they are not;
- and proposing the budget and managing it when approved.

The governor of the Bank of England is not elected. The head of the British National Health Service is not elected. Why should the Commission have to be? It is not a government or a "cabinet" in the British sense. Although sometimes called the EU's "executive," or even its "political executive," this is more in the sense of a civil service or administration. Many people—even the BBC—are sometimes misled by the terminology and equate EU institutions to national bodies with similar names and job descriptions. The EU institutional architecture is unlike that of national political systems.

Are the members of the Commission really bureaucrats? Though accepted practice in anti-EU British newspapers, to call the commissioners "bureaucrats" is wrong for two reasons: (a) they have responsibilities equivalent at least to a national cabinet minister, and (b) they are not career civil servants but are appointed for a limited term of office typical of a political office holder. You would not call the American Secretary of

State or the governor of the Bank of England a "bureaucrat." The term "bureaucrat" applied to commissioners is pure Brexit propaganda. Together with the epithet "unelected," it is calculated to arouse anger about the undemocratic nature of the EU in which, so the narrative goes, the Commission—"unelected bureaucrats"—pass EU laws. This narrative is wholly false and misleads the public because the European Commission does not pass laws except for secondary legislation and taking decisions under specifically delegated powers.[10]

It is equally false and demeaning to call the permanent president of the European Council, Donald Tusk, a former prime minister of Poland, a "bureaucrat." He is an office holder doing a high-level job, like Mark Carney or Cressida Dick (the Metropolitan Police Commissioner), who I have not yet heard called bureaucrats by the British press.

The ingrained habit of calling all top EU officials "unelected bureaucrats" sometimes leads British Eurosceptic papers to slip up and wrongly include members of the European Parliament in this category, as the *Daily Mail* has done with Guy Verhofstadt, who was most definitely elected, to the European Parliament, and is therefore *not* a bureaucrat.[11]

What about the Commission staff? There are roughly 33,000 European career civil servants and contract staff—from director generals (permanent secretaries) to clerical officers—working in the Commission. In their case, there is definitely no harm in their being "unelected," for they do the normal work of civil servants and do not take major decisions. It is the Commission proper, namely its 28-member board or "college," presided over by Jean-Claude Juncker, that takes the big decisions in the areas for which it is responsible.

There's no harm in calling the run-of-the-mill EU staffers or career civil servants in the Commission "bureaucrats," but given the pejorative connotations of the term—arbitrariness, concoction of overelaborate rules, pen-pushing and thumb-twiddling—it is a little unfair. Pen-pushing and bureaucratic meddling are not a true picture of EU civil servants, whatever Matthew Elliott in his Brexit bible, the "Great European Rip-Off," may say.[12] Ask any Whitehall civil servant in regular contact with the Brussels institutions his opinion of the EU civil service and they will testify to its quality. EU civil servants likewise have a high regard for most national officials dealing with EU business, including the British civil service. British newspapers would hardly label national civil servants "bureaucrats" unless they wanted to denigrate or abuse them.

"Eurocrat," with its connotations of untrammelled power, diktats, autocratic behaviour, and arrogance, is even more of a misnomer. The Commission or any other European Union institution for that matter does not have absolute power or anything like it.

What about another of the Brexit mantras that is repeated *ad nauseam* in the anti-EU press that "the Commission is unaccountable and unlike a normal government cannot be removed by the people in an election?"

In fact, the Commission's top officials, the 28 commissioners, are removable. If the Commission's performance is unsatisfactory, the European Parliament can pass a censure motion to remove it. This almost happened in 1999, but the Commission resigned as a body to forestall the censure motion. Parliament's threatened action was prompted by cases of misuse of funds by commissioners, most notoriously Edith Cresson, who had paid her dentist for studies for which he was not even remotely qualified. Mrs Cresson was prosecuted and punished for this behaviour and the money was returned. Action was also taken in other cases brought to light by whistle-blowers around the same time.

Parliament subsequently approved a new Commission, with a new president, Romano Prodi, but containing some of the former members, including the British member Sir Leon Brittan. Parliament required the Commission to undertake a major programme of reforms to prevent similar abuses by commissioners or staff members in future. The reforms were carried out between 2000 and 2003 under the supervision of the other British commissioner (at that time the big countries had two commissioners), Neil Kinnock. They laid the foundations for an internal management and control system in the Commission which matches the best standards found in any national administration, including that of the UK.

There have been other occasions when the Parliament has threatened to vote the Commission out of office, though the threat of action did not progress as far as in 1999. For example, in 2008, during preparation of the motion to grant the Commission "discharge" for its management of the 2006 budget, the Parliament's Budgetary Control Committee almost voted in favour of a censure motion because it felt the Commission was not doing enough to reduce irregularities (mainly technical errors) in connection with projects carried out by member state authorities with structural funds. The crisis was averted by the Commission agreeing to a comprehensive action programme to tighten up its supervision of structural funds in the member states. This has now considerably reduced the rate of error in these programmes. This is covered in more detail in Chap. 6.

The powers of scrutiny and censure the European Parliament holds in relation to the Commission are substantial and taken seriously by the Commission. Parliament's Budgetary Control Committee which scrutinizes the Commission's management of the budget is rightly feared by the commissioners who have to appear before it to defend their department's performance. A former commissioner for regional policy, now in the European Parliament, said at the time that she dreaded her annual appearance before the Budget Control Committee the most of all the meetings she had in the course of the year. Her department prepared hundreds of pages of briefing for her appearance before this Committee, as it had previously done for Michel Barnier when he was regional policy commissioner.

Parliament has real teeth and does not allow the Commission to forget it. To claim there are no checks and balances on the Commission's freedom of action shows a wilful ignorance of the real situation.

The Commission is also scrutinized by the EU's independent external auditor, the European Court of Auditors, in relation both to its management of the budget and the effectiveness and value for money of its activities. In the annual budget discharge process before the Parliament, the Parliament and the European Court of Auditors join forces in an adversarial proceeding in which the Commission is effectively in the dock.

Finally, the Commission is accountable to the top decision-making body of the EU, the European Council, the EU summits of prime ministers or presidents. The Commission takes its instructions from, and answers to, the member states' leaders, not vice versa.

It is surprising how some British politicians fail to grasp this fundamental fact and imagine the Commission can impose its will on the member states and the European Council or assert itself in taking an independent line to that of the national leaders. In believing this they have fallen for their own propaganda. The reality is that the Council of Ministers and the European Council, the institutions representing the member states, are the true top dogs of the EU and, like the Parliament, can and do hold the Commission to account.

4.3.2 Delegated Legislation and Other Powers

The Commission itself enacts some secondary legislation, equivalent to statutory instruments in Britain, and takes decisions in certain policy areas like competition policy, decisions which are enforceable EU law. This delegation of powers to pass regulations and take binding decisions is expressly stipulated in the treaties or more often in primary legislation passed by the legislative authorities, the Council of Ministers and Parliament. Just as the procedure for drafting a proposal for primary legislation involves extensive consultation of the member states and outside interests, so does the procedure for issuing a Commission regulation.

For example, in the early 2000s the author was involved in drafting a regulation—thus, a "Commission regulation"—addressed to the member states on the standards they had to observe in administrative checks and audits of projects funded by the structural funds. It took nine meetings of a committee comprised of civil servants from the then 15 member states over a period of ten months to agree the final text of the regulation. The text had been heavily amended in the course of its passage through the committee. As well as the meetings with the 15 member states' representatives in the committee, countless inter-departmental meetings within the Commission were required to refine its position in response to member states' requests for changes to the draft regulation. Such extensive consultations will be familiar to British civil servants preparing national legislation. To claim the Commission can act autonomously, without consultation of national authorities, interest groups and NGOs, and that it hands down "edicts from on high" is pure fantasy based either on ignorance or deliberate deception—I tend towards the first explanation.

A similar level of consultation, both in and outside the Commission, with member states, industry, and scientific and professional organizations, takes place with all delegated decisions and legislation by the Commission in fields as diverse as competition and pesticides. For some areas, the EU has created specialized agencies such as the European Food Safety Authority, the European Aviation Safety Authority, the European Medicines Agency, the European Chemicals Agency, and the European Environmental Agency. The European Commission has overall oversight over these agencies, but they operate largely independently under clear mandates set by EU legislation.

In competition policy, whose purpose is to maintain an open and level playing field for firms to operate in the European market, the Commission exercises powers conferred by the treaty and primary legislation to prevent or remove barriers to fair competition. No specialized competition authority has been set up. The Commission still, as it has done since the very beginnings of the EU in the European Economic Community, exercises these powers itself. It can bust cartels and fine the firms involved, block anti-competitive mergers, and force governments to reduce or abandon proposed subsidies ("state aid"). The Commission's competition policy is acknowledged to be effective, fair and world-leading.

It cannot be emphasized enough that the Commission and its subordinate agencies only exercise powers that have been specifically mandated to it by the treaties, which are approved by all the member states, and have been further defined in legislation that has likewise been approved by the member states' ministers in the Council of Ministers and nowadays by the directly elected European Parliament as well. Moreover, all these powers are not exercised in isolation but with close involvement of member states' authorities, professional bodies and NGOs.

4.3.3   Conclusion on the Commission

In conclusion, contrary to the Brexit myths fed to the public on a daily basis by the Brexit newspapers and Brexiteer politicians and therefore widely believed:

- The European Commission does not pass EU legislation, except subordinate legislation similar to British statutory instruments. The Commission's main role in the passage of EU legislation is as a drafter. The institutions that pass EU laws are the Council of Ministers and the European Parliament, whose democratic credentials will be discussed below.
- The Commission is not elected in the normal sense, but its president is now appointed under a democratic procedure linked to the elections of the European Parliament. All the members of the Commission are screened and confirmed by the democratically elected European Parliament. It is perfectly normal for a body performing tasks like the Commission's to be appointed and not elected.
- The members of the Commission are political appointees, who can be called public servants or officials, but hardly "civil servants" or "bureaucrats."
- The Commission has a fixed term of office, after which its members are replaced by new ones nominated again by the member states. So the idea that they are irremovable (perhaps like members of the US Supreme Court appointed for life) and can act without regard to the people who appointed them or to public opinion is mistaken.

- The Commission can be removed by a censure motion of the European Parliament.
- The Commission is accountable to the European Parliament, the European Court of Auditors, and ultimately to the EU's supreme decision-making body, the European Council of member states' leaders.
- The Commission is mandated by the European Council, the supreme decision-making body of the EU, to prepare new legislation or policies. It does not act in complete independence from the member countries of the EU, its political masters, or indeed autocratically. Nor, as will be seen below, does it control the passage of legislation through the legislative bodies. The legislation is often substantially amended during its passage or it may be blocked entirely and the Commission is forced to withdraw it. The Commission consults widely on draft legislation, particularly among member states' authorities.
- The secondary legislation the Commission issues only concerns matters delegated to it by primary legislation. The specialized agencies set up for certain tasks under the Commission's auspices and supervision likewise operate under the precise terms of primary legislation. The Commission exercises delegated powers itself in certain areas like competition in accordance with rules and criteria set out in the treaty and legislation. In all its activities, legislative and executive, the Commission is subject to mechanisms and mandatory procedures for obtaining authority from the member states and Parliament and for consulting member states' authorities, professional and scientific organizations and NGOs.

4.4   THE COUNCIL OF MINISTERS: THE INCONVENIENT LEGISLATOR

The Council of Ministers is a problem for Brexit propaganda, for its existence detracts from their claim that the "unelected bureaucrats" of the Commission decide EU laws. They react to this inconvenient fact by doing one of several things:

- ignore it completely and the part British ministers (usually elected MPs) played in enacting the EU rules they are attacking;

- play down its influence on legislation by denying it does more than just discuss and give an opinion on Commission proposals and claiming the Commission controls the process from start to finish and in the event of disagreement will settle maters by "stitch-ups" with big member states like Germany;
- if forced to admit that the Council does have a decisive influence on legislation, they object that its majority voting system is undemocratic, and exaggerate the frequency with which the UK is outvoted and its interests thereby harmed.

More on these distortions below after describing the reality of the Council of Ministers' role in EU lawmaking.

The official name of the Council of Ministers is the "Council of the European Union." Informally, it is often referred to simply as "the Council." It has but one task, to deliberate on and approve EU legislation, or take EU decisions, concerning a particular policy area. It consists of the responsible ministers for the relevant policy area from each of the 28 member states. Thus, it meets in varying formations, the "Agriculture Council" bringing together the member states' ministers for agriculture, the "Foreign Affairs Council (Trade)" composed of the member states' trade ministers, and so on. Each minister represents his or her national government in the deliberations.

The Council of Ministers is often confused with the European Council. The two bodies have completely different compositions and roles: the Council of Ministers is composed of specialist ministers and having the main task of passing legislation; the European Council brings together the leaders of the member states to set the EU agenda, define future strategy and take big or intractable decisions like the budget. The similarity of the names, and the fact that both bodies represent the member states at different levels and are serviced by the same secretariat with the same website, make confusion inevitable and cause people, particularly in Britain, to overlook the Council of *Ministers*, the legislator, entirely because they are focussed on the prime ministers' or presidents' body, the European Council.

The "Eurogroup" is a special "Council of Ministers" consisting of the finance ministers of the now 19 countries that use the single currency, the euro. The Eurogroup decides matters concerning the single currency. It operates in a similar manner to the Councils in other fields but has a permanent president appointed by the European Council from among its members. It was in almost continuous session during the sovereign debt crisis, when unlike other Councils it acted more as a preparatory chamber for management decisions taken by the leaders of the Eurozone member states themselves. The allegedly "undemocratic" nature of these decisions and their implementation is discussed below.

The ordinary legislative system of the EU, however, is clearly, even from the cursory glance we have given it so far—before looking at the second legislative chamber, the European Parliament—not undemocratic. The claims about its fundamentally undemocratic nature do not hold up.

- The "unelected" Commission does not pass legislation; it only proposes legislation except for some delegated matters.
- The Council of Ministers, the first of the EU's two legislative chambers, is composed of the responsible ministers from the member states' governments. Most of these ministers will be elected members of their parliaments; a few may not be MPs but appointed by the prime minister from the outside, such as from the House of Lords.

4.4.1   Decision-Making in the Council: Majority Voting and Unanimity

In a large number of areas, most notably Single Market legislation, the Council can vote on the laws or decisions that come before it by a "qualified majority." The rules for qualified majority voting changed in 2014. Previously, member states were each allocated a fixed number of votes depending on their size. For a qualified majority, 260 out of the total of 352 votes, from 15 member states, were needed. Now, a "double majority" system applies, under which 55% of the member states (that is, at present 16 out of the 28) must be in favour and those member states must represent 65% of the population of the EU. In some policy areas such as taxation, the accession of new member states, foreign and security policy, and workers' rights, unanimity is required. Majority voting implies certain countries being outvoted and leaving the meeting dissatisfied on certain points, so in the interests of cohesion the Council will attempt to achieve a compromise before going on to a vote. Currently, around 80% of Council decisions on laws and other matters can be taken by majority voting.[13]

Before and during the EU referendum, Leavers argued that majority voting in the Council of Ministers was undemocratic because Britain could be and often was outvoted and because its voting strength had declined over time because of new countries joining and the smaller countries had more votes than their size would justify, for example Germany and the UK with 29 votes compared with Malta's three, although Germany's population, for example, is 180 times bigger than Malta's. The latter argument has become academic now that the old weighted-vote majority system has been replaced with the single-vote, double majority one.

But the first objection is still relevant. Is it not undemocratic when instead of proceeding by consensus a vote is taken, with the consequence that one or more member states are outvoted and their interests are not fully taken into account in the legislation?

The objection to majority voting in the Council of Ministers relates specifically to the possibility of such voting in a supranational organization like the EU, for no objection is raised to majority voting in a national context like the British Parliament. The fact, however, is that Britain and the other member states have agreed to majority voting on certain matters in the EU Council and the possibility of being outvoted is part and parcel of such agreements. In Britain's case, it was Margaret Thatcher who agreed in the amending treaty, the Single European Act, to extend majority voting in the Council for Single Market legislation because otherwise vital laws to make the Single Market a reality would continue to be blocked.

Clearly, for purist advocates of Brexit on the ground that the ceding of sovereignty has gone too far such procedures are anathema and if they are necessary in a supranational organization in order to "get things done" then better not be a member of the club at all.

In reality, the objections are overdone. The aim is to approve laws reflecting the common good of the parties, and not in every detail the individual interests of each one. Being occasionally outvoted is part of the rough and tumble of politics. It happens at a single country level in national, regional, or local government—for example, in the House of Commons, the Scottish Parliament, or Birmingham City Council—and also between different levels of government, when, for example, local authorities are unhappy with a decision taken by the Westminster Parliament that prohibits them from raising council taxes above a certain percentage without a referendum, or when the Scottish government is prevented by Westminster from having a second vote on Scottish independence.

If such outcomes are not "undemocratic" between different levels of government in a single country, why should they be in relations between member states and the EU, provided the member states have agreed to the possibility by accepting majority voting in the treaty in the first place?

Furthermore, in the EU the hurdles for passing legislation in the Council are higher than simple majorities. In Britain, decision-making by simple majorities, with the losing side's interests being completely ignored, is eulogized as the very essence of our democracy. Proportional representation in elections has been rejected. But the form of democracy chosen in Britain is not the only form and a different form can be just as democratic, if not more so.

There is also the fact that the issues on which a member state is outvoted in the EU Council of Ministers are not always substantial; the member state can usually "live with" the final text. The occasions when a vital national interest is at stake like the proposed allocation of refugee quotas during the 2015 migrant crisis which was strenuously opposed by some central and eastern European countries are rare. For a sovereignty purist, any case of Britain being outvoted is unacceptable. For a pragmatist, most such cases are not a big deal, but part of the "swings and the roundabouts"; they are quite likely to be compensated for by being on the winning side the next time.

During the referendum campaign, "Leave" campaigners exaggerated the frequency with which the UK was the odd man out in Council discussions and ended up being outvoted and its vital interests therefore being ignored. In fact, the occasions it has been outvoted on important issues are less numerous than claimed. Britain has much more often than not been in the progressive mainstream of opinion in the Council and therefore generally on the winning side in votes. This is partly because of the greater staff resources it as a big country can invest in Council legislative proceedings so that it is able to influence the text of legislation before it comes to a vote. Another point is that the Council of Ministers is not the only channel for influencing legislation; there is also the European Parliament where Britain has its own MEPs.[14]

Being occasionally outvoted on the details of legislation is an integral part of democracy at any level and in the EU context it is a small price to pay for the benefits of cooperation, in terms of administrative efficiency and economic prosperity. In a highly complex and interdependent world, the administrative savings from jointly agreed technical legislation are undeniable—about which more in the next chapter.

As noted already, the argument about the not completely proportional allocation of votes between member states in the Council under the old majority voting system has now become academic. But it was anyway a little unreasonable. After all, in no national legislature can MPs' constituencies always be the same size. In Britain, moreover, the "first past the post" system without proportional representation means that smaller parties like the Liberal Democrats or UKIP do not win the number of seats the total number of votes cast for them warrants, leaving whole swathes of voters to all intents and purposes disenfranchised. On the contrary, it was arguable that the favouring of small countries in the EU Council voting system was more democratic than a strictly proportional one as it prevented a few big member states ganging up on the small ones and ignoring their interests. The US system also stipulates two senators for each state regardless of the states' size. Similar controversy surrounds the ratio between population size and representation by MEPs in the European Parliament, of which more below.

Another point is that despite their proportionately smaller voting weights should a vote be taken, the larger countries had a built-in advantage in the Council, in that they had more staff resources to allocate to the work there and therefore could exert greater influence on the final form of the legislation. So Britain's interests were unlikely to be harmed by the disproportionate voting power of tiny Malta.

As already noted, some EU laws and decisions, for example on taxation, cannot be passed by a majority vote but require all member states to agree. Moreover, such matters are often reserved for the European Council, the EU's top meeting of the member states' leaders. This is the case for admission of new member states to the EU and the medium-term budget. Mendacious claims were made about Turkish accession during the referendum campaign. It was asserted that the UK would not have a veto over Turkey's accession to the EU and that Turkish accession was "imminent." Both these claims were false though carried by the Brexit-supporting newspapers and repeated by all the protagonists in the Leave campaign. In fact, accession of new countries being a matter for unanimity Britain would have to agree, and that of Turkey was a long-term prospect lying at least 25 years in the future, because the accession negotiations had not progressed and had been stalled since the assumption of power by President Erdogan, because of what the EU saw as a reversal of the progress being made towards democracy and protection of human rights in Turkey. The conclusion drawn from these lies, that unless Britain got out of the EU soon it would be powerless to stop hordes of Turkish workers flooding on to our labour market and their families monopolizing the NHS, schools and other public services, was pure scaremongering.

4.4.2   *The Eurogroup*

Brexit supporters have made much of the treatment meted out to Greece and other countries during the euro crisis as an example of the EU's undemocratic and bullying nature. In his thought-provoking book, *And the Weak Suffer What They Must?*,[15] Yanis Varoufakis, who was Greece's finance minister during most of the hard negotiations with the EU and the IMF, levels his main criticisms at the austerity policies the two organizations insisted upon, which he considers wrong-headed, over-dogmatic and counterproductive. But secondarily, he also attacks the undemocratic nature of a supranational system that substitutes itself for national political choices of economic policy and imposes the collective will of the organization on a country, leading to severe hardship among its people.

Whether or not the austerity programmes imposed on Greece and other countries concerned, mainly Ireland, Portugal and Cyprus, were justified is for economic historians to debate. While they appear to have worked, the social cost was high and it is possible other policies might have caused less hardship.

It is claimed that forcing such policies on a country against its will and by the combined weight of a "Troika" of institutions—the Commission, the European Central Bank and the IMF—not provided for by any Treaty amounts to undemocratic bullying. On the other hand, the Growth and Stability Pact, governing the obligations of the member states in the Eurozone, permitted the Eurozone member states to sanction a member for non-compliance with the rules to deal with excessive deficits and debt levels, obligations which Greece had accepted when it adopted the euro. The measures were moreover decided and implemented completely transparently in accordance with the procedures. Officials from the "Troika" only prepared and provisionally agreed the measures, the Eurozone country leaders meeting in the European Council together with the IMF, and in some cases other interested countries such as the US, collectively decided them, and the Eurozone country finance ministers in the Eurogroup supervised their detailed implementation, together with staff from the Commission, the ECB and the IMF. The Commission also regularly reported to and debated with the European Parliament on the action, with the Parliament on one occasion organizing an excellent debate with the Greek Prime Minister Mr Tsipras which probably influenced the final settlement. So if there is substance in the criticism of disregard of democratic processes at national level, especially in view of the referendum Mr

Tsipras called just before the final meeting, which rejected the terms he was then forced to accept at EU level,[16] it is the deficient system of governance of Eurozone countries' economic policies prior to the crisis that is more to blame than the collective action of the Eurozone countries to deal with the crisis.

Nevertheless, the democratic oversight of the governance of the euro, given that these powers of the EU can have immediate and severe social consequences for euro member states, is clearly particularly important and requires greater safeguards than the routine, less acute work of the Council of Ministers. One of the proposals for improving the governance of the single currency, which is supported by President Macron of France, is a specific assembly for the Eurozone.[17]

4.4.3 Technical-level Discussions and Mandatory Consultation of Advisory Bodies

The meetings of the Council of Ministers on a particular draft law or decision are the tip of a pyramid of preparation by working groups of national civil servants. These working groups may meet many times to discuss the Commission's proposal. In all meetings, the Commission will introduce, present, explain and defend its proposal, contrary to Roger Scruton's assertion quoted above. At working level, it will be Commission civil servants who present and defend the proposal and discuss amendments; in the final Council meeting it will be the commissioner. Working party meetings will hear evidence from experts and receive reports from specialist advisory groups and technical and professional bodies both at national and European level. The final stage of the preparation of Council meetings is the weekly meeting of the permanent ambassadors of the 28 member states, the "Coreper," which sets the final agenda and decides which items will be nodded through and which will be discussed and possibly voted on. In many policy areas, the treaty requires the legislators to consult the two main advisory bodies, the European Economic and Social Committee and the Committee of the Regions. This widens the range of professional input into the legislative process, of which more in Sect. 4.6.1 below.

Commission proposals for EU laws are regularly amended in the course of their passage through the Council. Sometimes a proposal does not advance because the member states cannot agree and the Commission withdraws it. The claim that the Commission forces through half-baked proposals against the will of member states has no foundation.

Brexit supporters also claim that EU decisions and laws are often political "stitch-ups" between the Commission and the larger member states like Germany and France. True, such unorthodox procedures may be used on conflicted and intractable matters like the EU's multi-year budget framework, which for obvious reasons is fought over tooth and nail as it involves large sums of money. For example, it is no secret the French and the Germans have typically reached private deals on the share-out of the budget between the Common Agricultural Policy and other policies like research before the official European Council meeting. But such cases are not frequent and anyway they are not played out in the Council of Ministers but between the leaders at European Council level. The "stitch-up," if such there is, will be between the most powerful member states, like Germany, France and Britain. The Commission will be a participant, but not one of the protagonists.

Similar decisions directly by the national leaders, over the heads of their ministers, may occasionally be taken to unblock particular matters that are deadlocked in the Council, but the (directly elected) European Parliament will have to agree and so to the extent that there are "stitch-ups" the decisions are taken at political, not Commission, level. Apart from such exceptional cases, the procedure for considering legislative texts proposed by the Commission is meticulous and transparent.

4.4.4   Involvement of National Parliaments During the Passage of Legislation

The ministers responsible for the subject matter of an EU proposal are kept informed of its progress by their civil servants and they instruct their staff as to the line to take on particular issues. The various committees in the House of Commons and the Lords are also kept informed by ministers and their civil servants and can thus contribute to the government's positions on the draft legislation. Unfortunately, in Britain's main legislative chamber, the House of Commons, this prior parliamentary scrutiny of draft EU laws is often insufficient. The House of Lords is much better in this respect. It has an impressive record of scrutinizing EU legislative programmes and individual pieces of legislation *ex ante,* involving the taking of evidence from a wide range of EU and national officials and interest groups. The Cameron government, however, further reduced the time allocated to draft EU legislation in the House of Commons on the ground of pressure of other business. The huge volume of former EU business to be "repatriated" after Brexit and of old EU legislation requiring review after it has been transposed wholesale into domestic law by the Withdrawal Act will redouble the pressure of parliamentary business, at a time when the government is proposing to cut the number of MPs.[18]

If the prior parliamentary scrutiny of EU legislation is inadequate in Britain, that is its own fault, not the EU's. The solution to the bitter complaints of Brexiteers that EU directives are incorporated into domestic British law by statutory instruments signed off by ministers without discussion in the House of Common surely lies in Parliament's hands: arrange for better scrutiny in Parliament beforehand so that Parliament's views are better reflected in the EU Council before the legislation is adopted. Other countries are much better at this than the UK, even much smaller countries. Under the Cameron governments, it was as if the EU was assigned such low priority, and the staff involved were cut back to such an extent, that pending EU business was often ignored until it was too late and the government was surprised and angered by a *fait accompli* that had "passed under the radar."

4.4.5   *The Falsity of Brexit Propaganda That EU Rules Are Imposed*

The claims of Brexiteers quoted in Sect. 4.2 above, for example, Prof. Scruton's about EU laws being "handed down from on high," about Britain "having no say" in them and about their not being "openly discussed"—because, according to him, it is the Commission that decides everything in the EU—do not bear scrutiny. The same goes for Simon Heffer's tirade against the EU imposing this or that further burden on Britain without consulting us. Any Whitehall civil servant involved in EU legislation would quickly disabuse them of these misconceptions. But for people who do not believe in international cooperation that in any way diminishes national sovereignty, the reality is inconvenient. However sincerely held their beliefs, the standards to be expected of influential commentators in their contributions to public discourse should make them pause before making statements at odds with verifiable facts.

Even the BBC occasionally slips up. One of the few occasions when I was dissatisfied with the information it provides about the EU on its website was in an animation early on in the referendum debate about how the EU works called "The EU: All you need to know in under two minutes," published on 19 February 2016. The admittedly highly simplified animation understated the function of the Council of Ministers. It said the Council was the place where the member states "have their say." The phrase "have their say" is too weak: it usually means "express one's views," "give one's opinion," not "decide on." Also, the text did not say on what the Council expresses its views. Although the viewer might have inferred from the previous section about the Commission that the Council "had its say" on legislation proposed by the Commission, this was not explicit and the fact that the Council is a key actor in the passage of EU legislation did not emerge. The following section on the Parliament was much clearer, saying that the Parliament voted on almost all EU laws.

4.4.6   Secretariat, Rotating Presidency, EU Laws

The Council of Ministers has around 3500 permanent staff—EU civil servants—to prepare meetings of its working parties, Coreper (the meeting of the member states' permanent representatives to the EU) and the Council itself, to translate its documents, and to interpret speakers' interventions at meetings. The same civil servants service the meetings of the European Council, the member states' heads of state or government, which is the top EU decision-making body.

All the member states take it in turn to hold the "presidency of the Council" for six months each. This involves setting the agenda for Council of Ministers meetings, in consultation with the Commission and the previous and following presidency countries, and preparing and chairing meetings, supported by the Council of Ministers staff. Big countries like Britain are sometimes contemptuous of small countries struggling to shoulder this burden, but in fact they often manage better than expected and the enthusiasm, effort and national pride they invest in "their" presidency can sometimes produce impressive results in finding compromises that elude bigger countries. The revolving presidency certainly improves the cohesion and togetherness of the European Union, though it might not be to the taste of English nationalists like Jacob Rees-Mogg, as it does not properly reflect the more elevated status of the UK.

EU laws are either regulations or directives. Regulations are laws that are directly applicable in the member states without needing to be first incorporated into a law passed by their parliament. Directives are framework laws that lay down the objectives and main measures for action to achieve a certain purpose. They must be transposed into a national law before becoming enforceable. Member states thus have a certain flexibility when converting directives into national law.

The term "directive" in English is unfortunate. It gives an impression of an edict handed down by a superior authority without consultation or redress. It is a translation of the French *directive* but the French word has a different meaning from the English. In French *directive* means more a "guideline" or a "framework," whose details can be filled in by the member states as they think best fits their particular national conditions. The translations into other languages—German *Richtlinie*, Dutch *richtsnoer*, and Finnish *suuntaviiva*, for example—express the term's discretionary nature better. The English word expresses the opposite.

Most EU laws are passed by the European Parliament as well as the Council of Ministers (see below European Parliament). They are thus prefaced by the title "Regulation (or Directive) of the European Parliament and the Council," dated, numbered, and signed by both institutions, the Council of Ministers in the person of the member of the responsible Council of Ministers from the country holding the presidency at the time, and the European Parliament in the person of its president or a vice-president.

EU laws are published in the EU's official law gazette, the "Official Journal," in all the 24 official languages of the EU countries. All draft laws and decisions are also published in the Official Journal in their various language versions, as are many other notices about EU business. The websites of the Commission's directorates general also contain detailed information about proposed legislation and other developments, as do the sites of the Council and the Parliament. It is ridiculous to complain of a lack of transparency about EU affairs and member states being ambushed. The information is all there and easily accessible to anyone who cares to look. What is more, the information on EU websites is less subject to spin than is typical of national government sources, including those in Britain. Outsiders can obtain information from the EU through freedom of information requests. This system has been substantially improved and made more rigorous over the years.

Up to the early 2000s, Council of Ministers' meetings were held in secret. In response to criticism from the European Parliament among others, the Council began to open its meetings to the public and the Lisbon Treaty of 2009 made this mandatory for parts of meetings at which legislative proposals are discussed and voted on. Nowadays, such meetings are web-steamed on the internet, following the example of the Parliament, which broadcasts not only plenary sessions but also committee meetings and *ad hoc* hearings. Whether the Council of Ministers' meetings are as interesting as those of the Parliament is for the reader to judge.

Given time, the opening to the public and now web-streaming of Council meetings should dispel the myth that the "unelected bureaucrats" of the Commission decide legislation, whereas in fact it is the Council—ministers from the governments of all 28 member states, including Britain—that passes EU legislation and takes EU decisions. This would take away the excuse member states often use for decisions that prove unpopular by pretending they were not involved in the decision, thus using "the EU" as a scapegoat. It should also counter the frequent claims that much of EU legislation is decided by "stitch-ups" between the Commission and the Council.

It has been convenient for the Brexit movement and its cheerleaders in the press to deny the existence of the Council of Ministers and the involvement of British ministers in EU decisions. Their case that the EU is autocratic is weakened by the Council's greater visibility. Prof Scruton fails to mention the Council in his well-argued pleading against Britain's involvement in the EU. This omission is, to say the least, being economical with the truth. Robert Bootle, in his highly readable books, appears to have fallen into the common trap of confusing the European Council (the leaders' meeting) and the Council of Ministers (the legislative body). Their names are confusingly similar. He therefore largely ignores the legislative function of the Council (of Ministers).

4.5   THE EUROPEAN PARLIAMENT

4.5.1   Roles: Legislation, Budget, Treaties, Supervision of Executive; Democratic Legitimacy

The second legislative chamber in the EU is the European Parliament, which is directly elected. The powers of the Parliament with regard to EU legislation have been gradually extended in successive treaty revisions to the point where the Parliament has a right of "co-decision" on the majority of EU legislation. "Co-decision," which since the Lisbon Treaty has been called the "ordinary legislative procedure," gives Parliament an equal say over legislation with the Council. The procedure involves "ping-pong" exchanges of versions of proposals between the Parliament and Council until both agree and can sign up to the final text.

Apart from its legislative powers, the Parliament also has to approve the budget, treaty changes, trade agreements, and the accession or withdrawal of EU member states—which means it must also agree to the deal on Brexit. Another of its important responsibilities is holding the Commission to account for its management of the budget through the annual budget "discharge" procedure. As already noted, it can also "sack" the Commission and it vets prospective members of the Commission and can refuse to endorse them, just as the American Senate can do with presidential nominees for offices of state.

Thus, with the members of the second legislative chamber of the EU being directly elected, it can hardly seriously be argued that the EU legislative procedure overall is fundamentally undemocratic, though there may be room for improvement. The question of the "democratic deficit" and the scope for improving the democratic legitimacy of the Parliament is addressed below.

There have been objections to the disproportionate number of seats allotted to the smaller countries compared with the bigger member states, which means that for example Maltese voters (population 432,000, 6 MEPs) are proportionately represented by more members of the Parliament than the UK (population 66 million, 73 MEPs). In its judgment on the Lisbon Treaty in 2009, the German Federal Constitutional Court found this disproportion reduced the Parliament's democratic legitimacy.[19] But there is a good reason for giving small countries proportionately more members: a minimum number of MEPs is needed for a small country to be properly represented at least on the main committees of the Parliament, without which there is hardly any representation at all. As in the Council of Ministers, where under the old majority voting system smaller countries used to have a bigger number of votes than their size warranted, overrepresentation in their number of seats in the Parliament allows small countries to defend their interests better against domination by the big countries, and compensates for the less support they receive from their governments, which obviously have a much smaller administration.

The Parliament votes on motions for the approval of legislation by simple majorities. The actual voting on hundreds of amendments and then on the measure as a whole is tedious, but many of the debates, both in the plenary session held in Strasbourg and in the committee meetings in Brussels, are of a high standard, even for listeners who have to rely on the simultaneous interpreting.

The Parliament now shares power over EU legislation with the Council of Ministers as a second but equal chamber. The "co-decision" procedure undoubtedly improves the quality of legislation and though EU legislative procedures are criticized for their length compared with, say, those in Britain, it is questionable whether this criticism is justified if the resultant laws are more thoroughly prepared and more soundly based.

Far from sitting in an ivory tower, members of the European Parliament actively seek contact with interest groups, lobbyists, and business and civil society organizations both from Europe and outside the EU and in their own countries. They organize public hearings and seminars, carry out field trips abroad and commission research. Information gathering from the whole of Europe and beyond and from a wide range of interests and viewpoints is essential for well-designed policies on subjects of new and acute importance that have to be applicable throughout Europe.

To criticize receptiveness to lobbying as akin to corruption shows as much ignorance as its opposite, the claim of sitting in an ivory tower and being out of touch. Neither the Commission nor the European Parliament could function without inviting representations from interest groups, doing research and consulting widely.

The best MEPs are in regular contact with national trade associations, interest groups and national politicians. Experience shows that representations by national trade associations can succeed in obtaining changes to EU legislation necessary to protect national interests. This sort of justified and effective lobbying activity might not attract attention from the British right-wing press, which only focuses on the monthly grandstanding antics of Nigel Farage. But other countries do report such successful lobbying as a matter of national pride, which shows that the European Parliament is not as remote or out of touch as its ill-informed critics claim.

The information gathering and research done by MEPs is supported by staff allowances funding up to four people working for the member in Parliament or in his or her home country.[20] Members also keep in touch with home by travelling back most weekends, not just to rest but also to work by speaking at conferences, giving press interviews, holding meetings with local politicians, taking part in events, and holding surgeries to meet members of the public. Another means by which MEPs keep in touch with the general public is by obtaining responses from the Commission to petitions or complaints; representatives of the Commission are required to appear before the Petitions Committee to respond to them.

The permanent base of the European Parliament and its staff is now Brussels. All meetings of the committees, which do the bulk of the work of preparing legislation, are held in Brussels, while the plenary sessions for one week each month are held in the Parliament's other base in Strasbourg. MEPs have voted frequently to end these monthly peregrinations to Strasbourg and concentrate all Parliament business in Brussels, but France has always opposed this and the *status quo* was confirmed in the Lisbon Treaty of 2009. The matter is not just a matter of national prestige for France but there are historical reasons for originally choosing Strasbourg as the seat of the Parliament: the city lies in the Alsace, which has frequently changed hands between France and Germany and so is a symbol of French-German reconciliation. The British press portrays the monthly move to Strasbourg as a junket of wining and dining and high living at national taxpayers' expense, and nicknames the special trains that are laid on to transport the tonnes of documents and hundreds of parliamentarians between the cities as "gravy trains." The reality is different. For MEPs and the Parliament's staff the monthly trip to Strasbourg is just an inconvenience they have to put up with.

4.5.2   British Media Coverage, UKIP, and the Eurosceptic Fringe

The British media's coverage of the European Parliament is patchy and gives disproportionate prominence to the insulting harangues and behaviour of Nigel Farage and his fellow UKIP members and hardly any to the constructive contributions of hard-working Labour, Liberal-Democrat or Green MEPs.

The European Parliament has long had members who are Eurosceptic in the true sense of the word, that is to say people who while believing in the EU have misgivings about particular policies and trends and see a need for reforms in certain areas. Such members challenge or moderate moves to integration they consider unnecessary or excessive; they encourage pragmatism and act as a counterweight to the federalists. They thus perform a useful role in Parliament and represent a sizeable segment of the European population who are Eurosceptic but not anti-EU. They tend to belong to the main centre-right ("European Peoples' Party"), Socialist and Liberal political groupings, which are basically pro-EU.

In 2002, a requirement to use a form of proportional representation in elections to the European Parliament was introduced, which since the

2004 elections has led to a sizeable anti-EU contingent in the European Parliament. Members of Parliament who are not just Eurosceptic but against the whole idea of the EU pose a serious problem for the business of Parliament, as many are poor attenders and spend more time advancing their nationalist causes back home than working for the Parliament, their employer. In the 2014–19 legislative period, there were three of these strongly Eurosceptic/anti-EU political groups in the Parliament: the European Conservatives and Reformists group, which included the British Conservatives and the Polish Law and Justice Party; the Europe of Freedom and Direct Democracy group, containing UKIP and the Italian Five Star Movement; and the Europe of Nations and Freedom group, made up of the Austrian Freedom Party and Mrs Le Pen's National Rally (formerly "National Front") party, among others. These groups made up around 150—roughly a fifth—of the 751 members.

Fundamentally, anti-EU MEPs like those of UKIP are of doubtful usefulness in the European Parliament. Many of the current batch of Conservative MEPs who had long agitated for Brexit before they voted for it in the referendum also belong to this category. UKIP's *raison d'être* was to take Britain out of the EU and it had always used its European Parliament platform and the publicity the party gained as a result of it to advance the Brexit cause, more than to advancing the interests of the EU. UKIP and the French National Front have also used the staff allowances provided by the Parliament to pay assistants for purely national work.[21] Before the Brexit vote, UKIP MEPs and their anti-EU Conservative colleagues created an impression of useful activity in voting against EU integration moves. Since the vote UKIP has abandoned this pretence and reverted to its traditional activity of disruption and grandstanding, while the Conservative MEPs have concentrated on lobbying Parliament to get Britain the best possible exit terms on matters like financial services and data transfer.

The European Parliament is an institution that has a job to do in the areas listed above pertaining to advancing the interests of the European Union. MEPs who seek to undermine or even destroy the EU are hardly acting in its interests. They are occupying seats that could have been taken by people who would act constructively in the EU's and their own country's national interests, even though quite possibly in a Eurosceptic, reformist spirit. While they may well be sincere in their opposition to the EU, they are literally a waste of space in the European Parliament and have no place there. What would the House of Commons gain from 100 MPs elected on a mandate to get rid of the entire institution of parliament?

This "cuckoos in the nest" problem in the European Parliament is a democratic phenomenon peculiar to the EU. It reflects the fact that a substantial part of the European population is against the whole idea of a supranational tier of government above the nation state. The problem can only be rectified, or at least prevented from growing, by democratic means. Member states must invest more in the European Parliament elections. The mainstream parties must campaign harder to get their candidates elected and not, like the British Conservative Party did in 2014, virtually abandon the field to its own Eurosceptic right wing and UKIP. The 2019 elections saw the main pro-EU parties occupying the centre ground of European politics losing some seats to the Eurosceptic nationalist and populist movements that have grown up in many countries, but this was partly offset by an increase in seats for the pro-EU Greens and Liberals. An encouraging development was the increased turnout, which at just over 50% was the highest it has been in 20 years.[22]

4.6   The "Democratic Deficit"

4.6.1   *Progressive Strengthening of the EU's Democratic Legitimacy*

Since the 1970s many observers of European integration have criticized the European Community and latterly the European Union as suffering from a "democratic deficit," a lack of democratic legitimacy. There was certainly some truth in this observation before the introduction of direct elections of the European Parliament in 1979, a Parliament equipped with much enhanced powers to influence European legislation. Previously, the European Community had been governed by the Council of Ministers and the European Commission, with a Parliament appointed by national governments which was little more than a talking shop. The initiator of EU legislation, the Commission, was then, as now (except for the recently introduced more democratic procedure for appointing the Commission President), not elected but appointed by national governments, and the Council of Ministers, which adopted the legislation, represented only national governments and could bypass their national parliaments, and its meetings were conducted in secret.

After 1979, while the role of the directly elected European Parliament in shaping European laws had been increased, pressure mounted for further steps to democratize European policy-making. The EU was still seen as distant from ordinary people and its procedures as non-transparent, secretive, and unamenable to influence unlike their own parliaments. Dissatisfaction was shown by negative or disappointing referendum results on the Maastricht Treaty in Denmark and France in 1992 and the accompanying rise of Euroscepticism. There were several sources of complaint. First, the European Parliament did not have an equal say on proposed legislation with the Council of Ministers when it was only consulted. Secondly, its right to scrutinize legislation was limited to certain policy areas. Third, national parliaments had no redress when their governments agreed to EU legislation the parliament would have opposed. Finally, citizens of member states did not have direct access to the EU institutions to complain about wrongs or injustices.

Over time the EU addressed these complaints with a number of reforms: in the Maastricht Treaty the powers of the European Parliament were increased to the level of having an equal say with the Council of Ministers, or "co-decision," and in this and the successive treaties, Amsterdam, Nice and especially Lisbon, the scope of the co-decision (since Lisbon, the "ordinary") legislative procedure was gradually extended to virtually all policy areas.

The "subsidiarity" principle was also developed to assuage concerns about "mission creep" by the EU, extending its tentacles by stealth into ever more policy areas contiguous to those already within its remit. The subsidiarity principle was introduced in the 1993 Maastricht Treaty and its application extended by the Lisbon Treaty.[23] It states that the EU should only take action when it is necessary to act jointly and when action to obtain the desired result cannot be left to the member states acting individually, thus protecting national parliaments from the EU legislative authorities encroaching on their powers. A practical possibility of national parliaments to act against breaches of subsidiarity was introduced by the Lisbon Treaty, which provided for a certain threshold of member states' parliaments to object to EU legislative proposals. This power has been successfully exercised in one case when such action forced the Commission to withdraw a proposal to legislate on the right to strike action by trade unions.

In the 1990s, the EU began to involve itself more in human rights, which had gained importance in the accession of new members and in the new justice and home affairs provisions introduced by the Maastricht Treaty. In 2000, the Charter of Fundamental Rights of the EU was approved and came into force with the Lisbon Treaty in 2009. The Charter partly overlaps with the separate European Convention of Human Rights of the Council of Europe, which the EU is committed to joining as well. This, too, is helping to overcome the perception of the EU's remoteness. The Lisbon Treaty also introduced a right of "citizens' initiatives" or petitions to the European Parliament and required the Council of Ministers to open its meetings to the public when legislation was being discussed or adopted.

There are further things that could be done to lessen the objections to the democratic legitimacy of the EU. Euro-federalists propose measures like the election of the whole Commission by the European Parliament, not just the Commission president through the *Spitzenkandidaten* (top candidates) procedure; European-wide political parties campaigning in the European elections, with MEPs being elected from transnational lists instead of national quotas; and giving the European Parliament the right to initiate EU legislation, which is currently reserved for the Commission.

These proposals are unlikely to be implemented any time soon. They would require treaty changes. But there are things that can and should be done now within the present legal framework governing the European Parliament as they could help reduce the sense of alienation ordinary people feel regarding Europe and to prevent the growth of nationalism.

The first is to galvanize European Parliament elections into a real contest engaging the attention of national voters. The (up to 2019) steadily failing turnouts in the elections and the election of an increased number of Eurosceptics in some countries show a degree of voter apathy. The EU can play its part in changing this situation, but national governments and parties must invest much more in the European elections and show a much more positive interest and determination in getting their candidates elected to what should be publicly recognized as a very important institution, and not an irrelevance, which is the impression left by the currently lukewarm level of support in national political circles in countries like Britain. Brexit is the fruit of British political lethargy and apathy towards the EU of which the weak involvement of the government in the European elections was a symptom.

Secondly, the democratic deficit would be ameliorated by greater contact and cooperation between the European Parliament and national parliaments, which, as the German Constitutional Court has pointed out, are one of the sources of the EU's legitimacy. National parliaments are more powerful than the European Parliament in the majority of policy areas and possess clearer democratic legitimacy. The fact that the EU legislative authorities have the power to determine the law in certain areas does not remove the right and obligation of self-confident national parliaments to get involved more in scrutinizing EU legislative proposals and influencing them through their governments. There has been a tendency for British MPs to view the European Parliament as an inferior rival instead of as a partner. Other EU countries have been much better at influencing EU legislation through their own parliaments by means of proactive, timely interventions than Britain has. The British House of Lords has shown an admirable example in how to scrutinize proposed EU legislation with its EU Select Committee. The House of Commons should follow its example and not be too proud to call its government ministers to account over their stance on forthcoming EU rules and to lobby their MEPs and the Commission though consultative bodies.

Two advisory bodies that connect the public across the EU to the European institutions and increase democratic representation must also be mentioned here. They are the European Economic and Social Committee, which was set up under the original EEC Treaty, and the European Committee of the Regions set up in 1994 under the Maastricht Treaty. Both have memberships appointed from serving officers of civil society or local and regional organizations in the member states. In the case of the EESC, these are employers' organizations, trade unions, and other interest groups like farmers, consumers and NGOs, and in the case of the Committee of the Regions local and regional authorities. In both bodies, the members are not paid salaries but only expenses. They are an important two-way link with public opinion in their member states, passing grassroots messages up to the EU authorities and disseminating ideas and initiatives back downwards, and a forum for exchanging ideas and best practice horizontally between the countries of the EU.

Then there are the hundreds of regional representations and professional and trade associations that as often as not have no official role in the EU administration but maintain operations and offices in Brussels to represent their interests vis-à-vis the EU institutions, particularly with regard to legislation. They, too, indirectly at least, increase democratic representation. Democracy is not only something elected politicians do. Such organizations can disparagingly be called "lobbyists," but they perform an indispensable role in ensuring those preparing and deciding legislation in the Commission, the Council (through the member states' permanent representations), and the Parliament have vital facts at their disposal and are aware of their interests and specific concerns. They do this in ad hoc contacts with individual Commission officials, national seconded officials from member states' permanent representations, and MEPs, by sitting on the hundreds of specialist committees to advise the Commission or prepare its decisions, and by taking part in European Parliament hearings. The organizations range from the European Trade Union Confederation, through sectoral organizations like Euro-Commerce (wholesale and retail trade) and EUROFER (steel industry), to the some 300 representative offices of regions and local authorities, including the 16 German states and many British regions.

And what about the thousands of bodies and entities throughout Europe brought together by participation in common projects and programmes funded by the EU, like universities and research institutes collaborating on scientific projects as part of the Horizon research programme? What about the 2000 plus delegates from public and private bodies meeting at the Brussels "Open Days" on EU regional development activities? In a wider sense must not these people-to-people connections across member states also be recognized as reducing the gap between the people and the EU and thereby the so-called democratic deficit?

4.6.2 Supranational Organizations and Democratic Legitimacy: A Contradiction in Terms?

Eurosceptics often deny the very possibility of the European Union ever having democratic legitimacy, because that presupposes a European *demos* or nation, a common language, pan-European media, and a Europe-wide political discourse. They therefore consider there is no cure for the democratic deficit and, short of abandoning the European project altogether, call for a subsidiarity court to police subsidiarity and for a procedure to repatriate powers from the EU when member states believe they unduly infringe national sovereignty.

The German Federal Constitutional Court was questioned on such issues on several occasions in the 1990s and 2000s. In its judgments, it considered that a common nation and language, press, opinion-forming processes and political discourse are not a prerequisite for the democratic legitimacy of a supranational legal order. In its view, the EU does have legitimacy, indirectly via the mandates given to it by national parliaments, and directly through the mandate the peoples of Europe give to the

European Parliament. The legitimacy exists, though it needs to be strengthened.[24]

The German court's opinion is common sense and is borne out by developments since the questions were raised 20 years ago.

First, on the question of nationhood, the identity of a "nation" is debatable and its relationship to political units or "nation states" can change over time. Obviously, there are certain elements like language, culture, history, Parliament and the monarchy that make the UK a "nation," but what when due to immigration the nation becomes a multicultural and multilingual society? What about when previous separate nation states merge or when nation states split? In the case of the UK, can there never again be a Scottish "nation"? There used to be once apparently. And since when has Ireland been a nation? What are the criteria of nationhood? It has become a relative concept.

Cannot people have dual allegiances, both to a nation state and to a wider grouping like Europe, can they not feel both British and European? Of course, they can. In the modern world, to claim that people with allegiances to several countries are "citizens of nowhere" is ridiculous. Cosmopolitanism, mobility is becoming the new normal, and not just for a privileged few but for virtually everyone. People migrate, study abroad, visit countries on holiday, marry foreigners, and intermingle racially.

Language is not a criterion for the nation. Nation states are sometimes formed from different language communities. Take Switzerland. Even Britain has minority languages. Are the Welsh a nation? Or only Welsh speakers because they have their own language?

Some nation states have several languages but a common *lingua franca,* like India with English. Arguably nowadays, Europe, too, has a *lingua franca.* And it, too, is English. So could Europe ever become a "nation"? If not, why not? Perhaps it never will. But could it?

The case against the possibility of the EU ever gaining democratic legitimacy because there are no pan-European media or a common political discourse is also becoming obsolete. There are more and more television channels and newspapers that serve a European audience. Some British-based newspapers like the *Financial Times, The Economist,* and *The Guardian* have established a reputation for reliability and an influence right across Europe as well as further afield.

The information sources on the internet and social media by definition know no borders. National political parties have links with like-minded groups in other countries. The Socialist International is one of the oldest.

European Parliament political groupings, like the centre-right European Peoples Party, now meet to coordinate campaigns for European Parliament elections and to choose a joint candidate for the President of the European Commission. A European-wide political discourse and media landscape is gradually developing, even though in the bigger countries the national conversation remains mainly parochial.

Many other developments which are partly dependent on and partly independent of the EU are also bringing Europe closer together and making people in different countries more aware of what they have in common and of ongoing interactions, cooperation and interdependence between their respective countries and across the whole of Europe. These are things like easier travel, student exchanges via the Erasmus programme, and cultural exchanges in art and music. The use of English as a *lingua franca* (ironically now that Britain is leaving the EU) and a more integrated press and media landscape have already been mentioned.

4.6.3   Does a Democratic Deficit Matter?

Some have argued that the concerns about a lack of democratic legitimacy on the part of the EU are exaggerated.[25] For one thing, the EU's powers as a legislator and rule and decision-maker are limited; it enacts technical rules and takes decisions that under national systems, too, are nowadays usually delegated to administrative bodies or bodies not subject to the same degree of intensive public participation and scrutiny as legislation on taxes, social security, health spending and education, which are almost entirely the preserve of national parliaments, not the EU. Secondly, it is subject to severe constraints on its power to act independently, in the form of the treaties which only national governments can change, procedures requiring supermajorities for action often beyond the requirements in national legislatures, and a fiscal straitjacket decided by the member states which prevents the EU ever becoming a "European super-state."

The second and third objections—that the EU's action is severely circumscribed both legally and financially—are true. The member states rightly control what the EU can and cannot do and hold its purse strings. The first point, however, that EU legislation is largely technical and of the type not usually subject, or indeed amenable, to wide public participation and therefore usually delegated to administrative bodies, while still true to a large extent, requires qualification.[26]

The technical character of EU legislation is an important reason why most of what is done in Brussels does not interest the press: it is too arcane. But developments over the past 20 years have begun to change that more and more. For example, some EU legislation and decision-making can have immediate and identifiable effects on people's wellbeing and daily lives. This is true of the management of the single currency, especially in crisis situations. Hence the calls for a Eurozone parliament. It is also true of sweeping changes in major industries like energy, transport, and financial and digital services, such changes often being to protect consumers, as with data protection rules, or producers with musical copyright on the internet, or to protect the environment. There is clearly more public interest in such everyday matters being decided in EU legislation than there is in the standards for tractor seats or tariff schedules in the free trade agreement with South Korea, so democratic awareness and transparency does matter in an increasing number of cases. A "democratic deficit," if such it be, does matter.

4.6.4   Conclusion

Much has been done to improve the so-called democratic deficit. The European Parliament has become a fully fledged legislature and the Council of Ministers—that is, the member states' governments—is finally abandoning its secrecy and standing up to be counted for its responsibility in making EU rules and not leaving the EU as a scapegoat. The level of transparency with regard to EU legislation is arguably greater than in national legislatures including Westminster.

But some things need to be improved further. There is a crying need for greater involvement of national governments in the European Parliament elections. The longer the present public apathy continues, the faster populism, Euroscepticm and nationalism will grow and will endanger the whole future of the European Union. The EU's fate is largely in the hands of the member states. The same is true of the need to develop cooperative links and mutual support between national parliaments and the European Parliament, which have complementary tasks and should not be rivals but partners. The adversarial relationship between Westminster—the House of Commons, not the House of Lords—and the EU has been one of the causes of Brexit, as much as have the ridicule and disparagement of the EU and its "bendy banana" legislation in the British right-wing press over many years.

The improvements in the democratic accountability of the EU made so far give the lie to claims by Eurosceptics that the EU is a basket case and unreformable.

Taking a still wider perspective of the democratic representation of national interest groups, regions and NGOs in Brussels through bodies like the Economic and Social Committee and the Committee of Regions, lobbying organizations and contacts between national actors through EU funding programmes, it is hard to argue that the EU is out of touch with people in the member states or that the "democratic deficit" is still a serious problem. The exception is the organization of European elections, which needs to be improved urgently.

Rome was not built in a day and it must also be borne in mind that national democracies, too—even Britain's after devolution—are imperfect, as Nicola Sturgeon noted when asked on ITV's *Good Morning Britain* why she seemed to place more faith in the EU which was often criticized as undemocratic than in the democratic system of the UK.[27]

NOTES

1. El-Agraa, Ali. M. 2011. *The European Union: Economics and Politics,* 9th ed. Cambridge: Cambridge University Press.
2. Scruton, Roger. 2016. Democracy After Brexit. After the Vote. *BBC Radio 4 A Point of View.* 14 July. Published on *Conservatism Archive, YouTube.*
3. Lewis, Jane. 2016. *Stay or Go? All You Need to Know in One Concise Volume,* 22. *London: Connell Guides Publishing.* The book goes on, on page 23, to say that the European Commission is "the EU's principal legislative body," but that it submits its proposals for approval by the Council of Ministers and the European Parliament, leaving the picture unclear.
4. Heathcoat Amory, Edward. 2004. The lies of 1975 still haunt us. *Daily Mail.* 20 April.
5. *BBC News.* 2016. The EU: All you need to know in under two minutes. 19 February.
6. Heffer, Simon. 2016. Speech at conference in Peterborough entitled "No to the EU." 17 March. Published by *RobinHoodUKIP* on *YouTube.*
7. *Sunday Telegraph.* 2017. Brussels in denial over Macron's victory. 14 May.
8. Booker, Christopher. 1998. From better to worse—Twenty Things—20 daft EU laws that changed our lives. *The Sun.* 2 January.
9. Bootle, Roger. 2016. *The Trouble With Europe,* 3rd ed., 55. London: Nicholas Brealey. See also Lewis, Jane. 2016. *Stay or Go,* 22–23. London:

Connell Guides Publishing, who, like Bootle, apparently misunderstood the dual role of the European Council/Council of Ministers, the former made up of the member states' leaders taking major strategic decisions, the latter being the day-to-day legislative body composed of national ministers passing laws in consultation with the European Parliament.

10. *Daily Telegraph.* 2017. Give EU families in the UK open-ended right to stay. 30 May. The introductory words to the article concerning the first two working papers published by Commission's Brexit Task Force for discussion by the Council Working Party entitled "Essential Principles on Citizens' Rights" and "Essential principles on Financial Settlement" are "European Union bureaucrats are demanding..."
11. *InFacts.* 2017. Sorry Daily Mail, Verhofstadt ain't no "bureaucrat." 15 December.
12. Craig, David and Matthew Elliott. 2009. *The Great European Rip-Off: How the Corrupt, Wasteful EU is Taking Control of Our Lives.* London: Random House.
13. Di Franco, Eleonora. 2018. Unanimity and QMV. How does the Council of the EU actually vote? *My Country? Europe.* 21 April.
14. *FullFacts.* 2016. EU facts behind the claims: UK influence. 25 April.
15. Varoufakis, Yanis. 2016. *And the Weak Suffer What They Must? Europe, Austerity and the Threat to Global Stability.* London: Bodley Head.
16. Critics like Jacob Rees-Mogg (Rees-Mogg, Jacob. 2013. Debate in Oxford Union on the EU as a threat to democracy. 11 November. Available on *YouTube*) have claimed that this was not only undemocratic, but smacked of the EU's fundamentally anti-democratic instincts shown by its reaction to the rejection of its policies in referendums.
17. Fromage, Diane. 2018. A parliamentary assembly for the Eurozone? *ADEMU. ADEMU working paper series.* May 2018.
18. *BBC News.* 2018. Boundary changes: Final proposals published. 10 September.
19. Véron, Nicholas, and Anish Taylor. 2014. How unequal is the European Parliament's representation? *Brueghel.* 19 May.
20. *European Parliament.* Staffing arrangements: Parliamentary assistants.
21. See Sect. 6.4.
22. *BBC News.* 2019. European Elections 2019: Results in maps and charts. 27 May.
23. European Parliament. Fact Sheets on the European Union: The principle of subsidiarity.
24. The Maastricht and Lisbon judgments of 1993 and 2009, respectively: BverfGE 89 155 and BverfG 2 be 2-08.
25. Particularly Moravcsik, Andrew. 2003. In defence of the "democratic deficit": Reassessing legitimacy in the EU. Harvard University Centre for European Studies Working Paper 92.

26. Robert Cooper made a similar point and said that the obvious voter apathy in European Parliament elections bore it out. He therefore advocated returning to a system of appointing representatives in the EU's assembly: Cooper, Robert. 2014. The EU does not have a democratic deficit—it has a democratic surplus. *LSE blogs*.
27. ITV *Good Morning Britain*. 2018. Nicola Sturgeon: People Have a right to change their Mind. 8 October.

CHAPTER 5

"Taking Back Control of Our Laws": II. Sovereignty

Even if it is not true that EU laws are imposed on Britain by unelected and unaccountable bureaucrats in Brussels or that the system for making EU laws and running the EU is undemocratic, have we not ceded too much sovereignty to the EU when it reaches the point that our own Parliament is virtually emasculated and the EU interferes in every aspect of our lives? And is it right that our own courts are being supplanted by foreign judges in Luxembourg and Strasbourg and our own efficient administration by the bloated bureaucracy and incompetent, self-serving elites of Brussels? This chapter looks at the question of sovereignty, which is not all or nothing, as the Brexit rhetoric would have it, but a tradeable commodity that it makes sense to share and exchange, a commodity that grows with the sharing, a case where you really can "have your cake and eat it." The chapter finishes with those unassuming judges in Luxembourg, who are no doubt as perplexed at the bogeyman image they have acquired in Britain as its own Supreme Court judges are at being cast as the "enemies of the people," with their pictures plastered over the *Mail's* front page, for defending the sovereignty of Parliament.[1]

5.1 The Scope, Volume and Quality of EU Legislation, Now and in the Future

How much of the law applicable in Britain comes from the EU and does not originate from the British parliament? During the referendum campaign, the BBC *Today* programme ran a series entitled "The EU in ten

© The Author(s) 2019   151
F. Rawlinson, *How Press Propaganda Paved the Way to Brexit*,
https://doi.org/10.1007/978-3-030-27765-9_5

objects" showing the extent to which the rules governing consumer goods, food, working practices and other aspects of our lives are set in European Union legislation, not by Westminster. The series also appeared as video clips. They were a laudable attempt to show how widespread was the impact of the EU on British life and to correct some "Euro-myths," though the spots were rather too short and superficial, and not up to the standard of the well-researched "Reality Checks" on Brexit issues published on the *BBC News* website.

Rubbishing "daft" EU rules had become standard fare in British Eurosceptic newspapers since the 1990s, especially when the rules allegedly stopped Britain from keeping up traditional British customs like imperial measures, food specialities or English product names. Many of the claims were completely false, or they talked of proposals or ideas somewhere in the EU machinery as if they had already been decided. Accuracy or the possible justification for the EU rules did not matter as long as the article was funny and got people worked up about the level of EU interference in national affairs. "Euro-bashing" became a national sport, with no holds barred like pro-wresting. The EU Commission sporadically tried to debunk the worst of these "euro-myths," but to little avail: the reality was too boring. Many Brexiteers cut their teeth as journalists writing such stories.

That is not to say there was no merit in the charge of overregulation, especially during the flood of Single Market legislation during the early 1990s. Even the Europhile Douglas Hurd, Foreign Secretary in John Major's government, voiced sympathy with this view, which was thought to have been a factor in the Danish "No" vote to the Maastricht Treaty:

> People want to see decisions taken nearer to those whom they affect. The growing appetite in Brussels in recent years for promulgating rules which probe into the nooks and crannies of national life is clearly at variance with this trend.[2] (*Daily Telegraph*, 1992)

Between the late 1990s and the 2016 referendum, however, measured criticism turned into hyperbolic condemnation and a compelling case for leaving the EU:

> The EU is a "beast … which aims to devour our national identity" and "a very real dragon which threatens every single one of us throughout the United Kingdom."[3] (*The Sun*, 1996)

It is 25 years since Britain joined the Common Market. In 1973 we were told it was 'just a trading arrangement'. In fact, we signed away the right to run our country to Brussels, whose decrees now override our own Parliament and courts. Here author Christopher Booker reveals 20 ways in which they have changed our lives for the worse.[4] (*The Sun*, 1998)

The market became a community that became a union, that now wants to be the United States of Europe. Out went free trade; in came laws and regulations reaching into every part of our lives.[5] (*Daily Mail*, 2004)

The EU [...] has overweening power.[6] (*Daily Mail*, 2003)

Seventy per cent of our laws are made by unelected bureaucrats in Brussels.[7] (*Daily Mail*, 2003)

The *Daily Telegraph's* lament for the halcyon days before joining the EU when the UK controlled its own destiny is typical:

[Sir Vince Cable] might ask himself why more older people voted for Brexit. And the obvious answer is that these are the voters who can themselves remember what life was like before Britain handed increasing chunks of its sovereignty away to Brussels by joining the EU. These are the people who are most looking forward to a restoration of such sovereignty, because they have most experience of how much it matters, and how profound has been its loss.[8] (*Daily Telegraph*, 2017)

The claim that a democratic Britain has ceded almost total control of its affairs to an undemocratic EU which is on its way to becoming a European "super-state" is persuasive in the British historical context.[9] But it is a highly distorted image of reality.

As we have seen, the EU has evolved into a much more democratic structure than when it started out as the European Community. But what about the extent of the sovereignty the UK has ceded to the EU and is now exercised by EU institutions, democratic or otherwise?

First of all, measures like the percentage of UK laws affected by EU decisions—estimates of 60%, 70% or 80% are the most common figures cited by Brexiteers—are pretty meaningless as they suffer from counting and definitional problems. A *BBC News* "Reality Check" analysed such measures and concluded they are not a good guide to the amount of influence EU law has on UK law. The main problem is distinguishing new EU laws from mere amendments and administrative measures applying existing laws, like the hundreds of minor EU administrative regulations made every year in agriculture. Including the latter inflates the result. Yet quoting such misleading figures gave considerable traction to the Leave campaign's argument that Britain was totally controlled by the EU.

A former Treasury Solicitor, Sir Paul Jenkins, interviewed by the BBC's "Reality Check" team said the whole debate was a red herring.

> This is one of many areas in the EU debate where both sides describe meaningless nonsense as facts. The impact of EU law varies from sector to sector. In many areas—public order, crime, defence, health—EU laws have minimal impact. But in others—workers' rights, trade—the impact is much greater because the single market and the free movement of workers are at the heart of what the EU is about. The way we organize our NHS is not.[10]

To Sir Paul's list of areas in which EU law has minimal impact, one could add social security and education. The impact on foreign policy and taxation is also limited. Foreign policy and taxation are largely outside the EU control because any EU decisions or legislation require unanimity and therefore are hard or impossible to get through. Public order, health, defence, criminal justice, social security, education and foreign policy account for the overwhelming bulk of public expenditure in Britain, which represents around 40% of its GDP. In comparison, Britain contributes only about 1% gross of its GDP to the EU budget. On this financial measure alone, the EU's impact on British legislation would only be 2.5% (assuming public expenditure as 40% of GDP), but that is certainly an underestimate as much EU law does not have implications for the EU's budget though often it may have for national budgets.

The best guide to the extent of the EU's influence on the UK's affairs is provided by the review of the "Balance of Competences" ("competence" is EU-speak for "powers, responsibilities, authority," in short "sovereignty") between the UK and the EU which the Cameron Government carried out between 2012 and 2014. The 30 reports on different policy areas—two cover general issues—are around 3000 pages in length and based on thousands of interviews, consultations, written submissions, conferences, and workshops organized by the responsible Whitehall departments with experts and interested parties. They show the varying extent of EU involvement in setting the rules and practices in the various sectors. In some, it is extensive, in other, practically zero, as Sir Paul Jenkins rightly pointed out. As already noted in Chap. 2, the general conclusion of the review exercise was that the extent to which powers were exercised by the EU jointly was "about right" and in the UK's national interest—not to the UK's detriment as claimed by the Eurosceptic press and later by the Leave side in the referendum. The Competences review could have been used as ammunition by the Remain side to counter the Leave side's "60% of UK law from EU and all bad" message, but for political reasons, the Cameron government buried the results of this huge exercise and Leavers denounced it as the work of the Europhile Whitehall elite.

The degree of the EU's involvement in the different policy areas according to the Competences review is shown in Table 5.1. It also gives the review's conclusions as to whether the EU activity in the relevant policy areas is beneficial to the UK and whether changes are needed to rectify problems identified by the review.

The charge of overregulation, excessive bureaucracy and "red tape" in what the EU does will be addressed later in this chapter, while more detailed comments on another key issue in the referendum, immigration, will be made in Chap. 7. But a few general points can be made here.

First of all, it is worth repeating the conclusion of the review that the EU's exercise of the sovereignty ceded to it—or more accurately, pooled with the other member states of the EU and exercised jointly by them all—generally serves the UK's national interest reasonably well. It is possible to disagree with this assessment in respect of particular areas like fisheries or freedom of movement or with regard to particular aspects of certain legislation. But in the light of the opinions of the stakeholders and experts surveyed for this series of studies, it is untenable to argue that being in the EU has generally been bad for Britain. The considerable body of evidence assembled by the review exercise does not support this claim, nor the other assertion by Brexit supporters that Britain has been held back from reaching its full potential by the "dead hand" of Brussels.[12]

Secondly, the UK has managed to opt out from a number of policies—the single currency and the associated controls on budget deficits and debt, the Schengen free travel zone, asylum policy and justice and home affairs provisions. In the latter case, it can opt back into the arrangements it likes. This shows the EU is not the inflexible, centralizing bureaucracy it is portrayed as by the Brexit movement, but that it affords considerable scope for accommodating member states' particular circumstances and wishes, when they fight strongly enough to secure such exceptions, as Mr Major did with respect to the Maastricht Treaty (the euro), Tony Blair with the Amsterdam and Lisbon Treaties (Schengen, Justice and Home Affairs, asylum, and Charter of Fundamental Rights), and as Mrs Thatcher had done previously to secure Britain's budget rebate.

Thirdly, there is little or no EU involvement in large swathes of policy that affect people's everyday lives like social security, health, education

Table 5.1   Degree of EU involvement in policy areas and benefit to UK/need for change

	Policy area	Degree of EU involvement	Benefit to UK/Need for change
	Core single market policies		
1	Single market overview	Considerable	Beneficial
2	Free movement of goods	Considerable	Beneficial
3	Free movement of services	Considerable and more needed	Beneficial, further EU regulation needed
4	Free movement of capital and financial services	Considerable, increasing, UK-led	Beneficial, a UK priority
5	Free movement of people	Considerable	Generally beneficial but in UK controversial
6	Competition and consumer policies	Considerable	Beneficial
7	Foreign trade and investment	Considerable	Beneficial
	Sectoral policies		
8	Transport	Considerable, UK-led	Beneficial
9	Energy	Considerable, increasing	Beneficial
10	Environment and climate change	Considerable, UK-led	Generally beneficial, but subsidiarity needed in some areas
11	Agriculture	Almost complete	Beneficial, reformed as wanted by UK but some aspects criticized
12	Fisheries	Considerable	Arguably beneficial, but controversial
13	Food safety and animal welfare	Considerable	Beneficial
14	Public health	Slight except in niche areas (health insurance when abroad)	Beneficial in applicable niche areas
15	Digital information rights	Considerable and increasing	Beneficial
	Economic, monetary and social policies		
16	Economic and monetary union	Slight—UK opt-out from single currency	UK impacted by EU policies

(*continued*)

Table 5.1 (continued)

	Policy area	Degree of EU involvement	Benefit to UK/Need for change
17	Social and employment policy	Considerable	Beneficial but some rules criticized
18	Cohesion (regional) policy	Considerable	Beneficial but restriction of coverage being considered
19	EU budget	Complete, but overall size restricted and funding priorities subject to review by member states	Beneficial, especially given UK's rebate
20	Taxation	Limited (unanimity requirement)	Beneficial
	Justice and home affairs		
21	Fundamental rights	Considerable	Beneficial but controversial in UK
22	Civil judicial cooperation	Slight—UK opt-out	Beneficial where applicable
23	Police and criminal law cooperation	Growing, despite UK opt-out	Beneficial where applicable
24	Asylum and non-EU immigration	Slight—UK opt-out	Limited participation of UK judged beneficial
	Education, research and culture		
25	Education, vocational training and youth	Slight, voluntary cooperation only	Beneficial in niche areas like Erasmus
26	Research and space	Considerable	Beneficial
27	Culture, tourism and sport	Slight	Beneficial in niche areas where applicable (e.g. footballers' freedom of movement)
	External relations		
28	Foreign and security policy	Considerable but on cooperative basis (unanimity)	Beneficial
29	Development cooperation and humanitarian aid	Considerable but parallel national policy as well	Beneficial
30	Enlargement	Complete and completely under control of member states, each having a veto	Beneficial but immigration implications now make policy controversial in UK

Sources: "Review of the Balance of Competences between the UK and the EU," https://www.gov.uk/review-of-the-balance-of-competences; Emerson (2016)[11] and defence. It is an exaggeration to say that the EU probes into *all* the "nooks and crannies of national life," though Douglas Hurd was right that it reaches into many of them. Another area still hardly affected by the EU is tax policy.

The warning in the alarmist headline in the *Daily Express* of 15 May 1991,[13] about possible proposals to be put to the intergovernmental conference on economic and monetary union at the end of the year (on the future Maastricht Treaty), was premature, as the Commission had only announced that it was *looking at* income, energy or corporation taxes as a potential source of extra revenue to the EU budget in addition to the small percentage of VAT (Value Added Tax) receipts it already received. British governments have always strongly opposed ceding powers over taxation to the EU, so the strident tone was hardly necessary to stiffen the government's resolve against such a proposal. The reaction of Anthony Beaumont-Dark MP reported in the article ("Taxation is the bedrock of all democracies and once they have got the right to tax we will have sold our country") was and still is fairly representative of opinion in the UK and is widely shared in other member states, too, though usually expressed more moderately.

The EU concentrates its efforts on the cooperation between national tax authorities to establish transparency and prevent tax avoidance and fraud, particularly in the area of corporate taxation and taxation in the digital market.[14] Tax harmonization requires unanimity in the Council and is therefore exceedingly difficult. Ireland has successfully defended its 12.5% corporation tax rate from attacks for years. The Commission proposed a standard financial transactions tax in 2011 but failed to get all the member states to agree and only ten member states are likely to go ahead with the tax. Similar difficulties were encountered with a proposed carbon tax. However, VAT is an exception in that the EU has coordinated this tax since the 1960s because it is charged on goods easily traded across borders, and therefore the EU currently sets minimum rates and limits the scope for reductions.

The "tampon tax," the 5% VAT rate on female sanitary products, became an issue in the referendum. Leave campaigners were citing it as an example of needless Brussels meddling and David Cameron was under pressure to gain approval for reducing the rate to zero. He demonstratively raised the matter in a European Council meeting but was told the rules of the VAT directive did not currently allow zero rates on sanitary products. While it was relatively easy to gain approval for reduced VAT rates of 5% on certain specified items including sanitary products, even for such changes unanimity was required, and zero rates, like those in the UK on food and children's clothing, are exceptions agreed often after long and hard negotiations. The Commission said it was planning to introduce more flexibility in setting reduced and even zero rates in future,[15] but these proposals only appeared some time later.[16] The episode was a godsend for Leave in that it confirmed the public's false impression that the EU largely controlled taxes. The aggressive stance Mr Cameron adopted towards the EU did not help his subsequent credibility in the referendum campaign. Mrs May reinforced this misconception when she occasionally added "taxes" to the list of things—"our laws, our money, and our borders"—she claimed her deal with the EU would "take back control" of. It is even more blatant and mendacious an exaggeration than the other items on the list.

A fourth important point to make is that a high degree of EU involvement in a policy area does not mean complete control. Often there is a system of multi-level governance in which the EU institutions collaborate with national bodies in the public and private sectors. A case in point is "cohesion" policy, which is essentially regional development and social policies centred on training and inclusion. The EU (European Council, Council of Ministers, and Commission) sets the budget and the regulatory framework. The member states' central, regional and local authorities design and implement the development and social action programmes with invitations to tender projects for funding. The national authorities and the EU (Commission) together supervise and audit the spending. The EU Court of Auditors carries out external audits and reports its findings to the European Parliament, which assesses whether the Commission's management of the relevant budget has been satisfactory.

Another example of multi-level governance is competition. EU competition policy has four main areas with different degrees of EU and national involvement in each. In the first area, "state aid," which means all levels and kinds of government subsidies to businesses, the Commission has exclusive responsibility for assessing whether the subsidies are not unfair to other countries and for ensuring a "level playing field." National authorities have no role, as they are likely to be biased in favour of their own governments and companies. The situation is similar for the second area, monopolies, which are exclusive rights granted by governments to operate in certain markets usually in order to provide public services or to control sales of certain products like alcohol or tobacco. Here again, the EU acts alone, through decisions in individual cases taken by the Commission or through directives issued by the Council of Ministers and the European Parliament. The aim is always to liberalize such markets—to allow competition to operate—as far as possible, consistent with efficient provision of the services or attainment of the public health objectives of the controls, as the case may be. Incidentally, freeing up monopolies was a policy pioneered by the UK under Thatcher which the EU adopted and ran with. It has led to cheaper air fares and mobile roaming charges, securer electricity supplies, and more efficient cross-border payments systems, to name but a few of the achievements of the policy.

For the two remaining areas of competition policy, mergers, on the one hand, and restrictive practices and abuses of dominant position, on the other, there is a divided or shared responsibility between the Commission and national competition authorities. Mergers are examined by the Commission when they are large-scale and have a European dimension, while smaller and mainly national ones are examined by the relevant national competition authority according to its own national criteria. In restrictive practices, which cover both anti-competitive practices like cartels and predominantly beneficial practices like licencing or distribution agreements and joint ventures, and in cases involving abuses of market power by companies against weaker competitors or consumers, the Commission and national competition authorities and courts now share responsibility for enforcement. Previously, the EU (through the Commission) had exclusive jurisdiction, like for state aid and monopolies, but it has now delegated the power to investigate and adjudicate cases to national authorities and courts according to standard EU criteria. There is a "European competition network" to ensure consistency of interpretation of the law and mutual administrative assistance. National competition authorities and courts now adjudicate on ten times as many cases as the Commission, and the system is considered to work very well.

Fifth, it is not true that the trend is always towards more EU control, more centralization, and more harmonization. The examples just given of the return of decision-making in competition cases to national authorities and courts and the earlier one concerning the plans to allow member states greater flexibility in setting reduced VAT rates show that the movement can be in the opposite direction. And who knows whether, with the pressure on its limited budget, the EU will, in future, stop financing regional development in the wealthier countries and thus voluntarily repatriate this policy area also? The same repatriation could sometime happen with agricultural support, which would change the Common Agricultural Policy as we now know it unrecognizably. The division of power and sovereignty between the EU and its member states is thus not fixed but a dynamic picture.

Granted, until recently the trend was towards the EU legislating in ever more areas, because the member states saw a need for common rules in these areas. The 1992 single market programme led to a surge in legislation on product and social protection standards and to remove barriers between national markets and liberalize services. Then came a wave of EU activities on the environment. The introduction of the euro, and then ten years later, the onset of the world financial crisis and the euro and banking crisis, triggered similar spikes in legislative activity, designed to secure the single currency, in the Eurozone, and to reduce risks in the financial sector generally. There are now pressures to extend EU action to liberalize further services markets (until recently largely at the behest of the UK), to improve energy security, create a digital single market, coordinate asylum policy, and continue common action against climate change.

These peaks in legislative activity were and are not due to surreptitious "mission creep" or power grabs by the EU authorities, notably the European Commission, as the Brexit movement repeatedly claims. They respond to identified needs for joined-up action at the European level, often because of pressure from business struggling against competing national regulations. Cases in point are the merger control regulation which was added to the EU Commission's powers in 1989 following widespread pressure from business, and the liberalization of the electricity and gas market sector from the late 1990s onwards. Where necessary, the member states have amended the treaties in order to transfer new authority to legislate in new areas to the EU.

5.2   How Far Will EU Integration Go? Is It Moving Inexorably Towards a European "Super-State"?

Before answering these questions, we have to ask ourselves in what areas it is desirable for countries to cooperate in order to improve economic and social outcomes for their citizens. We have seen that the EU's involvement in fields of government policy varies from a high level of involvement to virtually none. There is a reason for that. International cooperation in certain fields is necessary or desirable because it increases economic and social welfare. In other fields, the benefits of cooperating are less significant and after a certain point diminishing returns set in because decision-making at the national or local level is better. It can be assumed that the EU will only continue to integrate as long as integration still yields positive benefits and that it will not pass the point of diminishing returns where decisions begin to be best left to member states. That is not because of any modesty or superior knowledge on the part of the EU institutions but because there are external constraints, checks and balances, preventing the EU gaining powers it does not need—of which more below.

Table 5.2 classifies the policy areas of the "Balance of Competences" review according to the need for the EU to be involved in those areas, judging by how much it is involved at present. In many areas, the perception of a need for EU action is likely to increase over time, causing an area to move up the scale from "Nice to have" to "Desirable" or "Necessary." But demotions are possible, too, as has already been mentioned. The UK's priorities for cooperation post-Brexit—whether with the EU or with other countries or organizations—are likely to be broadly similar, because there are inherent, objective reasons for cooperating in

Table 5.2   Degree of perceived current need for EU integration, by policy area

Degree of need to cooperate	Policy area
1. Essential	Internal trade, single market (including capital and financial services), free movement of people, environment, fundamental rights, cohesion policy
2. Necessary because related to policy area in category 1	Foreign trade and investment, economic and monetary union (single currency), competition, budget, enlargement, agriculture, fisheries
3. Desirable because related to policy area in category 1	Energy, transport, social and employment policy, food safety and animal welfare, digital information rights
4. Desirable—"nice to have"—standalone cooperation	Asylum and non-EU immigration, civil judicial cooperation, police and criminal law cooperation, consumer protection, foreign and security policy, development cooperation and humanitarian aid, research and space, taxation
5. Not necessary	Social security, education, public health, vocational training and youth, police and criminal law enforcement

certain areas. However, of course, for some areas more national control may be a priority.

A few points are worth mentioning in relation to this classification concerning issues that have come up in the Brexit debate.

A customs union with tariff-free and frictionless trade between members ("internal trade," category 1) makes it impracticable for the members to pursue their own external trade policy and set their own tariffs on goods imported from outside the territory (category 2) because that would require customs checks on such goods at internal frontiers within the territory in order to levy or adjust tariffs, and the trade could no longer be frictionless. A common external trade policy is therefore also required which prevents partners in the customs union striking their own trade deals. Some Brexiteers and Brexit-supporting newspapers[17] talked as if this linkage was an example of EU bullying, whereas it is an essential quid pro quo for treating the internal trade of goods originating from a country outside a customs union, once they have arrived in the union, the same as trade originating between its members.

Free movement of people to live and work in another EU country (category 1) is considered an integral part of the policy for welding the EU into a frontier-free economic and social area; hence, its high status in EU eyes, unlike in Britain where many people see only the downsides. Cohesion policy is also considered very important for integrating the poorer periphery of Europe into the centre through investment financed by redistribution of a third of the budget, largely to central and eastern Europe. Recent UK governments do not appear to rate regional development very highly, even within the UK, and many people fail to understand how regional development elsewhere in Europe (or development aid outside Europe) could possibly benefit Britain, which is very short-sighted, if not economically illiterate.[18]

Economic and monetary union (the single currency) is only placed in category 2 and not in category 1 because it does not currently cover the whole of the EU. It is the biggest step forward in integration since the single market, and like the single market has become a key policy for economic and social cohesion. It is also a problem child. The EU showed its mettle in defending the common currency during the euro crisis and has made huge strides in proofing it against further shocks since, but the euro is still work in progress which will inevitably involve closer integration of the Eurozone. The UK is not directly involved but has an interest in the euro's stability.

The environment and human rights (category 1) have assumed such priority relatively recently. The UK shares Europe's perception of the importance of the policies, in spite of strong currents of right-wing and libertarian thought against them in Britain.

Agriculture and fisheries (category 2) have a high profile because of their importance for food production, the environment and the single market, but fisheries raise questions of territorial sovereignty in the UK. The conflicting interests of Britain and the EU over fishing access and free trade will make it a bone of contention when the two have to reopen the compromises reached while Britain was a member and seek a new relationship post-Brexit.

For tax (category 4), as noted above, cooperation may well be desirable but it is not necessary and taxation will probably remain largely a national prerogative, with member states, even Eurozone countries, resisting EU attempts at harmonization. This is even the case in advanced federal systems like the US. For all the areas in category 5, efficiency and democracy demand that decision-making remains, as it always has been, in national hands, as will the bulk of the 90% of taxpayers' money in national budgets spent on them.

The answer to the question how far European integration will go is thus that there will be incremental increases in areas like services, including telecommunications and transport, Eurozone governance, environment, energy, consumer protection, defence, foreign and security policy, asylum policy, and research and space. There may be moves in the opposite direction towards renationalization of parts of agricultural and cohesion policy.

Will the European Union become a "European super-state"? There are several reasons why not.

The need for concrete treaty changes to transfer new powers to the EU is a constraint that prevents the sudden emergence of an EU "super-state" in the foreseeable future. Treaty changes require unanimous support from all member states and now involve referendums in many countries; such referendums are notoriously hard to win. The Cameron renegotiation in 2015 made much of gaining the UK an exemption from the commitment in the preamble of the Lisbon (and before that in the EEC) Treaty to an "ever closer union." But this was never, on its own, a legal basis for EU action. Concrete enabling provisions—agreed by all member states—are always required for new areas of EU activity.

Another check on the unbridled expansion of EU power is the subsidiarity principle introduced in the Maastricht Treaty to prevent the EU from legislating needlessly in areas and on details that should be left to the member states, and the right of a number of national parliaments to join forces to oppose EU legislation (the "yellow card" system) introduced by Lisbon Treaty.

A third constraint is the tiny budget. How could the EU become a "United States of Europe" with a budget representing only 1% of the member states' GDP? Federal governments typically have revenue of at least 20% of GDP.[19] The EU's finances are strictly controlled by its members. It has no power at present to raise its own taxes, nor can the European Central Bank finance the EU administration by creating money or borrowing. So, whatever the Brexit narrative, a European "super-state" is not on the cards any time soon. France and other countries are pushing for greater integration and a bigger budget in the Eurozone, but these ideas are at an early stage and would not concern Britain even if it stayed in the EU.

The plans for further integration of fiscal policy in the Eurozone exemplify a wider point that the more integrated EU that is likely to develop in the future will not necessarily concern everyone. The EU has always accommodated countries like the UK that want to go more slowly, as the extensive opt-outs it has secured and the "enhanced cooperation" (two-speed Europe) possibilities introduced by the Lisbon Treaty prove. That flexibility is unlikely to diminish and more likely to increase.

The "European super-state" feared by Mrs Thatcher is not on the horizon.

5.3 SOVEREIGNTY

If we vote Leave and take back control I believe that this Thursday can be our country's independence day.[20] (Boris Johnson)

We are leaving [the European Union] to become, once more, a fully sovereign and independent country. Our laws made not in Brussels but in Westminster. Our judges sitting not in Luxembourg but in courts across the land. The authority of EU law in this country ended forever.[21] (Theresa May)

5.3.1   Sovereignty as an Absolute

There is no such thing as absolute sovereignty. A case can be made that the UK has ceded too much sovereignty to the EU, but not that all our sovereignty has gone and leaving the EU will suddenly bring it all back again.

Just as it cultivated the myth that Britain was completely controlled by the EU, so the Brexit campaign fed voters the illusion that by leaving the EU Britain would become completely independent again. This is pure fantasy. No modern country is completely independent; all to a greater or lesser degree share their sovereignty with other countries, through membership of alliances, agreements and international organizations. It was and remains dishonest and counterproductive to pretend that Brexit will fundamentally change that. The black-and-white picture of sovereignty painted by Brexit-supporting politicians, commentators and newspapers is false.

First of all, how independent from the EU will the UK become under various conceivable versions of Brexit?

The "hard Brexit" advocated by some Conservative politicians and a group of free-trading businessmen and economists, in which the country would fall back on World Trade Organization (WTO) rules and at least initially not seek a preferential free trade agreement with the EU, would go furthest in reducing Britain's dependence on EU rules. However, it would not make the country completely independent of the EU because to continue selling their goods in Europe, British exporters would still have to comply with EU rules and standards. Given that nearly half of the country's exports go to the EU, the UK would be under pressure to continue shadowing EU rules in the future, at least on product standards, though there would be more scope for loosening other regulations.

Other Brexiteers favour a somewhat closer relationship with the EU through a preferential trade agreement like Canada's CETA (EU-Canada Comprehensive Economic and Trade Agreement). Under a free trade deal, the dependence on EU rule-making would be greater. Besides requiring the UK to comply with its customs regulations and product standards, the EU would seek to ensure a "level playing field" on matters like competition, subsidies, employment and environmental law that affect business competitiveness. They would try to prevent a low-cost production base on their doorstep undercutting their producers. There would be little scope for deregulation under this kind of Brexit.

The version of Brexit Mrs May finally plumped for, after spending the first 18 months of her premiership toying with a hard Brexit of the types just described, was a softer variety. This was the proposal discussed at a long cabinet meeting at Chequers, the Prime Minister's country retreat, in July 2018, which became known as the "Chequers plan." Its main features were incorporated into the agreed Political Declaration on the future relationship between the EU and the UK that is attached to the withdrawal agreement with the EU of November 2018.[22]

In the Political Declaration, the use of terms like "deep (or wide-ranging) cooperation," "compatible regulatory arrangements" and "equivalence" cannot disguise the fact that the planned relationship will keep Britain tied closely to the EU, implying less of a repatriation of sovereignty than would a free trade agreement. Mrs May changed tack towards a softer Brexit because a hard Brexit would have disrupted the frictionless trade and highly integrated supply chains that have grown up between the UK and EU countries over the past 45 years. The ideas for the future relationship outlined in the Political Declaration seek to minimize the disruption of trade and supply chains. They also go some way to maintaining an open border between Northern Ireland and the Republic of Ireland, which both sides had agreed was essential in order to retain the benefits of the Good Friday Agreement.

But though stressing that the relationship will preserve the UK's "regulatory autonomy," it is hard to see how in practice it will avoid Britain continuing, as during the transition period, to shadow EU rules without any longer having a say in making them.[23] Without any representation in the Council of Ministers and the Parliament any more, the country will be a "rule-taker."

It is planned to end freedom of movement of EU citizens to the UK (and of course vice versa), which has always been one of Mrs May's priorities since accepting the mandate "to deliver Brexit" on being elected as Conservative leader and becoming Prime Minister, and this is also stated in the Government's white paper on future immigration policy.[24] But the precise "mobility" arrangements that are agreed with the EU may end up being quite similar to the current ones given the labour shortages in Britain. The UK will no longer be subject to the common agricultural and fisheries policies, but will be constrained from departing very far from the EU rules for both these sectors by its desire to maintain access to EU markets for its farm products and fish. For fish, that will mean it continuing having to allow EU trawlers to catch a considerable share of the fish available in its fishing waters. On services, particularly the rapidly changing financial services sector in which the UK dominates Europe, the sought-for equivalence arrangements for market access need not be problematic in the beginning, but in the longer term the UK may find itself unable to exercise its freedom to diverge from EU rules and end up having to shadow them closely in order to maintain its equivalence status and market access, rather like for agriculture and fisheries. Similarly, the Political Declaration envisages the UK having the right to conclude its own trade deals, but how soon it will be able to do so will depend on how long it has to remain in the "single customs territory" (the "backstop") with the EU pending the development of alternative ways of keeping the Northern Ireland-Ireland border open.

Furthermore, in a large number of areas from science and innovation, youth, cultural and educational exchanges, space, police and judicial cooperation, and transport, to trade in nuclear materials, the UK wants to maintain the existing beneficial cooperation with the EU and to continue relying on EU agencies for approval of medicines, chemicals and airline safety. These cooperation arrangements will require long and detailed technical negotiations, and while it is true that they will be entered into voluntarily, once agreed they will impose obligations similar to those the UK is under as a member state.

The soft version of Brexit espoused in the Chequers plan and later put into the Political Declaration was not to the liking of many Brexiteers. Ministers, among them the Foreign Minister Boris Johnson and the Brexit Secretary David Davis, and later his replacement Dominic Raab, resigned. The Brexit-supporting press called it "Brexit in name only." Jacob Rees-Mogg and Boris Johnson complained it would turn Britain into a "vassal state," condemned to obey EU rules without having a say in making them, and indefinitely so, given that in theory the Northern Ireland "backstop" could keep the UK tied in a single customs territory without time limit.[25] Some intimated that staying in the EU might be preferable.[26]

One fact is clear with all the alternative versions of Brexit: they will all leave the UK partly dependent on the EU, so the facile, populist claim by Mrs May that Britain would again become a "fully independent and sovereign country" thanks to Brexit was always wrong, and in relation to her "deal" which seems likely to leave Britain so close to the EU that very little changes it is doubly wrong: only a small part of the sovereignty currently ceded to—or rather pooled in—the EU is regained.

On trade, the idea was that after Brexit, armed with newly won freedom and independence from the EU, the UK would strike free trade deals with other countries, which would supposedly help to replace the trade and services business the country may have to give up when leaving the EU. In time, it was suggested, these new relationships with rapidly-growing developing countries like China and India as well as with its closest ally, the US, and with trading blocs like the Trans-Pacific Partnership (TPP), would make Britain more prosperous than it was while a member of the EU.

But will the sovereignty regained from the EU really remain intact when it signs such trade deals with countries like China, India and the US? The answer, of course, is No. Trade deals will not come at zero cost to the UK's freedom to determine its own affairs and, as a relatively small country, it may well have to make more concessions than it likes, such as on immigration in a trade deal with India or on food standards with the US. So any sovereignty regained from leaving the EU is likely to be partly lost again.

Sovereignty and independence are thus relative. In a globalized, interconnected world[27] countries are obliged to cooperate, and cooperation entails obligations which constrain their freedom of action. Such constraints may differ in degree, but their nature is not substantially different when they result from an independently negotiated trade agreement or when they emanate from membership of a bloc like the EU.[28]

5.3.2   Form Over Substance

The May government continued to pretend that the type of relationship with the EU outlined in the Political Declaration amounted to "taking back control of our laws." In fact, Britain will only in theory be able to diverge from EU rules; in practice, to maintain market access it will have to adhere to them whether it likes it or not. What is more, it will no longer have any say in making the rules. This is an extreme example of the habit of giving precedence to form over substance that characterized the Brexit debate. It is a British habit. Take the countless changes over the years in the names of Whitehall departments like the Department for Trade and Industry. Or the form of legal interpretation the famous jurist Lord Denning struggled with which ignores the legislative history and purpose of a statute and looks only at the wording.[29]

An example of this tradition was the interpretation of Article 50 of the EU Treaty concerning the UK's financial obligations to the EU in the event of a no-deal Brexit that the House of Lords EU Committee adopted in 2017. The Lords concluded that the silence of Article 50 on financial obligations in the event of a member state withdrawing without a formal withdrawal agreement meant that the UK's obligations towards the EU were wiped out. The interpretation rested on a reading of Article 70 of the Vienna Convention on the Law of Treaties to mean that the provision by the EU treaty of rules on withdrawal, Article 50, made Article 50 alone applicable to financial obligations in the event of there not being an agreement, and as Article 50 was silent on the matter there were no such obligations. This interpretation is against common sense, as it presents a huge loophole through which any withdrawing member state could slip: just refuse to negotiate, leave without a deal, and escape any of the normal legal obligations that leaving a treaty entails under international law, just because the EU Treaty had left a loose end.[30] It is typical of British law's prioritization of form over substance, the ordinary meaning of statute, whereas Continental law takes a more teleological (purpose-directed), common-sense approach to interpreting imprecise legal provisions. The ruling, by a normally legally sound House of Lords committee, was seized upon by Brexiteers, and the Government, as proof that Britain did not owe the EU a penny, ignoring the practical consideration that the EU would hardly be likely to be cooperative on granting the UK a preferential trade agreement if it left without paying its debts.

What Britain is doing with Mrs May's framework for the UK's prospective relationship with the EU is replacing one form of cooperation, as a member of the EU, by another, being technically out of the EU but entering into more or less the same obligations, and gaining more or less the same benefits, as before, whether with the EU again or with other partners, but under different names. Substituting ad hoc arrangements, associate membership of agencies, or semi-voluntary shadowing of EU rules from the outside for full EU membership, and renaming single market regulations as "compatible regulatory approaches" and the Customs Union as a "customs partnership", is not regaining sovereignty but continuing to share it de facto in a disguised form. It is "old wine in new bottles." Hard-line Brexiteers and the Brexit press rightly called it "Brexit in name only." But the future relationships they themselves favour like a "Canada+" free trade agreement suffer from the same defect: such agreements, too, will entail, eventually, undertaking similar obligations to those the UK is ostensibly casting off by formally leaving the EU.

If becoming a fully independent and sovereign country again is not actually possible, and you had never actually lost much of your sovereignty to the EU in the first place, the secret is to dress up a new deal involving many of the same obligations in different language and to pretend it's substantially different. If a free trade deal with the EU or membership of the Trans-Pacific Partnership requires you to comply with their product standards and customs rules, just point out that trade deals are a completely different animal from EU membership. The packaging is the important thing, not the content. When President Obama urged the British people to stay in the EU, Brexit campaigners and the right-wing press called him a hypocrite because his country would never cede so much sovereignty to a supranational organization. But America is a member of many international organizations like the WTO and subjects itself to their authority. Even the TPP regional trade deal he was about to take his country into until his successor tore it up—and whose remnants Britain is now considering joining—is full of binding obligations.

5.3.3   The "f" Word

Federalism is a word that has been given a bad name in Britain, like "liberal" has in the US. The Eurosceptic press could think up no more damning a judgment of Jean-Claude Juncker, when he was being considered for Commission President, than that he was an "arch-federalist." However, the phobia of being in a federal European "super-state" is as irrational as attachment to the myth of absolute sovereignty. There seem to be two reasons behind the taboo associated with the "f" word: the feeling that there is a certain cut-off point beyond which power-sharing within a partnership tips the scales—the balance of power—away from the individual partner towards the partnership, and secondly confusion between form and substance, law and practice.

In practice, a federal relationship is similar to any relationship in which sovereignty is shared for some types of decisions which it is efficient to take collectively with one's partners, and is retained for other decisions that can better be taken by each partner individually. The current relationship between the European Union as a supranational body in which its members take collective decisions in some areas and the individual member states take individual decisions in others is already to some extent, in practice if not formally, a federal relationship. Admittedly, overall it is far from being as close as the fully-fledged federal systems in countries like the US,

Germany or Australia. But in some policy areas, like competition and, currently, agriculture, it is already a very close "federation"—at least as close as the situation in the US and virtually indistinguishable from it—while the "federal" relationship is extremely loose or is non-existent in fields such as education, social security or defence, areas that are fully or largely federated in the US.

In legal form, the EU is not, or not yet, and perhaps never will be, a "federation," but in practice, it already is, though much less close a one than the US, Germany or Australia. The point is that power-sharing is nothing to be afraid off and the sooner people abandon hang-ups about "sovereignty" and "federalism" and accept the sharing of decision-making with partners, allies and neighbours as a practical necessity, whether the relationship be called "federal," "multi-level" or anything else, the better.

5.3.4   Sovereignty Is Divisible and Not Immutable

The EU is a union of nation states, not a federation or a federal state. The member states are in charge. The European Commission is the executive but not the government of the EU. If one wishes to compare the EU to a country, it is the European Council—the EU "board" consisting of all the 28 (or 27) countries' prime ministers or presidents—that comes closest to a "government." The European Council is chaired by a President, currently Donald Tusk, but a "president" more in the sense of chairman not president of a country like the US or France.

When the former American Secretary of State Henry Kissinger asked in frustration "Who do I call if I want to call Europe?", he was right to feel confused, and the situation is not much different since the appointment of a European Council President.[31] Mr Kissinger would now have a counterpart he could call, the "EU high representative for foreign and security policy," Federica Mogherini, but she is responsible for only some areas of foreign policy and he might prefer instead to call the German or French foreign minister and his boss might phone Mrs Merkel, President Macron, or in days past, Mr Blair. It is they, the leaders of the member states, that ultimately hold the power and the purse strings.

As well as suspecting the EU of federal, "super-state" ambitions, some British traditionalists have an overly romanticized view of national sovereignty, the nation and the nation state, considering it somehow as sacred, unique, enduring, indivisible and immutable. This romantic view is belied by experience and (even recent) history. From time immemorial, countries have merged as a result of conquest or unification and countries have split, causing new countries to be formed that are bigger or smaller, as the case may be, than the countries that preceded them. Such changes lead to population transfers. A less romantic view of such processes is that people thereby come "under new management" like the employees of companies that merge or are taken over. Or in the case of people emigrating to another country far away and becoming assimilated into it, they are like people switching their employer.

Where does this leave the "nation state," the "nation," "nationhood" and "national sovereignty"? It shows that the social communities called "nations" with their own governments, their "national sovereignty," and their citizens are in fact highly variable entities, variable in their geographical extent and size, variable in their composition and the people that make them up, and variable in their system of government. It at least puts a question mark against the concept of "nation" as a long-term or enduring community with a distinct identity.

As well as due to changes over time in countries' boundaries ("territorial sovereignty"), political sovereignty is also divisible at a single point in time in relation to a single country.[32] The country may opt to entrust part of its government to a collective alliance with neighbours or with countries further away. Here, we have the situation of countries belonging to a political community or trading bloc like the European Union. But within the country itself, sovereignty may be delegated away from the central governments to sub-federal states or regions.

Both forms of delegation of sovereignty—upwards to a supranational body and downwards to regional or sub-federal entities—may make good economic and political sense.

The principles of delegation are analogous in business and in government. The delegation of sovereignty in government is not special. In business, management delegation usually denotes the situation where directors or managers leave decisions of lesser importance to lower ranking staff in order to concentrate on the big decisions themselves. It is delegation downwards through the organization to the appropriate level for the decisions to be taken. However, for some types of decisions it may be necessary or appropriate to go beyond the organization to an entity bringing together several similar organizations and to take the decision jointly through a form of cooperative arrangement. This is upwards delegation. In common with delegation downwards, it seeks the appropriate level for a decision, which in this case happens to be a level beyond the individual organization, that of an inter-organizational cooperative structure able to take a joint decision in the interests of all the individual member organizations.[33]

In government, the desirability of downwards delegation, or devolution, of power to regional and local levels is widely accepted as more efficient and more democratic, but discovering the optimal degree of devolution is difficult and implementing it even more so as central governments have a natural tendency to cling on to power and not to delegate. Failure to respond sufficiently to demands for regional autonomy, however, may create pressure for regions to secede, as we can see in Britain with Scottish independence and in Spain with Catalonia. "Control-freak" behaviour by government can be counterproductive.

Britain, lacking an internal power-sharing structure in the form of a written constitution which can contain pressures for further devolution, has not been particularly good at finding the optimum level of delegation between the centre and the regions. There is a strong centralizing instinct in the central government of Britain, particularly when the Conservative party is in power, perhaps due to the mystique attached to Westminster as the "mother of parliaments" and the reverence of all its traditions. It was Labour that brought in Scottish and Welsh devolution, against initial Conservative opposition. A Labour government also introduced regional development agencies in England, which the Conservatives promptly abolished once they regained power, although they have since created new mayors in the bigger English cities and devolved some powers to them, which is welcome. The Cameron government also launched the "Northern Powerhouse" initiative, a coordinated development programme for the North of England.[34]

The lack of devolution to the English regions, and the consequent lack of investment in old industrial areas in the North and Midlands, in stark contrast to the booming London and the South East, was a contributing factor in the strong Leave vote in these areas, despite this having nothing at all to do with the EU. In fact, the EU through its regional development spending and European Investment Bank lending was doing more to get investment to these areas than Britain itself was.

The Scottish independence movement is a reaction to the perceived lack of internal, downwards delegation of power within the UK. The Eurosceptic movement was the opposite. It was prompted originally by a feeling around the time of the Maastricht Treaty that the upwards delegation of sovereignty to the EU was going too far and the UK should resist further moves in that direction. But the rationale for some upwards delegation of powers to the European Community was generally accepted in that period; it was a matter of degree.

After Maastricht and the introduction of the single currency, opposition to European integration hardened and grew into a movement to exit the EU, and in the interests of their cause its supporters began to the challenge the very idea of delegating sovereignty to a supranational organization. They muddied the waters by presenting it as a black-and-white issue, as a choice between remaining in an organization moving inexorably towards a European "super-state" whose members had lost all or most of their sovereignty, and leaving the organization and regaining sovereignty completely. This was always a false choice but its simplistic message was sold to voters in the EU referendum campaign and Mrs May continued the deception.

The concrete benefits of cooperating as a member of the EU were played down, and the downsides in terms of loss of freedom to pursue Britain's own interests, and in the shape of overregulation and red tape, were exaggerated to make leaving seem like an obvious choice, a "no-brainer." The defence of the benefits of cooperation within the EU and the damaging effect of their loss was dismissed as fearmongering ("Project Fear"), so no serious debate took place.

5.3.5   Why Delegation of Sovereignty—Both Downwards and Upwards—Makes Sense

The government's "balance of competences" review described earlier would have been a perfect basis for such a debate, but the government, having practically disowned it as too pro-EU during a phase in which it was at pains to appear neutral in the Brexit debate, decided not to use it. The review had gone through the various areas of government activity one by one, examining to what extent sovereignty was delegated, how the frequently shared exercise of sovereignty in a policy area worked, and whether the balance of power between the UK and the EU resulting from the delegation was beneficial. The conclusion was that it was overwhelmingly in the national interest for the cooperation to continue broadly as it was now. Though in some policy areas like internal EU migration ("freedom of movement"), adjustments and reforms were called for, no need for wholesale repatriation of delegated competences was identified.

The facts thus told a different story than the Brexiteers in the referendum debate. International cooperation brings enormous benefits.

An often forgotten one is that cooperating countries do not fight one another. Churchill's dictum about "jaw-jaw" being better than "war-war" echoes a profound truth. In the long run, cooperation and war are alternatives. In the absence of cooperation, bad relations between two countries can quickly tip over into conflict. Brexiteers rubbished the contribution of European integration to peace in Europe and attributed this entirely to NATO, but they were ignoring history.

Another key advantage of cooperation or sharing—upwards delegation—of sovereignty is economic: reduced costs and increased prosperity. Cooperation can be a lot cheaper than doing your own thing. If it had been used, this argument might have carried weight in a referendum campaign dominated by arguments about money and the size of Britain's contribution to the EU budget, but it was not. The savings from delegating things to the EU are only now coming home to people as they hear about the numbers of new staff having to be recruited by public authorities to deal with extra work post-Brexit and the separate new bodies being set up to replicate services previously provided by EU agencies. A BBC News Reality Check article[35] responded to the question "We never talk about the economy of scale created by the EU. How much would it cost for the UK to duplicate all the EU agencies?" The reply was:

> There are dozens of EU agencies that the UK currently relies on, regulating everything from aviation and maritime safety, through chemicals and pharmaceuticals, to food and drink. Some people might say we don't need them, it's all just excessive bureaucracy. But without regulations on airline safety your planes can't take off, and without regulations on pharmaceuticals you can't buy and sell medicines. So it does matter. Building new institutions from scratch, training staff and developing expertise, will take considerable time and money.

The *Financial Times* of 17 May 2017[36] reported about the European Commission staff of inspectors and vets that inspect the health and hygiene of livestock overseas as part of the strict controls on food imported from outside the EU. It said that unless the UK reached a deal with the EU, it would be likely Britain would have to create its own unit of travelling inspectors to ensure the quality of food imports, and at present the country did not train enough vets. Quoting the president of the British

Veterinary Association, it went on to say, "The issue is one of several instances where the UK is set to take on bureaucratic work carried out at EU level."[37]

Ken Clarke wrote in similar vein in an article in the *Daily Telegraph* of 23 May 2014, misleadingly headlined "Britain ignited the bonfire of Brussels' bureaucracy. We must stay to finish the job."

> What [Leavers] fail to acknowledge is that the creation of the European Union and the single market was, in itself, one of the biggest deregulations in history. The separate regulatory regimes of 28 member states have in large part been swept aside in favour of a single body of regulations establishing common standards of food safety, health and environmental standards, consumer protection and so on. This makes the EU the most extraordinary platform for reducing regulation ever conceived.[38]

The extra costs of the new arrangements after Brexit not only burden public finances but impact on consumers as well, as British people will learn if leaving the EU results in their paying for travel visas, pet passports and higher mobile roaming charges, having to get international driving licences to be able to drive for long periods in Europe, or losing automatic health cover when abroad. Voters were not told that "independence" would come with costs and extra hassle. They were told Britain would be able to negotiate the same benefits at it had as a member, without the obligations, "both have its cake and eat it," in the famous phrase of Boris Johnson, now somewhat tarnished by contact with reality.

That trade increases economic growth and prosperity has been an axiom of economics since Adam Smith. The more frictionless the trade, the bigger is the economic gain. The 1988 Cecchini report estimated the effect on GDP in the European Community of the removal of regulatory barriers, which were still restricting trade within it, at at least 5% of GDP. These forecasts were largely borne out and removal of the remaining barriers, particularly in services and the digital market, will also have positive economic effects.[39] The single market is a buoyant marketplace. Its detractors who argue that the EU regulation that replaced national regulations stifles growth by increasing businesses' costs are in a small minority of libertarian, extreme free-trading economists.

Cooperation also increases mobility and convenience. Business and leisure become smoother, less time-consuming, less of a hassle—simpler customs procedures, lorries not being delayed at borders or passengers waiting endlessly in airport queues,[40] less bureaucracy and form-filling, no need to change currencies, and so on.

Many people also appreciate the interaction with other cultures that international cooperation allows, like more exciting food, a more varied cultural scene, more competitive sporting events, football leagues with more top players and managers, more diverse and successful universities, and more opportunities to travel, study and work abroad.

Improvements in mobility, convenience and cultural offerings make for a better quality of life. More will be said on the benefits of migration—as well as some drawbacks—in Chap. 7.

5.3.6   Cooperation Extends Sovereignty and Control

By cooperating, you can influence the decisions of your partners towards more desirable outcomes. Kim Jong-un has tight control of what happens in North Korea and has hitherto gained leverage over his neighbours by threatening nuclear attacks, though not entirely successfully as economic sanctions have been imposed on his country in retaliation. In the meantime, however, he seems to have learned that cooperation with China, the US and South Korea to influence the decisions they take affecting his country might actually increase his ability to govern and provide for his own economy.

Harold Macmillan expressed the same idea eloquently in his reflections on the benefits of joining the then European Economic Community in 1962[41]:

> Accession to the Treaty of Rome would not involve a one-sided surrender of 'sovereignty' on our part, but a pooling of sovereignty by all concerned, mainly in economic and social fields.
>
> In renouncing some of our own sovereignty we would receive in return a share of the sovereignty renounced by other members.

By leaving the EU, Britain will regain some sovereignty to determine its internal affairs but will lose the extended sovereignty it previously enjoyed owing to the leverage it had over its erstwhile partners. For example, any gain in sovereignty the UK secures by not being bound by EU decisions on agricultural subsidies will be partly offset by a loss of influence over EU Council of Ministers' decisions about, for instance, veterinary checks on meat or phytosanitary checks on food intended for export to the EU. To export its meat and food products, Britain will have to do checks which it had no part in determining, whereas as an EU member its minister and civil servants might have managed to shape the checks more to their liking. It will also lose the power to prevent its former EU partners in the Council from gaining competitive advantages in the form of waivers of rules or special treatment.

The British government is fully aware of this loss of control from leaving the structures of the EU and is therefore in the proposal contained in the Political Declaration attempting to maintain some of it by obtaining associate status in multiple EU bodies and agencies on a fee-paying basis after leaving. Under any of the other Brexit versions suggested the situation would be little different. There were real advantages in the extra sovereignty gained from membership; losing that control and having to get it back in roundabout ways afterwards hardly seems sensible.

National sovereignty is a not a finite cake. Cooperation makes the cake bigger. Or using the game theory analogy, international cooperation is not a zero-sum game, but a win-win situation.

5.3.7   The Penalties of Non-Delegation

Failure to respond to complaints of over-centralization of power in a country threatens the unity of countries like the UK. It led to the independence of Ireland in 1922 and could still lead to the secession of Scotland, especially if Britain ends up leaving the EU, against the wishes of a large majority of Scots in the EU referendum.

Supranational organizations like the EU that have previously had powers delegated upwards to them are subject to similar pressures. These pressures are a brake on unnecessary accumulation of power by such organizations and ignoring them could jeopardize the existence of the organizations. Thus, an organization like the EU that has had power entrusted to it by its member states needs to exercise such power sparingly and sensibly without encroaching on areas that properly belong to the sovereignty of the states. In some cases, it may mean the EU repatriating powers that have been transferred to it. This is "subsidiarity" in practice. "Subsidiarity" is just another word for good management practice whereby decisions should be taken at the appropriate level. The penalties for failing to practise "subsidiarity" curb any inclination the EU may have to forge ahead with integration against resistance from Eurosceptics and they force the EU to accommodate the desire of certain member countries to proceed more slowly than others.

5.4   RED TAPE

A high proportion of the British population is convinced that EU laws are essentially "red tape," or at least contain large amounts of that commodity and could therefore easily be simplified or abolished. So embedded in the British psyche is the view that bureaucracy is one of the defining characteristics of the EU that even the BBC is compelled to pay lip service to it.[42] The image of EU legislation being largely red tape or at the very least overly bureaucratic and of the liberating effect of getting rid of it or replacing it by simpler British-made laws was one of the most powerful arguments for Brexit. But is this reputation deserved?

There is some merit in allegations of overregulation by the EU.[43] I had plenty of experience of it myself, while working in the Commission department responsible for regional policy and having to grapple with badly written legal provisions that were confusing national officials and project managers and often leading to costly mistakes found by our own and external EU auditors. Before every new budget period, the department carried out "simplification" exercises in an effort to streamline the rule book. That said, the EU is not noticeably more bureaucratic than national administrations. The stereotype view in the British public and media about EU red tape is a considerable exaggeration. The level of prejudice towards the EU on this score that exists in Britain today is unique.

Many EU rules represent a considerable improvement in the quality of people's lives without the slightest bureaucracy. For example, Article 2 of EU Directive 2006/126 states simply that driving licences issued by Member States shall be mutually recognised. The result is that UK citizens can drive throughout Europe using their national driving licence without time limit, extra tests or having to apply for a licence from the other EU country.[44] What is bureaucratic about removing multiple layers of national red tape?

5.4.1   The Noble Sport of Brussels-Bashing—The British Press' Equivalent of Pro Wrestling

The anti-EU propaganda of the British press is largely to blame for ratcheting up the level of dissatisfaction with Europe about excessive bureaucracy. The beginnings of the British national sport of "Euro-bashing" date from Margaret Thatcher's time[45] and her quarrel with Europe over the budget. It took off in the early 1990s and never abated in intensity right through to the EU referendum. The four "Brexit" newspapers are past masters of this sport, but social media—which are even less accountable than the press—are becoming good at it, too.[46]

Like a sport, "Brussels-bashing" entertains the public and allows its practitioners to display high feats of journalistic prowess. However, it is a game with a serious purpose: to convert the spectators (readers) to the Eurosceptic beliefs of their proprietors and editors. It is a special genre in which, to keep up the sporting analogy, fair play (informing and educating the public) is not as important as winning (turning them into diehard Eurosceptics), by fair means or foul (misinformation).

The European Commission was alarmed at this trend as far back as 1996. Its President, Jacques Santer, complained in a Radio 4 interview about "anti-European propaganda, and even xenophobic propaganda, in the British press."[47] His comments were echoed by Kenneth Clarke: "Quite a lot of the press is owned by anti-European people and they go to great lengths to try and arouse prejudice in their readers to match that of their own political opinions."[48]

The London-based German journalist Ulrich Schilling wrote in *The Guardian* of 3 June 1996, "The *Sun*, the *Mail* and the *Express* are not harmless leaflets: they are read by 20 million people, and they may not always understand the special brand of humour which flavours *Sun* headlines."[49]

The British Foreign and Commonwealth Office published pamphlets to try to correct some of the worst "euromyths."[50] The European Commission also published myth-busting leaflets, entitled "Do you believe all you read in the newspapers?" and "Do you STILL believe all you read in the newspapers?", and its representative in Britain complained, "If you read a lot of English newspapers you will not find much to do with the reality of life in other countries or in the EU. There is no true assessment of the important role of Europe in helping to promote the wellbeing of Britain," adding that a survey on young people's attitude to the EU in Britain was symbolic of "the beginnings of a crisis in British people's attitudes towards Europe."[51]

Here are a few examples of headlines and key sentences of articles belonging to this typically British genre in newspapers in the 1990s and 2000s, with a few more recent ones thrown in. The supply hasn't stopped with the Brexit vote: the papers need to keep their readers fired up to fight the betrayal of Brexit being plotted by traitors in the "Establishment elite."

Eurocrat who wants to crunch our crisps. NEIN! Bangemann is determined to ban our flavoured crisps.[52] (*Daily Express*, 1991)

Eurobabble—If you thought Ecu was a new kind of vegetable read on.[53] (*Daily Express*, 1994)

Now They've Really Gone Bananas. Euro bosses ban 'too bendy' ones and set up minimum shop size of 5 and a half inches.[54] (*The Sun*, 1994)

From Better to Worse—Twenty Things—20 daft EU laws that changed our lives[55] (*The Sun*, 1998)

Wimbledon have been given a boost in their bid to move to Dublin by the European Union.[56] (*Daily Mail*, 1998)

Belgians view Euro method as an assault on their chips.[57] (*Daily Telegraph*, 2017)

Brexit to bring back Churchill's pint of fizz. When Britain joined the Common Market Brussels bureaucrats banned wine sales by the pint in favour of metric measures.[58] (*Daily Mail*, 2018)

Bring back the pint of wine—I can make sense of old measures. The pint bottle was barred by Brussels in 1973—one of those pointless bans that gave the European Union a bad name for prescriptive uniformity.[59] (*Daily Telegraph*, 2018)

The items quoted—a few of the thousands of similar reports in the Eurosceptic newspapers since the 1990s—illustrate certain of the characteristics of "Brussels-bashing."

1. The headlines and content of the articles are often funny and skilfully written, with scope for puns and double entendres. Journalists relish the opportunity the genre presents to show off their writing skills while entertaining and firing up their readers.

2. However, if satire can be graded on a scale between gentle, sympathetic teasing or ribbing and visceral, blistering attack, this *genre* is often closer to the visceral end of the spectrum. It has a serious purpose: to arouse indignation, outrage, and even hatred against its target, reinforcing the reader's negative preconceptions about it, in line with the editorial policy of the paper.

3. The stories are unverifiable because few readers will have concrete knowledge of the subject matter and the chances of the newspaper incurring sanctions for misreporting such esoteric and technical material are zero. Newspapers in Britain are accountable to no one. Readers' letters trying to get them to correct errors are immediately binned (or rather, more often nowadays with email, deleted). The

press' self-regulation body, the Independent Press Standards Organization, is pretty toothless. The journalist is accordingly under no pressure for accuracy or fairness. Fact checking will depend on the professional conscience of the individual journalist, and this will often collide with the pressure of deadlines and the dictates of editorial policy which prioritize a certain stance towards the EU over factual accuracy and balance.[60] In any case, studies of attitudes to fake news show that many people readily believe stories that agree with their preconceptions and reject facts that contradict these. Good "euro-myths" like that about "bendy bananas" are amazingly persistent. So why bother with boring facts? The "bendy banana" myth was "the euro-myth that would never die," according to David Charter in his book *What Has the EU Ever Done for Us?*[61] Boris Johnson used it in his campaigning and it was reported that a voter who intended voting "Remain" changed her mind when seeing a straight banana in a supermarket which reminded her of the "silly rules that come out of Europe."[62]

4. Balance and accuracy being a low priority, the articles rarely try to give the background that might explain and justify the EU action. The reporting is entirely one-sided, biased, skewed, pure "spin."

5. Hate-arousing stimuli, cues, and fear or outrage buttons like "Brussels bureaucrats," "unelected bureaucrats" and "eurocrats" are scattered liberally over the copy like cookie sprinkles. These much maligned—but, the papers would claim, deep-pocketed so fair game—individuals are scapegoated for laws the member states and the European Parliament decided, not them.[63]

6. The reports are often premature. A proposal or idea to do something is presented as a decision, something that will become law very soon. Cf. the crisps and Belgian chips items.[64]

7. Headlines can be mischievous. An example is that above the *Mail* story about Wimbledon (football club) moving to Dublin. It is guaranteed to arouse the ire of its London readers at "Brussels interference." Whilst it is true the EU social affairs commissioner, the Irishman Padraig Flynn, had expressed support for the plan, the *Mail* must have known that the EU had very little, if any, say in the matter, and the Commission's spokesman had indicated that it was a national, not an EU, matter.[65]

The feature in *The Sun* about "daft" EU laws referred to above is a prime example of the unverifiable assertions about EU red tape and lack of balance that are characteristic of Brussels-bashing. The article reproduced some of the claims in a book by Christopher Booker describing the large volume of legislation coming from the EU since 1992 to complete the single market. He says this is over 3000 laws a year on average and that "Without any control by parliament, our Government is forced to enact any law from Brussels," which, of course, is contrary to the clear facts.[66] However that may be, these "daft Brussels laws" have been bad for Britain:

> "Vast tracts of English countryside have been reduced to hedgeless, treeless prairies by the CAP.... The EU can now ban the export of British goods anywhere in the world. After the BSE scare we were forbidden to sell soap, candles or wine gums—even to countries which wanted to buy them... Our water bills have soared by billions of pounds a year, just to comply with over-the-top Brussels rulings—even though our water was already as clean as any in Europe."[67]

EU laws had also forced changes to the length of cricket pitches, led to traditional blue passports being replaced by standard red ones, and to health and safety rules limiting how much pregnant women and care workers can lift.

Would any *Sun* reader (or any *Times or Telegraph* reader, for that matter) bother trying to verify all this? Would they not tend to take the journalist's word for it, even though they might be a tiny bit sceptical about British water being "as clean as any in Europe," or about the totally nonsensical character of rules on the weight employers could require pregnant women or carers to lift, in the latter case, probably referring to the weight of bedridden patients in care homes? There is no attempt at journalistic balance, to explain the pros as well as the cons, something that *Financial Times* readers and BBC listeners would take for granted. *The Sun* has an admirable ability to explain complex issues to its readers in simple terms. The language of its leading articles, *The Sun Says*, is masterly. It is a great pity its anti-EU stance prevents it from explaining complex issues about the EU in a balanced way and, once in a while, saying something good about Europe.

The more recent story about the possible return of pint bottles of champagne after Brexit is a sequel to the long-running debate over metrication. The history of this debate is one of the subjects of David

Charter's book *What Has the EU Ever Done For Us?*[68] The discussion of metrication in Britain goes back to the nineteenth century and the switch from imperial to metric units was under way well before Britain's entry into the EC. British industry was wholly in favour of moving to metrication and the system was already in standard use in science. Thus, it was not a case of the EU forcing metrication on an unwilling Britain, though it was true that EU law was gradually moving Britain, with the support of successive British governments, to a situation where initially dual use of metric and imperial units (indication of weights and measures in metric units alongside imperial units) would be required, before phasing out imperial units and having only metric. The intention of the exercise, however, was not to force Britain to give up cherished traditions, but to remove obstacles to trade.

In 2008, the EU responded to the political furore surrounding the prosecution of traders weighing vegetables in imperial measures, dubbed the "Metric Martyrs," by giving up the attempt to get the UK to move to a single metric system. The current situation is that goods can have both metric and imperial units on their packaging, while the pint measure can be used for draught beer and cider and bottled milk.

The *Mail* and *Telegraph* articles of 28 February 2018 about pint bottles of champagne got many of their facts wrong, but worse than that they took up a position similar to that of the "Metric Martyrs" that Britain was being forced by the EU into something it didn't want. This is wrong. The weight of opinion in industry and government has always been in favour of metrication, because having parallel systems is costly; most manufacturers have to work in metric units because over 90% of British trade is with countries using the metric system; and the country will not after Brexit go back generally to imperial measures because it would not make economic sense.[69] The *Telegraph* even referred to the symbol of British freedom constantly invoked by Brexiteers like Farage and Johnson, the Magna Carta, which does refer to units of measurement but is hardly relevant in the twenty-first century. Apart from the usual blame put on "Brussels bureaucrats," whereas it is the member states who decide EU laws, the articles said the ban on pint bottles for wine began in 1973; in fact, it came in 1980, well after Britain joined, so it was not something imposed on the UK as a *fait accompli* right from the beginning.

The BBC, as usual, shed light on the darkness. A member of the Pol Roger champagne family interviewed on the *Daily Politics* programme on 1 March 2018[70] said French champagne producers had themselves proposed restricting champagne bottle sizes to the metric measures during the consultation preceding the issue of the 1980 legislation. This was because after the war there had no longer been much demand for pint bottles (the size Winston Churchill preferred), as drinking champagne by the glass had become common. But the Pol Roger spokesman said the firm was prepared to re-introduce pint bottles for the British market after Brexit.[71]

In the light of this statement by the maker of Churchill's favourite champagne, the *Telegraph* article's statement that the prohibition of pint bottles of champagne was "one of those pointless bans that gave the European Union a bad name for prescriptive uniformity" was false.

Readers of the Eurosceptic newspapers like to get in on the act, too, and the papers love to print their stories, because not only do they maintain the party line on the EU, they are often entertaining. Brussels-bashing is a sport anyone can play. In the *Daily Telegraph* of 1 January 1992, a reader wonders whether the disappearance of innards from chickens on sale in supermarkets is due to "yet another piece of EC legislative buffoonery," and another on 6 January 1992 speculates whether the EC is going to harmonize the information that has to be given on stamps. At present, British postage stamps do not carry the name of the country of issue, namely the UK, but only the head of the Queen. Will the Queen's head disappear?, he wonders. A glance at the letter pages of the *Mail, Sun* and *Express* shows a similar picture. Only in the rarest of cases do they print letters representing pro-EU views. The *Financial Times*, on the other hand, regularly publishes letters critical of its own columns.

Light mockery laced with wit, charm and feats of verbal acrobatics, a talent he has in common with his idol Churchill, characterized the dispatches of Boris Johnson during his time as Brussels correspondent of the *Telegraph* from 1989 to 1994. But colleagues on the Brussels beat and Commission insiders such as Chris Patten were critical of his penchant for embellishing his stories.[72] A Johnson report in the edition of the paper on 1 July 1992[73] about the visit of Jacques Delors with the whole Commission to London at the start of the British presidency was typically spiced with derogatory references to "the EEC's sprawling decision-making machine," and to EU figures who were unpopular in Britain for proposing rules considered by the libertarian *Telegraph* as too onerous, such as the environment commissioner Mr Ripa de Meana, who had proved "too meddlesome for British taste," and the social affairs commissioner Ms Vasso Papandreou, "who did so much to exasperate British ministers with her directives over pregnant women and hours at work." Mr Delors himself was taking over the responsibilities of Mr Ripa de Meana and was likely, Mr Johnson claimed, to "use the opportunity to prune vexatious euro-law, such as instructing farmers when they can shoot magpies."

Though Johnson's dispatches were light-heartedly satirical in tone, the cumulative effect of his regular mocking criticisms of the EU during a period of deep divisions in the Tory Party about the EU was probably considerable. There was a reckless irresponsibility about them, a nonchalance about the damage he might cause, a prankster's glee combined with an *agent provocateur*'s steely destructive intent. On BBC Radio 4's *Desert Islands Disks* in 2005, he said he himself had been taken aback by the impact his dispatches produced back home:

> I was chucking these rocks over the garden wall and listening to the amazing crash from the greenhouse next door over in England. It gave me this weird sense of power.[74]

This trait remained with him during the referendum campaign. He trotted out a huge repertoire of euro-myths, appealing to prejudices about Brussels interference, faceless bureaucrats, "fat-cat" salaries and scandalous waste, and at the same time conveying the nationalistic message of British exceptionalism and its independent future striding the world stage. It was populism worthy of Trump with his "Make America great again," "Drain the swamp," "Lock her up" and "Build the wall" slogans.

That is not to say Boris did not also send serious and balanced copy to London during his days in Brussels,[75] or that other *Telegraph* writers were not, in the early 1990s, still producing fair and balanced reports about Brussels legislation at this time. For example, the paper's agriculture correspondent, David Brown, on 1 January 1992, in an article headlined "Why potted shrimps may lose their tang," gave a neutral account of an EC hygiene regulation which was to come into force on 1 January 1993 and would ban boiling shrimps in sea water as is traditional in Morecambe Bay, so requiring trawlers to carry fresh water with them for boiling the shrimps. He did not play this ban up as an assault on British traditions, but explained why it was justified, the reason being that Morecambe Bay had a poor record on sewage pollution and despite a planned new sewage pipeline, the water in the bay was not expected to meet EC quality standards for fish processing. Yet, by mid-1992, balanced reports like this were already in a minority, and there were clear signs that the paper was moving to the uncompromising Eurosceptic line in its editorial policy that has been its hallmark ever since.[76]

It would have been a miracle if the constant stream of negative press stories about EU red tape had not helped turn British public opinion against Europe. Mixed in with the issues of immigration and unfair treatment over the budget, they helped create an animus of resentment and anger in a substantial part of the population, which influenced the referendum result. For many, the European Union was—and still is, because the propaganda continues—the enemy.[77]

5.4.2   How Much EU Law Is Needless Red Tape?

Well, after all, apparently not all that much. Otherwise Parliament would not have passed a law temporarily incorporating all EU regulations into UK law. "Temporarily," by the way, does not mean until a specific date, but indefinitely until Parliament gets round to reviewing it all, which could take years.[78] True, legislation in some areas like agriculture, trade and immigration, for which the government has definite plans to change the current rules after Brexit, will be replaced more quickly. But for the rest leaving the EU laws on the British statute book for the time being is not considered to be so damaging to British interests that it is essential to abolish them *tout-de-suite* on the "bonfire of red tape" promised by the *Daily Telegraph* and Boris Johnson.[79]

The nefarious EU rules being left untouched for the moment include those on health and safety at work, so that Littlejohn in the *Mail* will not immediately get to hear Big Ben chiming live again. The chimes have been stopped while Westminster Tower is being renovated to avoid them causing hearing loss to the construction workers doing the repairs. Littlejohn, not a scaffolder himself, thought this "snowflake" health and safety nonsense—all, of course, Brussels' fault—should be ignored.[80]

What other "useless red tape" could eventually be scrapped? David Charter gives a detailed account of the scope for scrapping EU rules in 15 areas and states the reasons for his conclusions, which are that many of the allegedly "intrusive" EU rules castigated by the newspapers are justified and are likely to remain in place. These include rules on air and water quality, renewable energy, flying, weights and measures, employment rights, domestic appliances, including vacuum cleaners and lightbulbs, and, by the way, even bananas. On the other hand, there may be changes in animal welfare, trade, agriculture, fishing and VAT rates, and Brits will get their "iconic" blue passports back.[81] There will be no wholesale return to using imperial units in science laboratories and factories, however.

It turns out, then, that the bonfires of "red tape" will be smaller than the libertarian *Telegraph* and *Mail* would like and they will keep having to relight them!

Indeed, in some areas like air safety, chemicals regulation, medicines approval and control of nuclear materials, the rules will be on the UK statute book permanently, as the government intends to leave these matters to EU agencies in future. The UK will have to pay for these services, showing that as a member Britain was after all getting something back for the "vast sums" it was sending the EU every week.[82] So it looks like the EU rules and the agencies applying them were not such a bad thing after all!

EU rules on energy-saving lightbulbs and vacuum cleaners were lambasted by the Brexit press and campaigners in the referendum as needless bureaucratic meddling.[83] Judith Woods, in the *Daily Telegraph* of 28 December 2018, in an article otherwise full of Christmas good cheer, lambasted "that stupid Brussels ban on proper light bulbs."[84] But this was not a Brussels edict. Successive UK governments had supported the changes. Studies are now showing how important such energy-saving measures are in reducing CO_2 emissions; they are having an even bigger impact than renewables.[85] They are examples of good EU rules which after Brexit will probably eventually, after review, be maintained. I doubt if the Brexit newspapers and campaigners will still remember to criticize them when in ten years' time they, or something very similar, are quietly slipped into British law permanently under cover of statutory instruments.

There has always been only one valid reason for opposing EU technical rules of this nature: that British-made rules are qualitatively better and cater better for British interests and consumer preferences. Clearly, this could make it worthwhile to produce goods to British specifications, despite the possible disadvantage of such products not being able to be exported freely to Europe and requiring manufacturers to produce to two different standards, which is costly.

A bad reason for going it alone would be that the underlying laws would be undeniably British, even though for the most part copied from and identical to the EU rules. I strongly suspect that Brexit-supporting newspapers and politicians have always been more exercised by the second form-over-substance consideration than by the first.[86] The evidence certainly does not support the view that British laws are intrinsically better than EU laws.

5.4.3   Is British Best?

In his speech in a debate in the Oxford Union on 11 November 2013,[87] Jacob Rees-Mogg gave only one, oblique, example of British laws being qualitatively better. It concerned a case in which he had tried to obtain redress for a constituent, a farmer, who was facing a fine under an EU agricultural regulation concerning a straying cow. Mr Rees-Mogg was unable to help his constituent because he was told by the responsible DEFRA minister that it was a matter of EU law. Mr Rees-Mogg asserted that British authorities applying domestic British law would have been more flexible. Sadly, this is not always the experience of many British people.

The difficulties of members of the public with British-made rules are recounted, day-in-day-out, on consumer programmes like BBC Radio 4's *You and Yours* and *Money Box.* A recent example concerned the mistakes regularly made by the NHS in imposing penalties on patients considered to have fraudulently claimed exemptions from prescription charges. Enquiries had found that about a third of penalty notices were cancelled as unjustified, but before that they had caused considerable distress to innocent patients. The main reasons for the mistakes were the rules' complexity—pharmacists did not understand them—and faulty computer programmes.[88] Other examples are the hardship caused in the roll-out of Universal Credit by design faults in the legislation, and by a public debt collection system under which debtors are being forced into bankruptcy by becoming involuntarily subject to huge charges and legal fees which double, triple, or quadruple their debts, for example, for unpaid Council Tax owed to local authorities.[89] Or take the shambolic introduction of new railway timetables in Britain in 2018 causing widespread cancellation of trains and people not being able to get to work. Or consider the work that voluntary organizations like local Citizens' Advice Bureaus do to sort out cases of unfair treatment of consumers by public authorities. These problems arise under wholly British-made laws.

Isabel Hardman recounts the disappointment of new MPs arriving at Westminster at how bad the scrutiny of legislation is in the House of Commons, due to the system of patronage and whipping that prioritizes loyalty over the effort an enthusiastic new member might want to put into getting the details of legislation right; the Commons depends on the Lords for serious amendment of poorly drafted bills.[90] The select committee system is a rare shining light in the legislative work of the Commons. Even to an outside observer, the output of the House of Lords has always seemed of better, more considered quality.[91] The government is proposing to cut the number of MPs and has made threatening noises to abolish the House of Lords should it not be more docile in the Brexit legislation.[92] If the Lords goes, God help us!

The coalition government of 2010–15 launched a creditable "Red Tape Challenge" to cut away unnecessary regulations. The headline of a *Daily Telegraph* article (see above) about this initiative by the then Minister without Portfolio, Ken Clarke, was "Britain ignited the bonfire of Brussels bureaucracy. We must stay to finish the job."[93] But the first part of the headline was, as usual in stories about the EU, misleading. Much of the red tape Mr Clarke was targeting in the initiative was domestic legislation, and he emphasized the effort the EU itself was making. The progress was not all at the behest of Britain. In fact, in implementing EU rules Britain has always had a rather bad reputation for overcomplicating ("gold-plating") them. And Mr Clarke also wrote that the single body of regulations created by the EU which offers common standards in place of the separate regulatory regimes of 28 countries was "one of the greatest deregulations in history."

Contrary to the myths of the EU's "sprawling decision-making machine" fed by the newspapers and by books like Craig and Elliott's *The Great European Rip-Off*, and contrary to the superficial impressions occasionally given by the media, including the BBC,[94] the EU's legislative procedures work well and produce relatively good laws. The consultation of interested parties and national administrations at all stages in the process, during drafting in the Commission and during scrutiny and adoption in the Council of Ministers and in the Parliament, is nowadays extremely thorough. National governments and parliaments follow the process closely and make an indispensable contribution to it through their officials sitting on working parties and standing committees and through their liaison services in Brussels. So do the lobbying organizations in Brussels who devote staff to the process. The lower house of the British parliament is less involved in monitoring the process of EU legislation than it used to be, but fortunately the Lords compensates for this by being unusually active. The MEPs themselves are well-resourced with up to four research assistants helping them.

With this degree of preparation, consultation and care, the resulting legislation should be well-thought-out and usually is. The well-oiled system specializes in lawmaking that advances integration and delivers benefits for the whole European Union which national parliaments cannot achieve individually. Often this legislation is in pioneering fields like the General Data Protection Regulation, which US experts think could become a model for them, too. The legislation rests on long-term action programmes and information platforms like the Lisbon Agenda and Europe 2020.[95]

British laws are not intrinsically of better quality than EU laws. They are almost certainly often less well prepared. In that case, what is the point of keeping up the appearance of sovereignty in order to be free to make one's own worse laws or simply to be able to stick "Made in Britain" labels on laws copied from the EU?

It is ideological nonsense to wish to take back control of *all* our laws. The pressure in advanced industrial countries to regulate more and more areas of people's lives—whether this is always a good thing is beside the point—means that national parliaments do not have the time to make good laws in all fields. They could not do it if they tried. Better to share some of this rule-making with others through supranational bodies like the EU, the OECD[96] or the ECHR (European Court of Human Rights), and sign up to international treaties and conventions that relieve them of part of the burden. In today's world, small- or medium-sized nation states like Britain are only viable if they espouse international cooperation.

5.5   Is the EU Fit for Purpose?

The myth is that the EU is a dysfunctional and failing organization, run by a bloated, incompetent, inefficient, overpaid bureaucracy and headed by a corrupt, self-serving elite. If this were true, it would be yet another good reason for leaving. But the reality is different.

5.5.1   Failing?

The EU has its share of problems: the migrant crisis, the euro, populism, governments defying long-established norms of behaviour, climate change, terrorism, an insecure world order, and, of course, Brexit. But it is not falling apart, and it has shown its resilience in getting through acute difficulties like the financial and migrant crises, such that more routine problems like stand-offs with member states over budget deficits or democracy appear routine by comparison.

5.5.2   *Dysfunctional?*

The charge of "dysfunctionality" again seems to refer to the difficulties the EU as an organization has experienced in managing recent internal or external crises, and to the failure to find a consensus within the whole group, with the result that the solution ends up being left to one faction within the group or indeed to a single dominant player, usually Germany. But such an ad hoc and haphazard method of problem-solving is hardly surprising in an organization in which power—quite rightly—resides with its member states and these are of different sizes and varying degrees of availability in a crisis, given their domestic concerns. Moreover, the crises were intractable and unprecedented. There was no playbook telling the EU authorities what to do; they often had to make it up as they went along. It would not have been a "stroll in the park" for anyone.[97] And a lot of hard work was going on behind the scenes, out of the media lime-light. For example, in 2008–09 during the acute phase of the financial crisis, the Commission was applying a rapidly devised framework for refer-eeing member states' bailing out of banks and industrial companies, so that the solvent banks and companies were not put out of business by the ones getting aid.[98]

The even more dangerous euro crisis was a rollercoaster. It demanded the utmost technical ingenuity and political decisiveness from the EU pro-tagonists and the IMF. Their action saved the single currency, for the time being at least, by containing the immediate threat of contagion and avoid-ing the turmoil of a Greek exit, and it laid the foundations of a system that puts the currency in somewhat better shape to withstand similar shocks in future. The austerity programmes imposed by the creditor countries led by Germany and the IMF were hard but, except for Greece, the bailed-out economies have now recovered.

Of a similar level of threat, though shorter, the migrant crisis of 2015–16 was also contained, despite deep divisions between the member states. The detractors of the EU's and Chancellor Merkel's action, such as Nigel Farage and some commentators in the British press, have yet to say how they would have handled this humanitarian emergency better, if at all. The faltering steps towards a common EU asylum system, the failure so far to reform the outdated Dublin rules,[99] despite the burning injustice they inflict on "frontline" Mediterranean countries, are not a symptom of the dysfunctionality of the EU as such but rather of the divisions between the member states on this issue.

Many British journalists cannot resist a sly dig at the EU holding so many meetings, as if this in itself was evidence of dysfunctionality. But at times of crisis the need for regular summits and emergency talks is obvious. It is populism to pretend otherwise. The persistence of an unresolved problem and the multiplicity of meetings to resolve it is not evidence of dysfunctionality but usually of the difficulty of the problem per se. The increase in the number of member states has certainly increased the difficulty of reaching agreement on certain issues such as migration, but not, so far, to the point of rendering the EU decision-making system as such dysfunctional. The fears on this score expressed before the enlargement of the EU to eastern Europe have proved to be exaggerated, problems over migration and democratic norms notwithstanding. The talk of an East-West divide or a North-South divide in the EU is an over-simplification. The real divide is between more integrationist and more nationalist forces, and such divisions exist in all member states, whether in east or west, north or south.

The legislative process in the EU is a well-oiled machine. In itself it functions well. However, strains emerge between the EU institutions and member states in crisis situations, when divergent national interests are often at stake. Collective problem-solving is then more difficult, though mostly still possible, and the resultant solutions are better than purely national ones. International cooperation is worthwhile despite all the difficulties. These do not make a supranational organization as such dysfunctional.

5.5.3   A Sprawling, Bloated Bureaucracy?

The EU institutions, particularly the Commission, are not bloated. The EU institutions altogether have around 55,000 permanent civil servants or contract staff. The Commission has around 33,000 staff, the European Parliament 7500 and the Council 3500. By no standards can they be judged to be overstaffed. Large local authorities in Britain often have comparable numbers of staff.[100] Whitehall departments altogether had around 380,000 staff in 2016.[101] The degree of responsibility borne by individual EU officials is often greater than in national administrations and surprises visiting national officials when they ask their host about his support staff and find he doesn't actually have any. From top to bottom, the organization is lean, the leanest of all being the Commission's excellent Legal Service. Extra responsibilities do not lead to increases in staff. After introduction of a standstill on recruitment driven largely by the Cameron government the Commission raised its official working hours back to 40 hours a week from the 37 and a half hours that had been in force since the early 2000s.[102]

5.5.4   Incompetent, Inefficient?

Again a completely gratuitous assertion. Virtually, all permanent staff are recruited through public examinations similar to those for the British civil service. The exceptions are experienced personnel headhunted for special roles. There are an additional 15% of temporary contract staff recruited through tests and interviews. The organization resembles an inverted pyramid in terms of the qualification levels of staff, with many people at the administrator level holding specialist qualifications and PhDs. The male/ female balance is better than in most national administrations, Nordic countries excepted. Typing pools and hordes of personal assistants are a thing of the past. Staff undergo annual performance reviews, which determine salary increments, although there is also a seniority element in pay. Appointments to middle and senior manager positions are decided on the basis of merit. Working in a commissioner's private office ("cabinet"), with its associated high level of responsibility and exceedingly long working hours, is a training ground for management positions, but staff can also work their way up through the ranks to top "director-general" (equivalent to Permanent Secretary in the British civil service) positions without cabinet experience. I have worked under a lot of very good managers in the European Commission.

The efficiency of the EU civil service has been enhanced by reforms introduced while Neil Kinnock was in charge of human resources policy in the Commission in the early 2000s. These include internal audit units in each department, a general Commission inspection service reviewing internal procedures, as well as annual management plans and performance reports for each department. The reforms followed a series of (quite minor) corruption scandal in the late 1990s.

A large proportion of the total staff are translators (of text) and interpreters (doing simultaneous interpreting at meetings, a very special skill). Translators and interpreters are paid at the top "administrator" level grade but there are fewer management positions in the language services. With the increased number of official languages (now 24), the number of language staff is insufficient to meet demand, so many documents are not translated by translators (though rough machine translation is increasingly used), but only into English and/or French, and speakers at meetings often cannot speak in their own language but have to use English or French instead. German is a third working language but English now predominates. Most ordinary officials have to work—read, write and speak—in at least one language, often English, other than their own.

5.5.5   *Why Are There So Few Brits in the EU Civil Service?*

Brexiteers used the underrepresentation of British nationals in the EU civil service as evidence of Britain's declining influence in the organization and also implied that discrimination might be at work. This made two arguments for Brexit out of a single statistic. The reality is different. First, contrary to what many seem to believe, EU civil servants work for the EU and have no administrative connection to the civil service of their country and are not conduits of influence from their national capital.[103] Thus, if there are less Brits, it is because less Brits have applied to join the service and passed the entrance examinations. There is no discrimination in recruitment. The EU institutions have tried to recruit more British officials, and have even organized special recruitment drives for British citizens in which it has relaxed the requirement for candidates to have a good knowledge of another EU language. The results have been disappointing. Good graduates seem to be attracted more to the City and there are also better paying careers in legal services.[104] The declining reputation of the EU in British public opinion may also be a factor.

5.5.6   *Overpaid?*

EU staffers are reasonably well paid but not excessively so considering their qualifications including language knowledge and the level of responsibility exercised. The basic salary scales (before deductions and the addition of allowances) are visible on the institutions' publicly accessible websites.[105] Comparisons with British salaries are made difficult by the British custom of giving annual salaries rather than the monthly rates usual in mainland Europe. The deductions from EU basic salaries and pensions are a Community income tax averaging between 12 and 25% (no local, say Belgian, income tax is paid), a special solidarity charge of 6 or 7% and contributions to the health insurance and pensions schemes.

The additions are a 16% overseas ("expatriation") allowance for officials living outside their own country (thus, not Belgians in Brussels) and household, child and education allowances. Parents can send their children free of charge to one of the four excellent European Schools in Brussels and there are similar schools for officials' children in other EU institution locations like Luxembourg. Not all Brussels officials use the European Schools, however, because Belgian schools are good too. Some officials send their children to other international schools or to the other national (such as British, French, or German) schools that exist in the Brussels area. Officials and their families can use a contributory health insurance scheme. Pensions (pension age between 65 and 67) are up to 70% of the final basic salary (after 30 years' service). EU officials and pensioners in Belgium pay normal Belgian taxes apart from income tax (see above). Retired staff continue to receive health insurance but not the overseas allowance. Staff can continue working after retirement in jobs outside the EU institutions and many do.

5.5.7 Top Officials (Juncker, Tusk, Commissioners, etc.): Self-Serving, Arrogant, Corrupt?

This, too, is pure myth which by dint of frequent repetition becomes, not only in the eyes of the public but in those of the journalists who come to believe their own propaganda, an alternative reality.[106] It was given sustenance by hatchet job books like David Craig and Mathew Elliott's *The Great European Rip-Off.*

What is the evidence of nest-feathering and corruption? Is it the amount commissioners spend in expenses on foreign trips, about which the *Telegraph* made a brouhaha in 2017, but which turned out to be a damp squib as the amounts were unremarkable and fully comparable to those of British ministers?[107] Is it the fact that Jose Manuel Barroso landed himself a big job in Goldman Sachs after retiring as Commission President? This, too, is unremarkable. Other former commissioners like the Irishman Peter Sutherland and the Frenchman Pascal Lamy continued their distinguished careers in public service as heads of the World Trade Organization—so beloved of Brexiteers—or the UN refugee agency (the late Peter Sutherland in both); as presidents or prime ministers of their countries; as influential members of the European Parliament; or as heads of their central bank. What is "self-serving" about exceptionally capable and motivated people continuing serving their country or the world in senior positions after their ten-year stints in demanding jobs in the Commission, European Council or Parliament? Or does the evidence consist solely of the cases of fraud committed by a few commissioners 20 years ago which caused the mass resignation of the Santer Commission in 1999 and led to stringent reforms in the Commission and the other institutions making such abuses practically impossible thereafter? In Britain, people making such allegations would be told to put up or shut up. But Brussels is fair game because if it answers back, it will be accused of political interference and shouted down.

Is the affable Juncker or the gentlemanly Tusk arrogant? Are their mild comments and little jokes at the U-turns performed by the British government in the Brexit negotiations and their occasional retorts to the insults and outrageous behaviour of Farage in the European Parliament "mocking"? How sensitive we have become! They made their comments in English, not in French, German or Polish, and their messages are usually admirably clear, not abrasive or evasive, and not playing to the gallery back home. Where is the British minister on a foreign visit showing similar courtesy to his counterpart in a European institution or member state or to a local TV audience by speaking even a few words in their language?

5.6   THE EUROPEAN COURT OF JUSTICE

The judges of the European Court of Justice (ECJ) must have been taken aback at becoming at the same time a *bête noire* of the Brexit movement and one Mrs May's *red* lines. The insults,[108] however, probably hurt less than the depressing ignorance surrounding the European Court of Justice that exists in Britain. The ECJ is confused with the European Court of Human Rights, a quite different institution that is not even part of the EU, and the extent of the ECJ's jurisdiction and influence on British law is exaggerated out of all proportion. Hyperbolic references to the need to end Britain being "ruled by foreign judges" are all too frequent.

What is the real situation and how did this distorted picture of the ECJ take hold in Britain?

The ECJ is an administrative and commercial court whose jurisdiction is strictly limited to the policy areas in which the EU has been given the power to enact legislation and take decisions. These include the single market, competition, the environment, employment and consumer rights, trade policy, economic and monetary union, and now also fundamental rights since the Charter of Fundamental Rights was incorporated into EU law by the Lisbon Treaty. As explained in Sect. 5.1 of this chapter, the inclusion of a policy area in the list of fields in which the EU has certain powers does not mean the EU has all the power. In many policy areas, both the EU and the member states have powers to legislate and take decisions at different levels and on different matters. In that case, there is a strict demarcation between the powers of each. In some areas like education, health, social security, taxes, defence, and justice and home affairs including immigration and criminal law and law enforcement, the EU has little or no powers and all or virtually all power is retained by the member states' authorities. The European Court of Justice only makes judgments relating to the parts of a policy area in which legislative and decision-making power has been expressly entrusted to the EU. It cannot adjudicate on matters outside its jurisdiction, and these are by far the majority. So the implication of Brexit slogans like "taking back control of our laws" that, while Britain is a member of the EU, British courts have to follow rulings of the European Court a lot or most of the time is nonsense.[109] In a lot of the areas of the law that are adjudicated by courts there is no EU law, so cases are decided entirely under British law. Only in certain specific cases do British courts have to take account of EU law as interpreted by the European Court of Justice. In those areas of the law, EU law is applicable in Britain; it has become a part of British law, and the two are indissoluble. Mixtures of laws of different origins, domestic and international, are not peculiar to the EU. International laws deriving from other sources under international conventions such as the European Convention of Human Rights or the Geneva Refugees Convention are also concurrently applicable in one way or another with UK law. Conflicts between different levels or sources of law are resolved in the same way as the even more frequent conflicts between different domestic British laws. There is a whole branch of law dedicated to the conflict of laws.

What does the European Court of Justice do in the areas in which it has jurisdiction? It has several functions: to provide a service of judicial review of EU legislation and decisions, on appeal from member states, firms and individuals in member states, and other EU institutions, and to rule similarly on cases brought by the same parties claiming that the EU institutions have failed to act where they should have acted; to hand down authoritative rulings to national courts on the correct interpretation of provisions of the treaties and EU legislation; to find on a referral from the European Commission whether a member state has failed to comply with its obligations under EU law (so-called infringement proceedings); and to award damages to parties who have suffered harm as a result of wrongful action by the EU institutions.

There are two courts: a higher court, the European Court of Justice proper, and a lower court, the "General Court."[110] The lower court hears appeals against—carries out judicial review of—decisions made by the Commission and its agencies and other EU institutions under delegated powers in areas such as competition; from its judgments there is a right of appeal to the higher court, the ECJ itself. "Preliminary rulings" on the interpretation of EU law are handed down by the higher court, the ECJ, which is the final arbiter of such questions, effectively a supreme court.

The ECJ has a reputation for fairness and competence. All its judgments, now including those of the lower, "General Court," are published in extenso in a special collection of European Court judgments. "In extenso" means what it says: at full length, complete, comprising the remedy sought, the background of the case, a summary of the arguments of the parties, the opinion of one of the "Advocates General" (a lawyer performing a role similar to *amicus curiae* who researches the case and makes a recommendation as to how the court should decide, which is not binding on the judges but which they take into account), and, finally, the reasoning behind the judgment, and the operative part of the judgment with the remedies or relief granted, if any. As in administrative or commercial court proceedings in the UK, most of the work is done in judges' and lawyers' offices, not in open court, though in Britain the oral part of the proceedings tends to be longer even in these areas of the law than in the ECJ.

The European Court of Justice works in Luxembourg.[111] The higher court, the European Court of Justice, has 28 judges, one from each member states, and 11 Advocates General. The General Court has 56 judges but no Advocates General. The total staff of the ECJ is 800.

The European Court of Justice does not "supervise" British courts, as has been claimed, evoking images of a corps of EU legal inspectors touring the country's courts to check whether they are applying EU laws and dishing out fines if they are not. The Court's judges and officials never leave Luxembourg except perhaps occasionally to take part in conferences. The ECJ only gets involved in cases before British courts when the highest appeal court in the land for the type of proceedings concerned raises an issue of the interpretation of EU law with the European Court. There is no "supervision" or even monitoring of performance, no implication that British courts are inferior. British courts are used to applying the hybrid domestic-cum-EU law that exists in many areas and do so competently and without fuss. In the area of competition, the EU law that predominates is applied routinely by British courts without the slightest interference from Brussels or Luxembourg, but with the help of a Europe-wide competition law support network.

Two things noticeably missing from the "debate" about the pressing need to free Britain from the malign grip of the ECJ are complaints from British judges and the British legal profession and evidence of the deleterious effect of the application of EU law on Britain and its people.

Why is it that it is only the Brexit-supporting politicians[112] and the newspapers that are so exercised about this and not the legal profession? The reason is that it is a storm in a teacup. It is part of the myth of absolute sovereignty, it has to be part of that undefined "prize" of "freedom" which Brexit is supposed to miraculously deliver.

The latter presupposes that the application of EU law is damaging Britain's interests. The cases in which Britain disagrees with the ECJ on the application of EU law are actually very rare and cases where the government felt it could not "live with" a ruling by the ECJ even rarer, if they exist at all. The objections to ECJ judgments voiced by newspapers tend not to be about the substance but to the fact that it is a matter of EU law at all and therefore adjudicated by the EU court not a British one.[113] It is part of the preoccupation with "form over substance" and Britain having to do everything itself even if someone else can do it just as well or better—control freakery.

It is submitted that the obsession with the ECJ is also partly a case of mistaken (or pretended mistaken) identity. The ECJ is regularly, and often wilfully, confused with the European Court of Human Rights, a body under the auspices of the Council of Europe which has nothing at all to do with the EU and which will not be prevented from ruling on cases in Britain by the UK leaving the EU. It is the ECHR's rulings in human rights cases that have sometimes aroused (overblown) criticism in Britain, such as cases concerning the human rights of prisoners (extradition of terrorists, right to vote, etc.). Mrs May herself was Home Secretary when the ECHR handed down many of these rulings and she took a dim view of them. During the referendum campaign she advocated leaving the European Convention of Human Rights because of what the government perceived as the overreach of the ECHR, but supported remaining in the EU. After the referendum, she ferociously opposed any residual influence of the ECJ in post-Brexit Britain but went quiet on the ECHR.

The confusion of the two courts by the Eurosceptic press often seems to be deliberate, a ploy to discredit the EU Court of Justice "by association." The ploy has certainly succeeded. In the public mind, the ECJ is indelibly associated with the "European court" that handed down the judgment which made it hard to extradite a terrorist being held in a British jail to the US because of his human rights. In the British alternative reality, the ECJ and the ECHR are one and the same, they are jointly and severally liable for the "snowflaky" judgements on Abu Hamza and on granting prisoners the right to vote.

I was sympathetic to the government's insistence in the Brexit negotiations that the jurisdiction of the ECJ should be limited in relation to EU citizens after Brexit. Not to do so would be something of an anomaly under international law and there are parallels in the European Economic Area (the EFTA Court) for having a special local court to adjudicate on such cases in close consultation with the ECJ. On the other hand, the objections of the government and Brexiteer politicians and newspapers to the EU court's having a say on the application of EU single market rules in post-Brexit Britain have verged on hysteria.

Finally, some British politicians with a close knowledge of the European Court of Justice criticize its record of "judicial activism" in pushing European integration forward through judgments comparing the commitments member states have entered into in the treaties with their actual performance. While such activism is generally frowned upon in Britain, which has to do with the British tradition of sticking to the letter of the law and not considering the intentions of the legislators,[114] opinion on the Continent is that the steady insistence by the ECJ on the member states' giving effect to the purpose and intention of the treaties has been completely justified, and in doing so the ECJ has only been doing its job as a constitutional and supreme court. Without active courts, governments tend to drag their feet and solemn commitments remain unfulfilled. British courts are fortunately more interventionist than they once were. This is partly due to the challenge of interpreting human rights provisions and questions arising from the UK's unwritten constitution, as in the *Miller* case about the right of Parliament to a say on the Brexit negotiations.[115] Jacob Rees-Mogg's claim that the ECJ must be corrupt for the sole reason that it ruled on a case concerning the justification of a salary increase for senior EU officials, which affected the salaries of its own judges, is hardly compelling. The salary increase was based on a method enshrined in the EU legislation.

In such a case, any supreme court—with no superior court above itself—would content itself with checking that the method was properly applied.[116]

NOTES

1. *Daily Mail*. 2016. Enemies of the people: Fury over 'out of touch' judges who defy 17.4 m Brexit voters and could trigger constitutional crisis. 4 November.
2. Quoted by *Daily Telegraph*. 1992. Flow of ideas is moving in our favour, says Hurd. 1 July.
3. *The Sun*, 23 April 1996, quoted in Wilkes, George, and Dominic Wring. 1999. The British press and European integration. In Baker, David, and David Seawright (eds.) *Britain for and against Europe? British politics and the question of European integration*, 185–205. Oxford: Clarendon Press.
4. *The Sun*, 2 January 1998, p. 8, referring to a book by Christopher Booker, *From better to worse—Twenty Things—20 daft EU laws that changed our lives*.
5. *Daily Mail*. 2004. The lies of 1975 still haunt us. 20 April (Edward Heathcoat Amory).
6. *Daily Mail*. 2003, editorial "Overmighty EU." 22 September.
7. *Daily Mail*. 2003, 13 October, p. 25, advertisement for the UK Independence Party entitled "The Truth about the European Union."
8. *Daily Telegraph*. 2017. Editorial. 11 June.
9. Mrs Thatcher believed this too: Thatcher, Margaret. 2002. *On Europe*. London: William Collins.
10. *BBC News*. 2016. Reality check: How much UK law comes from the EU? 8 June.
11. Michael Emerson (ed.), *Britain's Future in Europe: The Known Plan A to Remain or the Unknown Plan B to Leave*, 2016. Brussels: Centre for European Policy Studies.
12. Here, most Brexiteers are referring to the alleged overregulation by the EU from the mid-1980s onwards; few would question the benefit of belonging to the "Common Market" in the initial period after Britain joined in 1973.
13. Eurocrats aim for triple-tax 'tyranny'.
14. European Commission. 2018. Annual Activity Report 2017—Taxation and Customs Union. 6 June.
15. Schickler, Jack. 2016. Britain isn't powerless to cut VAT. *InFacts*. 6 April.
16. *Financial Times*. 2018. Brussels to allow more flexibility over VAT rates. 18 January; *Parliament UK. House of Commons Library*. 2019. VAT on sanitary products. 14 January.

17. Admittedly not Liam Fox, the former trade minister, who knows better.
18. This is part of a widespread short-termism problem in Britain, seen with HS2.
19. El-Agraa, Ali. M. 2011. *The European Union: Economics and Politics*, 9th ed. Cambridge: Cambridge University Press.
20. Boris Johnson, televised Brexit debate in Wembley Stadium, 21 June 2016.
21. Theresa May, speech to Conservative party conference, 2 October 2016.
22. Council of the European Union. 2018. Political declaration setting out the framework for the future relationship between the European Union and the UK. 22 November.
23. This incidentally conceded something which Brexit-supporting politicians, commentators and newspapers have often denied: that, as a member state, Britain *does* after all have some say in the making of EU laws!
24. *Gov. UK*. 2018. The UK's future skilled-based immigration system. 19 December.
25. The former Governor of the Bank of England Mervyn King, who supported Brexit, termed the relationship "fiefdom" and "perpetual subordination": *Bloomberg*. 2018. May's Brexit Deal is a Betrayal of Britain. 4 December.
26. Nigel Dodds, leader of the Northern Ireland DUP party in the British Parliament, said the same on 29 March 2019 in explaining why the DUP still had not voted for Mrs May's withdrawal agreement that day.
27. *The Economist*, 19 January 2019.
28. "You can decide to give away your sovereignty in new ways but, in practice, you can't decide to keep it": Simon Kuper. Opening shot—Brexit: Britain's gift to the world. *Financial Times*. 2018. 23 September.
29. Lord Denning. 1979. *The Discipline of Law*, 9–22 The interpretation of statute. London: Butterworths.
30. House of Lords EU Committee. 2017. Brexit and the EU budget. 4 March. The report said that "The UK will not be strictly obliged, as a matter of law, to render any payment at all after leaving [without a withdrawal agreement]." The Committee's opinion was based on that of a minority of the international law experts it consulted plus the view of the committee's own standing legal adviser. It is unlikely such a narrow interpretation would be supported by the European Court of Justice.
31. Mr Tusk is one of leaders of the EU on a par with the Presidents of the Commission and the Parliament, but he is not a primus inter pares and not the "head" of the EU, though he can speak with a certain authority. See *Reuters*. 2009. EU Says it has Solved the Kissinger Question. 20 November.

32. The Political Declaration, para. 4, uses "sovereignty" in this territorial sense in the phrase "[The future relationship] must ensure the sovereignty of the United Kingdom and the protection of its internal market," a clear reference to the territorial union of Northern Ireland with Great Britain, breaking which would be like an "annexation" of territory.

33. Even where decisions are taken collectively by the delegating organizations within the inter-organizational body, one can speak of "upwards" delegation and not "sideways" or horizontal delegation. The latter would be a situation where an organization delegates a decision, for example, to a different organization at the same level.

34. This seems to have run out of steam since its main supporter, George Osborne, left the government after the referendum. Whether this is due to Brexit monopolizing all the government's energies, or to the fact that regional development has never been high on the Conservative party's list of priories, is unclear.

35. *BBC News*. 2018. Chris Morris. Reality check: Year to go: Your questions on Brexit answered. 29 March.

36. "Unappetising Brexit dishes up food safety dilemma for Britain."

37. See also letter to *Financial Times* of 27 July 2017 headlined "EU's provision of public goods has served UK well."

38. Users of the "Mifid II" (investment funds) rules may disagree with the last sentence as the new rules are rather voluminous and complex. But so is the corresponding US law.

39. Pataki, Zsolt. 2014. The cost of non-Europe: Checchini revisited. An overview of the potential economic gains from further completion of the European Single Market. September 2014. European Parliamentary Research Service.

40. There was huge disruption and inconvenience to travellers when stricter passport checks were introduced suddenly in 2017: see the case described in Chap. 3.5 above.

41. Danzig, Jon. 2016. 100% sovereignty means Britain losing power. EU Rope blog. 15 June.

42. For example, the writer of an article posted on the BBC Travel section of the *BBC News* website on 3 December 2018 about the Schengen system asked her readers to "bear with her" while she described the series of treaties leading up to the system which, being the EU, naturally "screams of bureaucracy." She went on to refer to the "inevitable bureaucracy" that caused the final abolition of border checks to take as long as ten years, from 1985 to 1995. She provided absolutely no examples of this alleged bureaucracy in her otherwise factual and informative article.

43. The Germans call it *Regelungswut*, legislative frenzy. Even British Europhiles like Douglas Hurd acknowledged the tendency of the EU to "probe into the nooks and crannies of national life." See Note 2 above.

44. *InFacts*, 31 January 2019.

45. In fact, even Harold Wilson was complicit in spreading mischief-making myths about the EU planning to introduce a standard "Euro-loaf" and "Euro-beer" and impose the use of metric units during the first EU referendum campaign in 1975: George, Stephen. 1994, 2nd ed. *An Awkward Partner: Britain in the European Community*, 87. Oxford: Oxford University Press.

46. The Leave campaign used the technology to good effect by targeting customized propaganda messages about "EU bureaucracy," "edicts" and "waste" at people identified by data analysts as likely to be susceptible to them. They apparently managed to get many people who had never voted before to vote in the referendum—and naturally to vote "out."

47. *Today*, 3 May 1996. See Wilkes, George, and Dominic Wring. The British Press and European Integration 1948–1996. In Baker, David, and David Seawright (ed.). 1998. *Britain for and Against Europe*. Oxford: Oxford University Press.

48. Ibid.

49. Morgan, David. 1995. British Media and European Union News. The Brussels News Beat and its Problems. *European Journal of Communication* 10 (1995), pp. 321–343.

50. FCO (1993) and (1995), "The European Community: Facts and Fairytales" and "The European Community: Facts and Fairytales Revisited"; EU Commission (1994) and (1996). See also *EU Observer*. 2019. Why the UK government failed to tackle the euromyths. 2 April, by Charlie Pownall, who was involved in the efforts to rebut the myths.

51. *Daily Telegraph*. 1998. No more EU please, we're British, say youngsters. 1 March.

52. *Daily Express*, 29 April 1991.

53. *Daily Express*, 26 June 1994.

54. *The Sun*, 21 September 1994. See also Wilkes, George, and Dominic Wring, op. cit., and Charter, David, 2017. *What has the EU ever done for us? How the European Union changed Britain: What to keep and what to scrap*, 29–40. London: Biteback.

55. *The Sun*, 2 January 1998.

56. *Daily Mail*, 7 February 1998.

57. *Daily Telegraph*, 21 June 2017.

58. *Daily Mail*, 28 February 2018.

59. *Daily Telegraph*, 28 February 2018.

60. Morgan, Wilkes and Wring, ibid.

61. Charter, David. 2017. *What has the EU ever done for us? How the European Union changed Britain: What to keep and what to scrap*, 29–30. London: Biteback.
62. Ibid.
63. Aka "faceless," "mindless" bureaucrats. See, for example, *Daily Telegraph*, 1 March 1998, "Christopher Booker's notebook," in which he blames "mindless" officials, "who know nothing about the animals whose cause they think they are promoting," for concocting rules requiring unnecessary rest periods for pigs after ferry journeys, which in fact inflict misery on the animals. This is unfair to EU officials as it implies that they alone are responsible for such rules. In fact, the Commission officials are just a cog in the legislative wheel. If these rules are indeed cruel to the pigs being transported for slaughter abroad, DEFRA and the British agriculture minister who were involved in drafting and approving them in Commission management committees and Council of Ministers meetings surely share the blame. See *BBC News*. 2017. European live animal trade raises major welfare concerns. 18 September.
64. In the text of the chips article the *Telegraph* admittedly does point out that the Commission denied any intention of proposing a requirement to blanch chips, as part of new safety measures to prevent the formation of carcinogenic compounds in fried snacks; it had merely included a recommendation to this effect in its draft legislation which was yet to be approved by the member states. But the headline would reinforce the perceptions most *Telegraph* readers are bound to have about EU "red tape" and those who merely skimmed the article would be misled.
65. As the EU Commission spokesman Willy Helin, quoted in the article, tried to make clear: "As a prima facie case, the EU would have no objections to the move. Ideally we would like to see the situation resolved between Wimbledon and the Irish football authorities."
66. Ironically, since the Brexit vote Booker appears to be have become a convert to joining the EEA (European Economic Area), which really *would* involve accepting EU rules without having had a say in them. Ellis, Walter. The strange case of "Begretter" Christopher Booker. He was the patron saint of Leave, now his model of a bespoke Brexit lies in ruins. *Reaction*. 27 March.
67. *The Sun*, 2 January 1998.
68. Charter, ibid. See also *BBC News*. 2016. Could Brexit lead to a comeback for pounds, ounces and yards? 21 September.
69. *BBC News*, ibid.
70. *BBC News*. 2018. UK will allow Imperial pint bottles of champagne again. 1 March.

71. Who know, if Britain were to stay in the EU, and if the government pushed hard enough, perhaps it would be able to get an exception for pint measures of wine like it has for beer, cider and milk.

72. *New Statesman.* 2017. Martin Fletcher. The joke's over—how Boris Johnson is damaging Britain's global standing. 4 November.

73. *Daily Telegraph*, 1 July 1992.

74. BBC Radio 4's *Desert Islands Disks*, 30 October 2005.

75. Such as that of 1 July 1992, "Major must pedal hard to keep the EC 'bicycle' on the road," about the challenges of Britain's EU presidency.

76. See, for example, the editorial on the same day, "Lamont gives in," about the government's acceptance of a minimum 15% VAT rate throughout the EU.

77. James O'Brien, *LBC* radio, 14 November 2018, wondered "Why do people hate the EU so much?" and said he thought he had found part of the answer: fake news stories in the Brexit newspapers. He read out a long list of British newspaper headlines above such stories about proposed EU laws. The list had been sent to him by the blogger Tom Pride. See also remarks by Germaine Greer in Chap. 3.2.3 above and *BBC News*, 26 July 2018, "Vote Leave's targeted Brexit ads released by Facebook."

78. Some Conservatives proposed a five-year "sunset clause" after which ex-EU laws not yet reviewed would automatically lapse, but Parliament rejected this suggestion: Charter, ibid., 163.

79. For example, *Daily Telegraph.* 2017. Cut the EU red tape choking Britain after Brexit to set the country free from the shackles of Brussels. 28 March.

80. Littlejohn, Richard. 2017. How little Hitlers of elf'n'safety succeeded where the Fuhrer failed: How Big Ben fell victim to one of the greatest tyrannies of our age. 15 August.

81. They were never banned anyway, see Charter, ibid., 139.

82. Leave campaigners pooh-poohed any benefits or, when they were forced to admit there were some, claimed Britain would in future get them for free.

83. Vacuum cleaners made it on to the *Daily Express*'s list of "The EU's top ten pointless decisions the UK can now get rid of," and *The Sun*'s "10 ways to say 'Up Yours to EU'": see Charter, ibid., 41 and 191.

84. *Daily Telegraph.* 2018. 'Tis time to enjoy this calm before the political storm blows up again. 28 December.

85. *BBC Radio 4, Today*, 3 January 2019, interview with Simon Evans of the environmental analysis website *Carbon Brief*, who had authored a report which highlighted the reduction in electricity consumption due to high energy efficiency standards for lightbulbs and domestic appliances like refrigerators and vacuum cleaners. Its author said EU product standards on

light bulbs, fridges, vacuum cleaners and other appliances had played a substantial part in reducing energy demand and thus CO_2 emissions. This contribution had been overshadowed by the emphasis placed on renewables, which tended to receive the headlines. See *BBC News*. 2019. Climate change: LED lights could dent UK energy demand. 3 January.

86. The same doublethink seems to underlie the idea that changing from being a member state agreeing common rules with its partners to adopting EU rules without any say in making them ("compatible regulatory approaches") will make the UK a "sovereign and independent" country.

87. "The EU is a Threat to Democracy," on YouTube.

88. *BBC Radio 4*. 2019. *You and Yours*. 12 January.

89. *BBC Radio 4*. 2019. *Money Box*. 2 January.

90. Hardman, Isabel. 2018. *Why We Get the Wrong Politicians*, 84. London: Atlantic Books.

91. The reports of the House of Lords Committee on the European Union are influential throughout Europe because of the high quality of their research and the EU institutions take their usually well-founded criticisms seriously. Its report concluding that the financial obligations of the UK to the EU would be extinguished if it left without an agreement was a rare lapse.

92. The sight of Mrs May listening in to a debate in the Lords on the withdrawal bill as a clear warning to them to toe the government's line, or else, was one of the low points in her handling of Brexit. Others were her rabble-rousing speech at the 2016 Conservative party conference demonizing "citizens of nowhere" and her Home Secretary's proposing the naming and shaming of employers employing too many immigrants. The daily incantations of empty Brexit slogans by Mrs May and much of her government did not bring much credit to politics in this country either.

93. *Daily Telegraph*, 23 May 2014.

94. Such as the monthly shots of Nigel Farage grandstanding in the Parliament or programmes like the *Newsnight* one about the Parliament before the referendum, which was memorable for John Sweeney speaking excruciatingly bad French to a French MEP and the biased report by a member of the Vote Leave campaign comparing the Westminster and Strasbourg Parliaments, whose most profound observation that the EU procedures took longer, and by implication were therefore less efficient.

95. Though criticized for not reaching their targets such action programmes create benchmarks for performance and data that provide an immensely useful basis for future legislation. Cf. Bootle, Roger. 2016. *The Trouble With Europe*, 61–62. London: Nicholas Brealey.

96. The latter is active, for example, in areas like shipbuilding subsidies, tax harmonization and tax avoidance.

97. Headlines of *BBC News* items like "Why is the EU struggling to …?" suggest this. For example, this was a headline in items about the little matter of the migrant crisis in 2015—the biggest migration in Europe since the Second World War!

98. The Commission played a similar referee's role in the coordinated restructuring of the steel industry in the 1980s, the "Davignon plan."

99. A reform opposed by Britain, among others, because it would no longer be able to return as many irregular migrants to the country they first entered the EU, usually Greece or Italy. See Chap. 7.

100. For example, Birmingham City Council had 12,000 in 2015, not including schools: *BBC News*. 2015. Birmingham City Council: 1200 job losses in 2016–17. 9 December. The UK Border Agency in 2016 had 17,000 staff.

101. The British government is recruiting 30,000 new civil servants to cope with the increased workload brought about by Brexit, around the same number as the whole staff of the European Commission.

102. For middle and senior managers in the EU institutions the official working hours are, as in any organization, largely academic, despite official, tongue-in-cheek admonitions to maintain "work-life balance."

103. Though they will often have good relations with their compatriots working in the country's permanent representation in Brussels.

104. A similar phenomenon is observable in recruitment to the British Foreign Office, once the jewel in the crown of a Whitehall career.

105. *Brussels Times*. 2016. Myths and truths about the salaries and taxes of EU officials. 20 June. Open Europe has calculated that the average annual salary for a non-Belgian official in Brussels (i.e. including the 16% overseas allowance) is around €91,000. Monthly basic salaries are around €7300 for a middle manager and €18,000 for a director-general (equivalent to permanent secretary in Britain): ibid. See also EuABC.com. Salaries for staff, Parliament members, and Commissioners.

106. *Daily Express*. 2018. Brexit Live: MPs rage at EU over snub—Free UK from SINKING MONOLITH. 22 September.

107. *Daily Telegraph*. 2017. How much did these 28 commissioners spend on travel? August 10.

108. The "tin-pot" judges of the two courts in fact have rather high legal qualifications, and while they are "unelected," this is also the case in most countries of the world, including Britain. Nevertheless, no doubt thanks to the referendum and the Brexit press, one of the FAQs in Google about the ECJ now seems to be whether its judges are elected. European Court judges can be consoled and reassured by the fact that at least the *Mail* does not yet call them "enemies of the people" as it has the judges of the British Supreme Court, which was virtually an incitement to violence. For Michael Gove, the ECJ is a "rogue court" because of its judicial activism

in human rights cases: *Daily Telegraph*. 2016. Gove: We will make Britain safe after Brexit. 7 May.

109. Newspapers and politicians will protest that they didn't say that, but it is often the clear message conveyed.

110. Formerly known as the "European Court of First Instance."

111. Not Strasbourg, as columns in the *Daily Telegraph* have occasionally claimed, probably confusing it with the European Court of Human Rights, which *is* based in Strasbourg. For example, Fabricant, Michael. 2017. Hard Brexit will protect this liberal nation. In *Daily Telegraph,* 16 June.

112. Including, stridently, the Prime Minister Mrs May, when she lists removing the UK from the jurisdiction of the ECJ as one of her "red lines" for delivering on the "instructions of the British people."

113. For example, Johnson, Boris. *Daily Telegraph*. 2015. Britain's own legal system should trump the one sitting in Brussels. *Daily Telegraph*. 18 October.

114. A restrictive approach that can lead to injustice, Lord Denning. 1979. *The Discipline of Law,* 9–22. The interpretation of statute. London: Butterworths.

115. Elliott, Mark. 2017. Analysis: The Supreme Court's judgment in Miller. *Public Law for Everyone.* 25 January.

116. Being able to quote Latin phrases like "*nemo judex in causa sua*" does not make a lawyer.

CHAPTER 6

"Taking Back Control of Our Money": The Cost of EU Membership

The belief that the UK was being treated unfairly over its contribution to the European Union (EU) budget dates back to the early and mid-1980s, when Margaret Thatcher fought with her fellow leaders to obtain a rebate from Britain's annual budget contribution, on the ground that it received back relatively little in the way of agricultural subsidies compared with the big agricultural countries like France. She finally won the rebate but a suspicion that the EU was not being fair to Britain lingered on in the public psyche.

In the late 1980s problems with the Common Agricultural Policy (CAP) came to the fore. The share of the budget going on the CAP soared and the European Commission acquired a reputation for poor budget management. Production surpluses of the main farm products were leading to vast quantities being put into store, creating "butter mountains" and "wine lakes," or to unwanted crops being left to rot in the fields or wine being "denatured" into industrial alcohol to stop market prices from collapsing. Export subsidies, another key part of the system to stabilize prices, were subject to widespread fraud and involved the dumping of the expensively produced, subsidized EU produce on developing countries' markets, which harmed their own fragile agricultural sectors.

By the mid-1990s, the EU had reformed the CAP to overcome these problems and had put the budget back on to a sustainable footing by reducing the share of agricultural spending from 80% to approaching 40%. But towards the end of the decade the EU was shaken by a series of

© The Author(s) 2019

F. Rawlinson, *How Press Propaganda Paved the Way to Brexit*,
https://doi.org/10.1007/978-3-030-27765-9_6

(relatively minor) corruption scandals in the Commission, and under pressure from the European Parliament the Commission had to resign. The Commission immediately took stringent measures to "clean up its act" and these have been effective, as will be described in Sect. 6.3. But the EU's reputation was damaged and continued to be fragile at least for the following ten years, with allegations by internal whistle-blowers, and European Court of Auditors reports of irregularities in regional fund spending in member states, frequently in the headlines.

By 2010 the internal management and control systems in the Commission were as good as those of any advanced administration, and spurred by the European Court of Auditors it had made huge strides in fraud-proofing the management and control systems of member states with which they spend EU budget funds. But public opinion in Britain had not caught up and the EU was still fair game for criticism of misman-agement and waste from Eurosceptic politicians and the press. The Cameron government saw political advantage in blackening the EU's image further. To appease the right wing, which was constantly "banging on about Europe," and keep Conservative voters from defecting to UKIP, and at the same time to bolster his own government's credentials for financial responsibility, David Cameron repeatedly took up campaigning stands against the supposedly lax budget management in the EU. He led calls for cuts to the budget, pointing to cases of waste.[1] He took sides against the Commission in its attempts to get the European Court of Auditors to tone down the criticism of its budget management, given the marked reduction in the incidence of irregularities in member states' spending of EU funds, although Britain itself was no paragon in this regard.[2] And in a press conference he vented his fury at the Commission over a bill for an additional budget contribution which was justified by a rise in the UK's GDP, but apparently came as a surprise to the Government.[3] While these stands played well with the party and the voters, they rein-forced, unfairly, the bad reputation the EU had in Britain for poor budget management and waste. Even worse, the overblown outrage over the additional budget contribution revived the sense of being ripped off by the EU that had simmered beneath the surface since Mrs Thatcher's stand-off with the EU over the rebate. Books like *The Great European Rip-Off* by David Craig and Matthew Elliott[4] had already rammed the message home.

The result was that by the time of the referendum a large proportion of the British public was convinced the EU wasted most of the money paid over to it and was extorting exorbitant sums from Britain. The propaganda had worked: the myth that the EU was corrupt, its accounts were a mess and it was ripping us off, "stealing our money," had become the accepted reality.

To fight back against a bully that is not only dominating your life but taking your hard-earned money as well is the most natural reaction in the world, and these two core messages of the Brexit movement proved a powerful brew. They lie behind the persistence of support for Brexit across the country since the referendum despite the growing evidence that it will turn out to be an act of self-harm.

This chapter looks at the facts hidden by the slogan of "taking back control of our money"—the budget and where it goes, the British contribution, waste, fraud and corruption, the auditing of EU accounts, and finally what Brexit will cost.

6.1   The EU Budget

The European Commission, which manages the EU budget, describes how the budget differs from national budgets: "The EU budget is unique. Unlike national budgets which are used in large part for providing public services and funding social security systems, the EU budget is primarily an investment budget. It provides a longer-term planning horizon and stability, which is a prerequisite for investment planning. The current EU budget covers 2014–20 and allows the European Union to invest around €1 trillion over that period."[5]

Budgets are the most difficult decisions in politics. The EU has a system that restricts the big arguments over money to once every seven years. The seven-year budget or "Multiannual Financial Framework" (MFF) is decided before the start of each budget period. The budget is then drawn down in annual instalments, which keep to the previously decided limits per types of spending and so are less controversial. The EU is able to do this because the budget is quite small, predominantly relates to capital spending, and does not involve decisions on taxes: the EU has no tax-raising powers. Decisions on the long-term budget, the "MFF," and annual budgets follow the typical pattern of EU decision-making on major issues: the European Commission makes a proposal and the European Council and the European Parliament amend the proposal and decide the final budget.[6] As usual, the Commission—the EU's civil service—is responsible for managing the budget and it answers to the European Court of Auditors, the member states and the Parliament for that management.

The total 7-year budget for the 2014–20 budget period is €1087 billion. This represents around 1% of the combined national income of EU countries and around 2% of their combined public spending. In other words, the total government spending by the EU countries is 50 times greater than the EU budget. Spread over 440 million people (minus the UK) the current long-term budget costs each person €0.89 per day, about the price of a cup of coffee.[7] In fact, it is under half that because the calculation is based on gross contributions, disregarding the moneys returned to the country from the EU budget to pay for agriculture, regional development, R&D, etc.

The EU budget for 2019 is shown in Fig. 6.1. There are separate limits for commitments and payments. Commitments are allocations to projects or programmes. Payments are mostly made in arrears, so there is a time lag between commitments and payments; also, some commitments are cancelled. That is why the limits for commitments and payments differ.[8] The types of things financed under the various headings are shown below.[9]

1. **Smart and Inclusive Growth**

   a. **Competitiveness for growth and jobs**: includes research and innovation; education and training; trans-European networks in energy, transport and telecommunications; social policy; development of enterprises, etc.

   b. **Economic, social and territorial cohesion**: covers regional policy which aims at helping the least developed EU countries and regions to catch up with the rest, strengthening all regions' competitiveness and developing inter-regional cooperation.

2. **Sustainable Growth: Natural Resources**: includes the Common Agricultural Policy, common fisheries policy, rural development and environmental measures.

3. **Security and citizenship**: include justice and home affairs, border protection, immigration and asylum policy, public health, consumer protection, culture, youth, information, and dialogue with citizens.

4. **Global Europe**: covers all external action ('foreign policy') by the EU such as development assistance or humanitarian aid with the exception of the European Development Fund (EDF), which

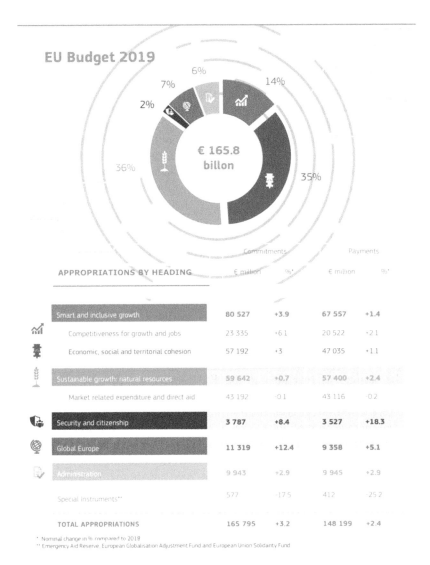

Fig. 6.1 EU budget 2019 (Source: European Commission)

provides aid for development cooperation with African, Caribbean and Pacific countries, as well as overseas countries and territories. As it is not funded from the EU budget but from direct contributions from EU Member States, the EDF does not fall under the MFF.

5. **Administration**: covers the administrative expenditure of all the European institutions, pensions and European Schools.

The structure of the budget is shaped by history and by the powers that have, and have not, been allocated to the EU for it to exercise on behalf of the member states. The large share of agriculture is a relic from the time when the industry was five times as important as now in terms of GDP, employment and household expenditure and reflects the decision taken in the 1950s to allow free trade in agricultural products and for that purpose to establish a uniform support system and finance it predominantly from the European Community budget. Other priorities have been added in the course of time, first cohesion policy, then R&D, and latterly asylum and border management. The absence of allocations for the big spending items in national budgets, social security, education, health and defence, reflects the fact that these are not, except to a very limited extent, EU competences. The member states have not seen fit to allocate the EU powers in these areas and there does not seem much need to do so (see above Chap. 5, Sect. 5.1).

The EU budget is growing only very modestly. The Commission has proposed for 2021–27 an increase to 1.2% of Gross National Income (GNI) but is unlikely to secure it in spite of the European Parliament's favouring a large EU budget.[10] The member states ultimately hold the purse strings.

The sources of revenue for the EU budget are customs duties on imports of goods from outside the EU, a percentage of member states' VAT receipts, a direct contribution from each member state based on a uniform percentage of its Gross National Income, and some smaller sources such as taxes on EU officials' salaries and fines imposed on firms for breaches of the competition rules. The GNI-based direct contribution represents roughly two-thirds of total revenue. Some member states receive a reduction in the contributions they would normally have to pay under the calculation method because of special circumstances. The UK receives by far the biggest such rebate.

The contribution system related to economic strength means that the more prosperous member states pay more into the budget than the less prosperous ones. As for payments from the budget, the amounts the member states receive back depend on their eligibility particularly for agriculture and regional funding, and their success in winning funding that is put out to tender (R&D, for example). The falling scale of contributions according to GNI and the progressive effect of the eligibility for regional funding[11] gives the EU budgets a redistributive effect. The better-off countries are net contributors, the poorer countries net beneficiaries. Thus, the main net contributors—or "net payers"—are Germany, the UK, Denmark, the Netherlands, Sweden and Austria, while the main net beneficiaries or recipients are Poland, the Czech Republic, Slovakia, Hungary, Bulgaria, Romania, Greece and Portugal. The redistributive element of the budget is an expression of solidarity between member states of differing economic strength.

Why do net contributor countries like Germany agree to this system? The reason is that they, too, benefit from the transfer payments to poorer member: they can sell more goods and services to the beneficiary countries during the investment phase of projects and later on when rising prosperity generates extra demand, and they benefit from the effect of economic growth in the poorer countries dampening pressure towards mass migration to the richer countries.[12]

The structure of the EU budget, its small size, its deliberately redistributive element, which brings indirect benefits to net contributor countries like Britain, and the other direct and indirect benefits that the budget helps to bring about, ranging from tariff-free and frictionless trade and travel, collectively provided public goods, to defence and security cooperation, and peace, were not explained to the wider public in Britain in the run-up to the referendum or during the campaign. The Brexit movement in typically British fashion focussed attention only on the "bottom line," the gross budget contribution, ignoring all else.[13]

6.2   THE UK BUDGET CONTRIBUTION: £350 MILLION A WEEK—AN EXERCISE IN POPULIST ECONOMICS

Probably the most effective slogan used by the Leave campaign was that about Britain's budget contribution painted on the side of the official Leave campaign "battle bus." It said: "We send the EU £350 million a week: let's fund our NHS instead. Let's take back control."

The figure itself was exaggerated. In addition, the slogan oversimplified the facts in several ways. First, it omitted to mention that part of the "£350 million" flowed back to the UK for spending on things like agriculture. It was a gross figure; the net figure was less. Secondly, it looked only at a nominal transaction, paying sums to the EU. It implied that stopping paying would be like switching off a tap; the water that did not flow through the pipe when the tap was switched off would all remain in the reservoir. But economic relationships are more complex. The real effect of a nominal change is a combination of the direct effect of the change (saving the "£350 million") and indirect effects, such as on trade, GDP, tax revenue and administrative costs. All these indirect effects—to continue with the water analogy—affect the volume of water remaining in the reservoir. Thirdly, the slogan reduces the entire relationship of Britain with the EU to a direct financial one, implicitly denying any intangible, non-financial, or not easily quantifiable benefits of membership.

In political campaigning, it is undoubtedly necessary and legitimate to simplify facts and figures to make sense to ordinary voters. But it is patronizing—infantilizing—voters to omit essential caveats and qualifications that people would understand like gross and net, and the indirect consequences of actions as well as their direct effects. In the newspapers and the EU debate itself, the boundaries of what is acceptable simplification were widely overstepped into the domain of wilful obfuscation, misleading the public, populism, post-truth politics, and lies.[14]

The £350 million itself amounted to the *theoretical* total contribution the UK *would have been due to* pay to the EU *had it not been granted a rebate* of 66% of the difference between its gross and net contributions (net contribution = gross contribution *less* payments received back). The rebate was won in 1984 and Britain has received it every year since. The rebate, of around £110 million a week, is not "sent" to the EU. It remains in the Treasury's accounts. The rebate is a legal entitlement enshrined in EU law and an equivalent amount—the exact amount is calculated later when Britain's receipts from the EU budget are known—is stopped from the UK's contribution and not paid over to the EU.[15]

The remaining £240 million a week (i.e. the theoretical contribution of £350 million minus the £110 million rebate) is a *gross* figure, roughly the amount Britain sends to the EU as its budget contribution without taking into account what it receives back from the EU for agricultural subsidies and regional and science grants. Deduct these and the *net* figure actually paid to the EU without receiving anything back in return comes to around £160 million a week.[16]

Boris Johnson and others tried to defend the £350 million figure both during the campaign and afterwards. They claimed including the rebate was fair because the Treasury does not fully control this money, which was rubbish: it is an accounting reserve for a theoretically unpaid amount and the Treasury will use it elsewhere just like a bank does a bank deposit.

Regarding the £80 million that was now sent to the EU and returned for agricultural, regional and science payments, Johnson & Co said that in future, the UK would have "control" of this amount because then it might not use the money for those things, but might spend it instead on things like the NHS. But this argument is belied by the Brexiteers' own claims during the campaign that agricultural, science and regional payments would not be affected by leaving the EU and by the commitments the government later gave to maintain this funding at least until 2020. So, as it will most likely continue to be spent on the same things after Brexit, the money currently sent to the EU and received back would *not* be available for spending on the NHS.

£160 million a week (£9 billion annually) is a less impressive figure than the £350 million on the side of the bus. Despite objections from independent bodies like the Office of Budget Responsibility[17] that the figure was exaggerated, the Leave campaign continued to use it. In a BBC documentary Dominic Cummings, the leader of the official Leave campaign organization Vote Leave, said the message they were getting across was that we were paying the EU a large amount of money, the exact amount did not matter.[18] This was tantamount to saying that in politics lying does not matter because the end—winning—justifies the means. That is how populists and demagogues gain power. Johnson and others' later denials of the obvious implication of the slogan that the UK would have £350 million extra a week to spend once it left the EU were unconvincing.[19] Even Nigel Farage said it was "a mistake."[20]

So much for the headline (nominal) figure of money "saved" by no longer paying it into the EU budget. What about the indirect economic effects of leaving? What are they and will they offset all or part of the amount "saved" in budget contributions, leaving it smaller than anticipated or indeed negative, or will they be positive and not only not reduce the budgetary saving but yield financial benefits over and above the saved budget contributions?

Forecasts by the Treasury, the Bank of England and other bodies are that leaving the EU will lead to a reduction of GDP and a fall in tax revenue.[21] This will not only be in the short term due to temporary disruption of trade, but in the longer term as well. Depending on the form of Brexit, the reduction in GDP by 2030 could range from 2% to 8%. A reduction of GDP of even the lower magnitude would completely wipe out the saving in EU budget contributions. The Leave side in the referendum and Brexit-supporting economists and newspapers dismissed such forecasts out of hand. They believe that Brexit will ultimately, after some initial disruption, boost economic growth and hence also the tax revenue available for public services. However, this is a minority view, partly based on adoption of an extreme free-trading model which could have a severely disruptive effect on the UK economy.

Some additional administrative costs which were completely ignored in the referendum campaign, and continue to be ignored by the Brexit camp whenever they are not too obvious, have emerged since the referendum. One is the "divorce bill" agreed as part of the withdrawal agreement negotiated by Mrs May covering the UK's share of outstanding unpaid commitments and other liabilities. Included in the divorce bill is a payment for the privilege of remaining in the EU single market and customs union during a transition period between Brexit and the introduction of new trading arrangements.[22] The divorce bill including the payment for a transition period up to the end of 2020 was put at approximately £39 billion. During the referendum it was repeatedly said that the divorce and the new trading relationship would be agreed in the two years between giving the EU notice of leaving and actually doing so. A second administrative cost consists of the payments the UK will have to make to the EU to continue receiving the services of EU agencies and participating in EU science and educational exchange programmes after Brexit. Finally, there is the cost of at least 30,000 new civil servants for work connected to Brexit and the cost of setting up new national bodies or expanding existing ones to do work previously done by EU bodies which the government wants in future to do itself.

A rough "back-of-the envelope" cost-benefit analysis of the direct impact of Brexit on British public finances is attempted in Sect. 6.5.

The climate of short-termism and emphasis on the "bottom line" and commercial viability prevailing in Britain is not conducive to investment in infrastructure or public services.[23] During the referendum campaign the prevailing short-termist mindset made it hard to argue that there were indirect, let alone intangible benefits of EU membership and the general message of the Leave side was that there were none, so being in the EU was a waste of money. The effect of the EU on helping to maintain peace in Europe was scoffed at: this was all thanks to NATO. If benefits were undeniable like cheaper roaming fees or Erasmus student exchanges, Leavers just had to claim that the same benefits would be available after Brexit or to deny they were thanks to the EU at all, and they were believed. [24]

To keep Leave supporters and Brexiteer MPs on board, the May government has mimicked the populist economics of the Leave campaign with mendacious claims such as that part of the planned increase in spending on the NHS would come from a "Brexit dividend"[25] and that the withdrawal agreement and planned soft Brexit would mean "taking back control of our money" and no longer paying "vast" sums to the EU (see Sect. 6.5). This populism wilfully insults the intelligence of voters and marks a new nadir in British politics. The Brexit press continues to aid and abet this deception.

6.3   AUDIT AND FINANCIAL MANAGEMENT

The European Commission is responsible for the proper management of the entire EU budget. Around 80% of the budget is spent in the member states on EU-coordinated programmes and measures. The bulk of the latter is agricultural support and structural and investment funding and is paid over to national authorities who pay it on to farmers and project promoters. For this expenditure the member states share responsibility.

Ensuring that EU funds are properly managed by national authorities when the Commission is at one remove from the action is difficult. The Commission has less than 5% of the staff of the member states' authorities managing this spending and it must confine itself to a supervisory role. Although it has taken time, the Commission has steadily improved its supervision of the spending of agricultural and structural and investment funds in member states.[26] The European Court of Auditors (ECA) audits the Commission's accounts, revenue collection and expenditure every year and publishes a report, on which the European Parliament bases itself for assessing the Commission's management of the budget. The Parliament exerts strong pressure on the Commission to further improve its supervision.

In its annual report for 2017 the Court of Auditors states with regard to the Commission's accounts:

> The EU accounts for 2017 were prepared in accordance with international public sector accounting standards and present, in all material respects, a true and fair view of the EU's financial results for the year and its assets and liabilities at the end of the year.
>
> We are therefore able to give a clean opinion on the reality of (i.e., 'sign off') the accounts, *as we have done every year since 2007.*[27]

With regard to revenue collection, the Court found that it was free of material error.[28]

On expenditure, the Court issued a qualified opinion, because the overall level of error found by the Court in the projects it audited was, at 2.4%, just above the 2% threshold for a material level of error. Half of this expenditure, however, was below the 2% threshold for a material level of error. This included direct aid to farmers, student and research fellowships, and administration (salaries, pensions and allowances paid by EU institutions and bodies). The other half of expenditure in which there was a material level of error, of 3.7%, was mainly on investment in regional and rural development and training schemes, research projects, and development aid. However, the Court reiterated that about half of the 2017 expenditure audited was free of material error and that therefore, overall, error was not pervasive.[29]

"Errors" or irregularities in expenditure mostly concern breaches of the rules and conditions applicable to the type of spending concerned; in relation to investments, the commonest errors are including ineligible costs in cost claims and breaches of the public procurement rules on fair Europewide competitive tendering. These rules are unfortunately but necessarily rather complicated. The level of error in expenditure has steadily declined in all categories. In 2016 spending it had been 3.1% and in that of 2015 3.8%. The incidence of fraud (deliberate rule breaches to obtain funds fraudulently or misusing them) is low. The European Court of Auditors found suspected fraud in 13 of the 703 projects it audited for 2017 expenditure.[30] That is a rate of 0.2%. The cases of suspected fraud reported to the European anti-fraud agency Olaf are at a similar level.[31] Errors or irregularities that are not clearly deliberate lead to the EU and national funding being partly or wholly withdrawn from the projects concerned.[32] When fraud is detected it is the subject of criminal prosecutions.

Thus, the claims that have been repeatedly made, and are still made, in British newspapers that the EU's accounts are not audited, that its auditors have never "signed off" the accounts, or that money "goes missing" from the accounts have always been and still are false. [33]

- The Commission's management of the budget has been audited by the Court of Auditors since 1994.
- The Court of Auditors has signed off the accounts every year since 2007, as the statement quoted above shows.

- No money has "gone missing" from the accounts. If it had, the Court of Auditors would not sign them off. The people claiming this are probably referring to badly planned projects that turn out to be "white elephants" so that the funding has to be recovered or written off.[34] That is different from "losing" money in the accounts, which really would be mismanagement.

As long ago as 2006, the British House of Lords European Union Committee published a report on "Financial Management and Fraud in the European Union."[35] The report said that the failure of the ECA to give a positive audit opinion on the EU's accounts until then (since 1994) had been misunderstood, which had caused a lot of bad publicity. The adverse opinion did not necessarily indicate that high levels of fraudulent or corrupt transactions had taken place,[36] but was due to the different basis of the opinion. Sir John Bourn, Comptroller and Auditor General at the UK's National Audit Office, told the Committee that were he required to issue a single Statement of Assurance [= positive audit opinion] on the UK Government's accounts in the same way as the Court of Auditors does for Europe's accounts, he, like the Court, would be unable to do so. The Committee considered that the ECA's decision to give a single audit opinion on the accounts as a whole made a positive opinion difficult to achieve, and that it would be preferable for the Court to issue separate opinions on the accounting and on each of the spending areas, in much the same way that the National Audit Office in the UK issues separate audits for each government department. This would give a more accurate picture of the state of financial management in the European Union and make comparison with other public bodies easier.[37] The Committee also noted:

> During our enquiry we heard considerable evidence on the Commission's financial management. None of that evidence supports the allegation that there is a significant element of corruption within the Commission.[38]

The European Court of Auditors soon afterwards changed its practice on the lines suggested by the Committee and began to give separate audit opinions on the accounts, revenue and different types of expenditure. The result immediately showed that the accounts and revenue collection were in order, but unacceptable error rates remained on some expenditure effected in member states, and subsequently these were steadily reduced through improvements in management and control systems.[39]

The myths about the poor financial management and unaudited accounts in the EU were thus comprehensively disproved around 2006–07. But the Brexit-supporting newspapers and politicians have never stopped repeating them because, however false, they fit into the propaganda narrative that Brussels is playing fast and loose with taxpayers' hard-earned money.

6.4   Waste, Corruption

For the Brexit newspapers and their columnists, it is axiomatic that the EU mismanages and largely wastes its budget and is a hotbed of corruption. Here are two recent examples of these tropes repeated in *Daily Telegraph* columns by writers who should, and actually probably do, know better:

> [Centre-right eurosceptics] profoundly dislike much about the EU, including its … *unforgivable corruption*.[40] (Allistair Heath, emphasis added)
>
> The reasons why [the EU] is so bad at trade policy are the same as the reasons why it is *bad at* just about everything else: *managing its own budget*[41] (Roger Bootle, emphasis added)

And in a *Telegraph* editorial:

> [We] have long grown used to the idea that the EU is a gravy train whose stewards loll about at the expense of the passengers, otherwise known as taxpayers.[42]

What are the facts? First about alleged waste. The EU budget is mostly spent on investment, training, research and agricultural support carried out in the member countries and a small amount in addition on administrative costs. Regarding expenditure in the member states, when the European Court of Auditors finds cases of badly planned or poorly executed spending that does not fulfil its intended purpose (like the Spanish airport or the Italian dams mentioned in note 34) or was larger than necessary, it counts the expenditure as made in error and adds it to the "errors" calculation that it later publishes in its annual report. As we have seen, the incidence of "error" in EU spending has been sharply reduced to the point where it is either immaterial or only just above the materiality threshold.[43] This means that on this strictly accounting measure there is practically no waste in EU expenditure.

It is of course perfectly possible for anyone to argue that spending that conforms to all the rules and conditions of a public spending programme or a political or administrative decision is wasteful because one does not agree that the government should be financing such things or financing them in that way. This is "wasteful" in the sense of not cost-effective, not "value for money." In that sense, some people would consider the whole or some aspects of the HS2 rail project, grants for renewable energy, certain social security benefits, or subsidized rural bus services to be a waste of public money.[44] On the first, strict definition, however, the evidence is that EU spending is not significantly wasteful. The curious can see for themselves on EU websites what the money is being spent on.[45]

Mr Cameron's objection to the European Parliament publicity material seems to have been based on his own—or more likely his entourage's—subjective judgment of the value for money of a glossy brochure saying what the Parliament does. If so, it is a little odd, even arrogant for a British politician to say so. Do not British government departments advertise themselves, partly in order to counteract unfair criticism in the media similar to that which the European Parliament is subject to on a daily basis? Whether or not it was value for money, there is no evidence that money had been wasted in publishing the brochure, so Cameron's intervention was based on a value judgment.

This is not to deny that there have been EU policies that were open to justified criticism as not cost-effective or "value for money" and even as wasteful in the strict sense. The prime example is the original Common Agricultural Policy which by supporting market prices as a means of maintaining farmers' incomes and stable food supplies led inevitably to overproduction and huge surpluses which cost enormous sums to dispose of. The policy also led to genuine waste by facilitating fraud. The changeover to direct income support started in the mid-1990s has achieved the same objectives at much lower cost, so that the present policy is harder to criticize on "value for money" grounds.

The European Parliament is also often accused of waste because of its dual seats in Brussels and Strasbourg and its generous expenses for MEPs. The first issue is also a question of cost-effectiveness or value for money, not of waste in the strict sense, although the hostile press keeps making unsubstantiated assertions that the trips also involve extravagance by MEPs and officials—on the "gravy trains" and in the expensive Strasbourg hotels and restaurants—and that is probably why British people are so exercised about it.

Clearly, it is not cost-effective to drag MEPs and staff off to Strasbourg for four days every month, incurring unnecessary costs for travel, accommodation, office space and meeting rooms. They have a perfectly good building, accommodation and facilities in Brussels where they work for three weeks in the month. But at France's insistence the EU has had to agree to continuing this arrangement and it is now enshrined in the Lisbon Treaty. The choice of Strasbourg as the first seat of the Parliament had a symbolic significance. It is in Alsace, a region Germany and France used to fight over constantly until they were reconciled after World War II. The European Parliament base in Strasbourg is a sacred cow for the French, a matter of totemic national prestige, something "worth dying for"—much like for many British having separate football teams representing the four nations of the United Kingdom, not having identity cards, keeping the pound sterling, or going back to blue passports is important.

MEPs' expenses are a different matter and one on which Parliament has in the past left itself open to charges of waste in the strict sense. There are two issues, travel expenses and staff allowances. The rules for reimbursement of travel expenses have been tightened up. Previously, MEPs were reimbursed for travel costs at a flat rate, not the actual fares, which allowed them to travel on low-cost airlines and pocket the difference. This has now been changed to reimbursement of actual travel costs up to a maximum beyond which Members must pay the excess themselves. The new rules are applicable to all MEPs and they must submit tickets or boarding passes as proof of travel. MEPs are also paid attendance allowances when they come to the Parliament and critics have suggested they should only get the allowance if they attend meetings at the Parliament or work in their offices afterwards. However, this would be unreasonable as they may well have Parliament-related business outside the Parliament building, which would be hard to check. The British House of Lords is criticized for the same reason.

For staff allowances there have been cases of MEPs claiming such expenses fraudulently. The staff for whom MEPs can claim an allowance to pay their salaries are supposed to assist the members in their work for the European Parliament, but some MEPs have claimed the costs of staff working on tasks unconnected with the Parliament, but related for example to party political work in the home country. The cases have often concerned Eurosceptic MEPs who do little day-to-day legislative work for the Parliament,[46] but have availed themselves of the opportunity to finance their political activities back home by getting the Parliament to pay for them. Parliament systematically makes MEPs pay back allowances that have been misclaimed for staff doing non-parliamentary work.[47]

While there used to be some merit in charges of waste in connection with the Parliament's expenses system, the problem has now been tackled. It is pure myth, however, that the whole Parliament, MEPs and staff, live it up during the Assembly's monthly peregrination to Strasbourg. There is no evidence for this. The newspapers still peddling this nonsense are betraying their journalistic principles.[48]

The *Daily Telegraph* on 11 August 2017 ran a major splash about the excessive travel expenses run up by the 28 members of the Commission, the "commissioners." It comprised a double-page spread with particulars of all the commissioners' total travel expenses over the first two months of 2016 (based on a freedom of information request), a front-page story, four other articles and comment pieces, and an editorial.[49] The story was headlined "EU chiefs in expenses scandal," but the amounts of the expenses appeared in fact reasonable considering that EU commissioners make many international trips and given their cabinet minister-level rank cannot be expected to travel economy or stay in second-rate hotels, and may be justified on occasion in chartering planes. A Commission spokeswoman told the paper that the officials worked throughout their flights and "the levels of luxury would disappoint you." The author can vouch for the fact that ordinary Commission officials' travel expenses are minutely vetted and the amounts are not particularly generous.

As for corruption, there have been problems in the past with MEPs having conflicts of interest through close links to lobbying organizations and even being ready to accept money for pushing through changes in legislation.[50] The European Parliament is tightening up its rules on MEPs meeting lobbyists.[51] In 2014, Transparency International, the independent anti-fraud and corruption campaigner, found that although the EU institutions were vulnerable to corruption, there were effective systems in place to prevent it.[52]

Angered by the "Remain" tendencies of many members of the House of Lords and their attempts to amend Brexit legislation, newspapers occasionally claim that members of the Lords are motivated to do so by money rather than wisdom. It is true a few of them are former EU commissioners and MEPs in receipt of EU pensions, and some have estates for which they receive farm subsidies. But the insinuation of these Lords having a major conflict of interest when voting on Brexit legislation is perhaps more a reflection of the mercenary inclinations of the newspaper owners than those of their lordships.[53]

6.5   THE COST OF BREXIT FOR PUBLIC FINANCES— TAKING BACK CONTROL?

The discussion of the financial impact of the EU on Britain has since Thatcher been one-sidedly focussed on a tiny element of this relationship, the country's contribution to the EU budget. The Brexit slogan of "taking back control of our money" and the mendacious claim that leaving would save us £350 million a week that could be better spent on things like the NHS were populist economics, plausible but fallacious, because they ignored the wider impact of Brexit on the economy which would have a knock-on effect on tax revenue and therefore public finances. As Brexit unfolds, we are also seeing unforeseen or previously concealed extra expenditure such as the "divorce bill," future payments for access to EU programmes, the costs of replicating services previously provided by the EU but to be "repatriated," the planning for no deal, and the recruitment of additional civil servants. In this light, the Prime Minister's talk of "Brexit dividends" and saving "vast sums" from our contributions to the EU budget is even more blatantly false now than it was when Johnson & Co were spouting such populist nonsense during the referendum campaign at a time when few people knew any better.

The effect Brexit will have on the economy is disputed. The consensus of opinion, however, is that for all Brexit scenarios it will be negative and forecasts differ only in the level of the reduction in GDP predicted. In late 2018, the Treasury, the Bank of England, the National Institute of Social and Economic Research, and a consortium comprising the London School of Economics, King's College London and the Institute for Fiscal Studies on behalf of the think tank "The UK in a Changing Europe" produced forecasts. As noted in Sect. 6.2, depending on how close Britain remains to the EU after Brexit, the loss in GDP could range from 1–2% to 8%. The latter study forecasts that the cost to public finances within 10 years in the case of Mrs May's Brexit deal being implemented could be between 0.4% and 1.8% of GDP, or between £10 billion and £50 billion a year.

Given that the forecast impact on GDP growth and tax revenue is disputed, let us just look at the costs and benefits of Brexit for Britain's public finances that are already known or reasonably certain. Estimates are asterisked and are on the conservative side. The time scale is until 2030 (Table 6.1).

Table 6.1 'Direct' costs and benefits of Brexit for Britain's public finances until 2030 (not including impact on GDP) (£bn)

Category	Cost	Benefit	Notes
Saved EU budget contributions		80	10 X 8bn/year
Divorce bill	39		
No-deal contingency planning	3		
Extra civil servants, replicating EU services	24*		12 X 2bn/year
Participation in EU programmes	10*		10 X 1bn/year
Commitments for agriculture, regional policy and science	14*		2bn/year until 2020, 1bn/year thereafter
Total	90	80	

This shows that disregarding the effect on the economy and tax revenue, the impact of Brexit on public finances up to 2030 will be negative. Only an increase in GDP claimed by a minority of forecasters could turn this into a positive. The majority opinion is that the hit taken by the economy as a result of Brexit will reduce tax revenue and thereby the money available for public services by considerably more.

NOTES

1. For example, European Parliament glossy brochures.
2. *Daily Telegraph*. 2013. EU auditors must tone down criticism of Brussels spending, says Herman van Rompuy. 13 September. The UK's management of EU regional spending in Britain was not particularly good and it has also been fined for allowing customs fraud: *Politico*. 2018. Brussels demands UK pay €2.7 billion in lost customs duties. 3 August.
3. See Sect. 2.5 above.
4. Craig, David and Matthew Elliott. 2009. *The Great European Rip-Off: How the Corrupt, Wasteful EU is Taking Control of Our Lives*. London: Random House.
5. EU Commission. 2018. The EU budget: Where does the money go?
6. Thus, not the "bureaucrats" in the Commission like Jean-Claude Juncker, contrary to the widespread perception in Britain.
7. Confirmed by *BBC News*. 2018. Reality Check: Will the EU cost people more than a daily coffee? 2 May. See also *BBC News*. 2016. Reality Check: Where does EU money go? 24 May. To combat fake news circulating about the cost of the European Parliament, in 2018 Italian MEPs tweeted that the real cost per EU citizen per year was under €4, compared with the over €17 a year that the Italian Chamber of Deputies cost each Italian:

Europarlamento, 8 October 2018, "Eurocamero costa meno d'un panino l'anno a europei."

8. The majority of the estimated £39 billion "divorce bill" in the withdrawal agreement which Mrs May negotiated with the EU is for payments of commitments made before withdrawal that will still be outstanding thereafter.

9. European Commission. 2018. Growth, solidarity and security in Europe and beyond. EU budget—factsheet—2019. December 2018.

10. European Commission. 2018. IP-18-6631. 4 December.

11. For example, the allocations of Structural and Investment Funds for the 2014–20 period range from €3389 per head of population in Estonia to €102 per head in the Netherlands.

12. UK Government. 2013. Balance of Competences Review: Cohesion policy. 13 October.

13. For example, Christopher Booker, in *Daily Telegraph.* 1998. Farms can kick the subsidy habit. 1 March, comparing the amount handed over to the EU for the CAP and the smaller amount British farmers get back.

14. Davis, Evan. 2018. *Peak bullshit—and what we can do about it.* London: Abacus.

15. Dominic Cummings was "bullshitting" when he argued before the House of Commons Ways and Means Select Committee that it *was* "sent."

16. That is 0.4% of the UK's GDP.

17. Not to mention the Treasury, the BBC and the Remain campaign.

18. Cummings, Dominic. 2017. How the Brexit referendum was won. *The Spectator.* Coffee House. 9 January.

19. See Head of Office of National Statistics and Lichfield, John. 2017. Boris Johnson's £350 million claim is devious and bogus. *The Guardian.* 18 September; *BBC News.* 2016. EU referendum Reality Check: Would Brexit mean extra £350 million a week for NHS? 15 April.

20. *ITV Good Morning Britain.* 2016. Nigel Farage admits NHS claims were a mistake. 24 June. Available on YouTube.

21. UK Govt. 2018. EU Exit: Long-term economic analysis. November 2018. Cm 9742; Menon, Anand, and Jonathan Portes. 2018. The economic consequences of the Brexit deal. *UK in a Changing Europe.* 27 November; Hantzsche, Arno et al. 2018 The economic effects of the Government's proposed Brexit deal. *National Institute of Economic and Social Research. 26 November; BBC News.* 2018. Brexit will make us worse off, government forecasts warn. 28 November.

22. Brexit was originally supposed to happen on 29 March 2019 with a transition period until the end of 2020.

23. Witness the strong opposition to high-speed rail investment and the neglect of rural bus services. On the latter see James O'Brien. 2019. James O'Brien's monologue on rural bus services has listeners gripped. *LBC.* 22

January. See also Radio 4's *PM* programme of 21 September 2018 in which a lady listener asked whether as the UK left the EU it had received any tangible credit for all the infrastructure it had helped to provide throughout Europe. She seemed to assume that investments in poorer regions financed from the EU budget only benefitted the country receiving the investment; it apparently did not occur to her that the wealthier countries of the EU like Britain and Germany that pay for the projects through their net contributions to the EU budget could benefit also. The benefit for the net payer countries lies in the potentially increased exports of goods and services to the recipient countries, both during the construction phase of projects and afterwards through the increased economic activity in these less wealthy countries generated by the investments. Slovakia, for example, has seen its GDP per capita almost double since it joined the EU in 2004—*Financial Times.* 2016. Anti-migrant rhetoric dominates Slovakia vote. 4 March. Investments in poorer regions probably also help to reduce the need for intra-EU migration, which many Brits would regard as a benefit.

24. A Scottish student and Leave supporter interviewed on Radio 4's *Today* during the referendum campaign did not believe Erasmus was an EU programme and that Brexit might affect access to it: Norway was a member, so Erasmus obviously could not be an EU programme!

25. *BBC News.* 2018. Reality Check: Brexit—Will a dividend help pay for increasing the NHS budget? 20 June. Eaton, George. 2018. There is no "Brexit dividend" to spend on the NHS. *New Statesman.* 17 June.

26. EU funds provided for projects in candidate countries and under the migrant deal with Turkey are also closely supervised. See *Financial Times.* 2016. Syrian refugees: cash dispute. 12 May. Thus, Charles Moore's statement, in the *Daily Telegraph.* 2016. We should resist Turkey's thin-skinned president rather than pander to him. 7 May, that the €3bn being paid for Syrian refugee camps is "pretty much unsupervised" is incorrect.

27. European Court of Auditors (2018), Summary p. 10, emphasis added.

28. Ibid.

29. Ibid., p. 12.

30. Ibid.

31. European Commission. 2011. Commission Anti-Fraud Strategy – COM (2011) 376, p. 6.

32. European Commission. European regional and urban policy. Glossary: Financial corrections.

33. *BBC News.* 2016. Reality Check: Has the EU had its accounts signed off? 12 May. *Daily Telegraph.* 2014. EU auditors refuse to sign off more than €100bn of its own spending. 4 November.

34. For example, Castellón airport in Spain (*Daily Telegraph.* 2011. Spain's white elephants—how country's airports lie empty. 5 November) or dams

in southern Italy that two years after being built still had no water in them because of drought.

35. House of Lords. European Union Committee. 2006. Financial Management and Fraud in the European Union: Perceptions, facts and proposals. 13 November.

36. Ibid., para. 146.

37. Ibid., paras 149–150.

38. Ibid., para. 160.

39. As with EU expenditure, the UK NAO's audits of British government expenditure continue to show high error rates for some departments like the Department of Work and Pensions which lead it to qualify its opinion on their accounts: National Audit Office. 2018. 2017–2018 annual report. See also Gray, Brian. 2007. In defence of the European Commission. *Accountancy Daily*. 1 June; Gray, Brian. 2007. In the hotseat—Gray's Euro vision. *Accountancy Daily*. 1 November.

40. Heath, Allister. 2018. There is one Brexit fault line that could see the Tories torn asunder. *Daily Telegraph*. 11 January.

41. Bootle, Roger. 2018. We must seize the opportunities of Brexit, not kow-tow to a Davos elite. *Daily Telegraph*. 29 January.

42. *Daily Telegraph*. 2017. EC expenses jamboree rot starts at the top. 10 August.

43. The requirement for competitive public tendering helps keep costs down.

44. The British government's £660 billion of expenditure a year also involves waste: see Bacon, Richard, and Christopher Hope. 2013. *Conundrum: Why every government gets things wrong—and what we can do about it*. London: Biteback.

45. See, for example, the huge amount of information on individual projects it is financing on the European Commission Directorate General for Regional and Urban Policy's homepage.

46. They are against EU legislation *per se*, so why bother?

47. See cases C-84/18 P Montel v. Parliament and T-624/16 Gollnisch v. Parliament in the European Court of Justice.

48. The famous "gravy train." *Daily Express*. 2018. Brussels gravy train to Strasbourg breaks down. EU off the RAILS. MEPs stranded as Brussels' £150 million 'gravy train' to Strasbourg BREAKS DOWN. 11 June.

49. *Daily Telegraph*. 2017. How much did these 28 commissioners spend on travel? 10 August.

50. In 2011 several MEPs resigned after being caught in a sting operation by the *Sunday Times* in which they had agreed to get laws amended in return for payments: *BBC News*. 2011. Fourth Euro MP named in lobbying scandal. 28 March; *Financial Times*. 2011. MEP resigns over allegations of

lobbyist payments. See also *Transparency International*. 2018. Side jobs of MEPs raise ethical concerns. 10 June.

51. *Politico*. 2019. Parliament adopts transparency rules on MEPs meeting lobbyists. 31 January.

52. *Transparency International*. 2014. First EU integrity report highlights risks of corruption in European institutions. 24 April; *Politico*. 2014 Transparency International report says the EU is vulnerable to corruption, but not to the extent that the public believes. 24 April.

53. *Scottish Daily Express*. 2018. Brexit wrecker lord and his EU handouts. 10 May.

CHAPTER 7

"Taking Back Control of Our Borders": Is the EU to Blame for Immigration?

Immigration arouses emotional reactions in people—disquiet at the challenge of having to engage with people of a different culture and language, concern about changes in the community, resentment at perceived preferential treatment of immigrants and about pressure on services, feelings of insecurity and fear, and even racism and xenophobia. These, even the latter, are natural reactions but in most people they can be lessened or overcome by contact with the people entering their community, with whom they find they can get along and even become friends, and by pro-active government policies to cushion the effects of immigration on communities. In time immigrants blend into the host society and become indistinguishable from residents of longer standing. They talk the same, adopt the same habits, intermarry, and become as attached to place as the original native population. Admittedly, for some immigrant communities, integration can be slower and harder. These tend to be the communities most different in culture and racial make-up from those of the host country, and they may remain a segregated parallel ethnic group for a long time, partly by choice, partly by force of circumstances. Inequality and barriers to social mobility in the host country exacerbate the difficulties of immigrant groups to integrate.

In Britain, concern about immigration was a major factor in the Brexit vote. Surveys put the belief that Brexit would lead to lower levels of immigration as the main reason why people voted Leave, ahead of concerns about sovereignty. The concern about immigration was justified. It was

© The Author(s) 2019
F. Rawlinson, *How Press Propaganda Paved the Way to Brexit*,
https://doi.org/10.1007/978-3-030-27765-9_7

running at around 300,000 people net a year. But the Brexit movement exploited the discontent to strengthen support for leaving the EU. Lack of investment due to the austerity policies of the government, outbreaks of terrorism and a refugee crisis elsewhere in Europe reinforced anti-immigration sentiment in old industrial and in rural areas. The pro-European side failed to engage sufficiently with the Leave side to counter its misinformation and allay the concerns of the population with concrete proposals and forceful economic and social arguments in favour of managed immigration.

Concern about immigration was whipped up into a pretext for Brexit; it was not a justification.

- Uncontrolled immigration from the EU was only partly to blame for high net migration into the UK. The rest—around half—was immigration from outside the EU. This Britain already controlled. The Leave side kept very quiet about the latter "controlled" but very high net migration.
- The Leave campaign stoked up fears of further mass migration by lying that Turkey and further Balkan countries were about to join the EU and Turks and Albanians could soon be flooding the British labour market, and that Britain would not be safe from the thousands of refugees from the Middle East making their way northwards to Germany and beyond. Campaigners also talked up the threat of terrorists slipping in with the migrants or getting in with Turkish passports when Turkish citizens no longer needed visas to travel in the Schengen free travel area, although Britain was not in Schengen and therefore had entry controls.
- Many British industrial and service sectors including the National Health Service (NHS) depended on EU migrant labour. Therefore, encouraging voters to believe that after Brexit immigration would suddenly stop (and even that existing migrants would be sent back home), as some in the Leave camp gave to understand, was a deception. The argument that migrant labour was pricing native Britons out of jobs was only marginally true. Moreover, EU migrant workers represented not a drain on the exchequer but a gain as they contributed much more in tax revenue that they took out in benefits.
- To manage EU migration better it was not necessary to leave the EU. There were many ways of limiting EU migration within EU rules such as compulsory advertising of vacancies and changes in benefit rules but the government had failed to use them because it

preferred to have an ultra-flexible labour market for business instead. Also, before the referendum the government had negotiated an additional "emergency brake" which could be activated in the event of surges of immigration placing severe strain on public services. Moreover, it was partly the government's fault if there was a strain on public services in the areas most affected by immigration, as it had not invested to relieve the pressure. It had scrapped a Labour government scheme to assist such areas and had refused funds available from the EU.

The chapter will start by looking at the extent of immigration in Britain and how the country got into that situation. It will then cover the pre-existing attitudes to immigration in the country, the refugee crisis in Europe and the coverage of immigration and the migrant crisis in the press, and conclude with the outlook for a new immigration policy after Brexit.

7.1 State of Immigration in the UK

The population of the UK in 2017 was around 66 million.[1] About one person in every seven, some 9.38 million, or 14% of the population, was foreign born.[2] In 2017 there were around 5.7 million foreign-born residents who were not UK citizens.[3]

For the past 20 years the UK population has been steadily growing. Between 1998 and 2017 it increased by 7.5 million (58.5 million to 66 million). Of this increase, around 3.4 million was due to natural change, while 4.1 million was due to new net migration.[4] Net migration, which has not been below 100,000 in any year since 1997,[5] though it fell during the financial crisis, reached a peak of 336,000 in 2015–16, before falling to 282,000 for 2016–17 and 248,000 in 2017–18. Net migration from outside the EU has tended to be a bit more than that from within the EU; only in 2015–16 were they roughly the same.[6] International students are included in the net migration figures (see next section).

Between 2005 and 2015 a third of the net migration (1.5 million) consisted of immigration from the eight central and eastern European countries that joined the EU in 2004 and 2007. The Blair government opened its labour markets to workers from these countries immediately after accession, expecting only a low level of immigration.[7] In the event, with other EU countries like Germany deciding to delay opening their markets to these workers for up to seven years, over 100,000 arrived in Britain in the first year and the flow hardly abated thereafter.[8] Though overall the volume of non-EU migration was greater, the wave of immigration from central and eastern Europe was the single biggest inflow of people in Britain's history and attracted negative publicity about allegations of welfare tourism and social dumping (see Sect. 7.2 below). The wave left the Poles with an estimated 831,000 people as the biggest foreign-born community in Britain in 2015.[9] The distribution of immigrants throughout the country is uneven. London is home to 13% of the UK's population but a third of its EU citizens. Manchester and Birmingham, too, are "super-diverse" areas.[10]

Some 11% of the people working in Britain are citizens of other EU or of non-EU countries. The total number is around 3.5 million, of which 2.3 million (7% of the workforce) are from the EU and 1.2 million from outside the EU. Of the 2.3 million EU nationals, 1.3 million are from central and eastern Europe, the majority of them Poles.[11] Some sectors are heavily dependent on migrant labour. For example, 150,000 EU nationals work in the health and care sector, according to the former health secretary Jeremy Hunt.[12] In the food manufacturing sector, central and east European citizens alone accounted in 2017 for 25% of the workforce.[13] The dependency ratio in central and eastern European communities is much lower than for comparable British-born workers: among the former the number of people working for every non-working person (retired person or child) is 3.9 against 1.8 for British-born workers.[14]

On top of the official figures, there could be up to 1.2 million migrants in Britain illegally, according to the former head of immigration enforcement at the Home Office. He puts the numbers who overstay their visa, remain in the country after having their asylum applications refused, or enter the country illegally, at 150,000 to 250,000 a year.[15] Most of these will not pay taxes and some will be involved in illegal activity.

After the EU referendum net migration from the EU to the UK halved to under 100,000 and new arrivals from central and eastern Europe were almost cancelled out by the people returning home.[16] In 2017 the Polish prime minister expected up to 200,000 Poles to return home that year.[17] The main reasons for migrants returning home were an improving economy and labour market in their home countries and the fall in the value of sterling after the referendum. Another factor was the targeting of anti-immigrant sentiment at central and eastern Europeans during the referendum campaign which made them feel less welcome.

Why has Britain been so attractive a destination for EU migrants? The main reason is that government economic policies have prioritized open and flexible labour markets able to tap into immigrant labour where nationally there are shortages. Large-scale immigration from the EU and elsewhere has been a "default option," both to secure workers for low-wage occupations and to cater for increasing demand for highly skilled staff which the national education and training systems cannot satisfy.[18] There were many things the UK could have done in the tax, benefits and regulatory sphere that were perfectly permissible under EU law to reduce this attraction, but it had not done so.[19]

As we shall see in Sects. 7.2 and 7.4 below, the large-scale immigration from central and eastern Europe, while convenient for business and good for economic growth, has aroused tensions in society and fuelled opposition to the EU which the Leave campaign were able to exploit in the referendum. But mass emigration to the west has also caused social problems and demographic crises and impeded growth in the countries of origin of the migrants, particularly in southeastern Europe.[20]

7.2   CLIMATE OF OPINION TOWARDS IMMIGRATION— TOLERANT COEXISTENCE STRAINED BY SOME REAL GRIEVANCES, BUT ALSO BY ENGINEERED ANGER AND FEAR

Negative feelings about immigration—immigration which leaving the EU was thought likely to reduce—were one of the main reasons why people voted for Brexit in the referendum.[21] However, up to the end of the first decade of the 2000s migration had been a taboo subject among most of the population because of its association with race.[22] Avoiding public discourse about racial prejudice and discrimination is not a good idea. We are all subject to subconscious bias and failing to confront it can help perpetuate injustices and leave the field to extremists.[23]

However that may be, until the end of the first decade of the 2000s the public reaction to high rates of immigration had largely been one of tolerant acceptance. A change in public mood coincided with the onset of the recession following the global financial crisis and the assumption of power by the Conservative-led coalition government in 2010. Before the 2010 election David Cameron had floated the idea of capping net migration to the "tens of thousands," that is, a maximum of 100,000, and a commitment to this effect was included in the Conservatives' 2010 election manifesto. Although the target was never reached, it was repeated in the 2015 manifesto and Mrs May reaffirmed the target before the 2017 election as well.[24]

During her time as Home Secretary in the Cameron governments Mrs May showed she was serious about the task of getting immigration down. In her 2015 Conservative party conference speech she said high migration year after year made it difficult to keep a cohesive society because it overwhelmed public services.[25] She also steadfastly refused to remove international students from the immigration figures because of the chance of their overstaying their visas[26] and presided over a restrictive asylum policy and a "hostile environment" towards illegal immigrants. The latter has involved making employers and landlords liable to fines for employing or letting property to illegal migrants and sending vans with warning slogans to tour areas known to harbour large numbers of such immigrants.[27]

Government efforts to reduce migration are popular. While some of the public support for a restrictive policy on immigration may be based on misinformation, there are also justified concerns. The main ones have been the strain placed by high levels of immigration on schools, the health service and housing, the impact on communities, and the effect of immigration of depressing wage levels and displacing UK-born workers. In 2017–18 the Migration Advisory Committee revisited these issues on the basis of existing literature and newly commissioned studies and representations from stakeholders.[28] The main conclusions were that overall the negative effects of EU migration were quite or very limited, albeit noticeable in a few sectors. There were also positive impacts, for example on public finances and health and social care services. Here are the main findings:

- In housing, EU migration had increased house prices and migrants represented an increasing fraction of new tenants of social housing, which given the insufficient level of new social housing being built meant that to some extent they were reducing opportunities for other potential tenants.[29]
- In health and social care services, migrants contribute much more to the health service and the provision of social care in financial resources and work than they consume in services.[30]
- In education, migrant children and the British-born children of migrants are a higher fraction of the school population than migrants are of the school workforce, but there is no evidence that migrants

have reduced parental choice or the educational attainment of UK-born children.[31]

- On the provision of extra government financial resources to areas receiving large numbers of migrants, the Committee was not convinced that sufficient attention was paid to ensuring that increased immigration brought forth the extra resources needed to manage the consequences of the immigration.[32]
- The effects of immigration on communities are hard to measure because of their subjective nature, which means there is a risk they are ignored. But there is no evidence it has an effect on crime or, on the whole, on the subjective well-being of communities, though that would depend on whether people had a positive or negative view of migrants.[33]
- Regarding public finances, migrants pay more in taxes than they receive in benefits.[34]
- In the labour market, migrants have no or little effect on the overall employment and unemployment outcomes of the UK-born workforce, though the impact may vary across different groups, with more negative effects for the lower-skilled. In terms of wages, migration is not a major determinant of the wages of the UK-born workforce, though lower-skilled workers may face a—generally small—negative impact.[35]

More generally, about population increases adding to pressures on the labour market or public services, the Migration Advisory Committee report reminded us that the extra population contributes both to the supply of and demand for labour and services and that migration cannot be seen in isolation from other policies, such as housing or public infrastructure provision.[36] As noted above, the Migration Advisory Committee is sceptical about whether the UK has devoted sufficient resources to areas bearing the brunt of extra migration. Mrs May seemed resentful of the need to allocate extra resources to, for example, providing extra school places just to cater for the extra migration.[37] The record of recent UK governments in investing in regions still suffering from past industrial decline or facing new challenges such as immigration has been poor, although the need for austerity after the financial crisis is a partial excuse. The "Northern Powerhouse" initiative is a lonely exception.[38] The UK has in the past failed to take up allocations from the EU structural and investment funds which could have helped provide such investment.[39]

Apart from government neglect, the discontent at the level of immigration in old industrial areas may be partly due to the consciousness of decline among the white ethnic majorities in such areas and to the continuing segregation of some immigrant communities of longer standing than the new EU migrants. Eric Kaufmann, in his book *Whiteshift: Populism, Immigration and the Future of White Majorities,* argues that rises in immigration have made the white working-class feel less secure in their ethnic and cultural identity; this should be recognized and not be equated to racism.[40] David Goodhart sees the declining status of non-graduate jobs among the bottom 50% of the population who have tended to stay put in their communities (the "Somewheres") as a cause of discontent with rapid social change due, among other things, to immigration.[41]

Others disagree that the white population, in particular, is disadvantaged in working-class areas. They maintain that there is a solidarity among the whole of the working class, both whites and immigrants, towards the economic problems such areas are facing. The question is about more than economics or culture; it is also about politics being capable of ensuring the provision of the public goods needed for viable communities, redressing inequality, tackling marginalized groups—some of which may tend to be white—and providing a safety net for the needy.[42] Lack of integration especially of established Muslim immigrant communities with the mainstream can also cause tensions.[43]

At the 2016 Conservative party conference Mrs May, newly installed as prime minister, delighted many of her party faithful—and Nigel Farage—by coming down firmly on the side of a restrictive immigration policy in the "sovereign and fully independent" country Britain was about to become through Brexit. But she adopted needlessly divisive language, echoing David Goodhart's distinction between the "Somewheres," rooted in a single community, and the footloose "Anywheres," whom she described as "citizens of nowhere" and likened to the exploitative "international elites." The aspersion this seemed to be casting on anyone internationally oriented enough to migrate to another country rightly upset many people, as it was a caricature: migrants and expatriates are not parasites and are not automatically disconnected from the people around them or from their native country; they have multiple allegiances.[44] The proposal floated by the Home Secretary Amber Rudd at the same conference to require employers to publish the numbers of foreign staff was in a similar anti-immigrant vein and was quickly dropped after widespread protests.

Among the Brexit-supporting newspapers, there is a difference on the issue of immigration between the *Telegraph* and the rest. The *Telegraph* often takes a moderate line, while the position of the three tabloids tends to be against immigration and often closer to UKIP than to the Conservative party. On the more critical wing of the *Telegraph* is the former editor Charles Moore, who writes on 24 June 2017 of mass immigration being "a huge shifting population, not all of it legal, searching for somewhere to live, and the consequent strain on services." For years, he writes, governments have declared that they are bearing down on immigrant numbers, yet they have failed and the non-immigrant majority fears that nobody knows what is going on.[45] Allison Pearson, in a column entitled "Brexit doesn't have to spell doom for the NHS" on 14 June 2017, writes that the sharp fall in the number of nurses from EU countries being registered in Britain may be less due to Brexit than to the tougher language tests that have been introduced, which are no bad thing as patient safety is at stake. Less EU doctors and nurses will mean the government will finally be forced to increase its training of British-born medical staff. After all, the UK had nurses before we joined the Common Market, she says.[46] The *Telegraph* is ambivalent about mass immigration. On the one hand, it can be positive about successful immigrants fitting into and contributing to British society;[47] on the other hand, it can stoke up fears of invasions through quite misleading headlines on a par with the Farage and Gove scare stories during the referendum campaign (see Sect. 7.4 below).[48] Ruth Davidson, in an article urging a serious debate about immigration policy, criticized the "'Britain's full up' brigade" and "those claiming that there isn't a nurse with a British accent left in the country," but it was met with a flood of letters from readers clearly supporting the Charles Moore and Allison Pearson view of immigration.[49]

Other *Telegraph* columnists like Ambrose Evans-Prichard and Allister Heath on the libertarian, free-trading wing of Conservatism take a completely different line and are opposed to restrictions on migration and particularly to Mrs May's *idée fixe* of ending free movement.[50] So is Fraser Nelson, editor of *The Spectator* and a regular columnist for the *Telegraph*, who criticized the then Home Secretary Amber Rudd for misinterpreting Brexit as a vote for closing the border rather than embracing a more global future.[51]

The *Mail*, *Express* and *Sun* have engaged in consistently one-sided reporting of large-scale migration: they have campaigned against it and have had no qualms about deliberately spreading misinformation where it suited their anti-EU agenda. They have been more circumspect and fairer in relation to immigration from Commonwealth countries, however.[52] "Benefits tourism," the claim that EU migrants were coming to Britain not to work but to take advantage of its generous benefits system, was a long-running, but basically false story.[53] It was comprehensively debunked by Oxford University's Migration Observatory.[54] The *Mail* later had the effrontery to use this "revelation," that the figures of EU migrants claiming benefits were quite low after all, as an argument to show that the concessions on migrant benefits painfully extracted from the EU by Mr Cameron—largely in response to agitation from newspapers like the *Mail*— would not be effective at cutting migrant numbers. Therefore, leaving the EU was the only option.[55]

The sending of child allowances abroad by EU migrants was another subject of relentless campaigning by the tabloids, which led the Cameron government to demand changes from the EU in the pre-referendum negotiations. Similar stories calculated to arouse anger against the EU were about the camps of immigrants in Calais waiting for a chance to slip across the Channel, after making their way up from the Mediterranean unimpeded through the border-free Schengen zone. This story tied in neatly with the scare stories in the Brexit press about the EU and in particular its open borders representing a terrorism threat to Britain. It would also ring a bell about another way the EU—actually European Court of Human Rights, but in Brexit mythology, it's the same thing (see above Chap. 5, Sect. 5.7)— is endangering Britain by preventing it deporting Islamist preachers.

Migration Watch UK, an influential immigration pressure group, also campaigns incessantly for lower immigration.[56] Thus, with the *Telegraph* being ambivalent and the rest of the Brexit press hostile to EU migration, moderating public discourse and keeping it evidence-based, as the Migration Advisory Committee and the Migration Observatory, newspapers like *The Guardian*, *Financial Times* and *The Economist*, and the BBC try to do, is an uphill and lonely struggle. Reasonable debate is drowned out by emotion and rabble-rousing rhetoric.

Just as the campaigning for the EU referendum was getting underway, a migrant crisis in Europe blew up which added fuel to the Brexit fire surrounding immigration. Up till then, the Brexit movement had channelled anti-immigrant sentiment mainly into opposing EU migration. Now it could turn to account, as part of the case for Brexit, the risk of Islamic terrorists hiding among the refugees making their way from the Mediterranean up through mainland Europe and potentially as far as Britain. It could also use the prospect of visa-free travel for Turks and even the eventual accession of Turkey to the EU—part of an agreement the EU made with Turkey to stem the flow of refugees across the Aegean—to stoke up fear of a further wave of indirectly EU-sourced mass immigration into Britain, which this time would mainly be of Muslims. Islamophobia, like racism in general, is a taboo subject in Britain. The link specifically to Muslim immigration had to be discreet and implicit.

Britain does not have a political party that is as overtly and vehemently against Muslim immigration like the Alternative for Germany (AfD) party or Geert Wilders' Freedom Party in the Netherlands.[57] Even UKIP was not specifically Islamophobic at the time of the EU referendum, though there was an undercurrent of anti-Muslim sentiment linked to concerns about cultural identity and Islamist terrorism.[58] Similar attitudes occasionally surface in the Conservative party, though the party's public face is firmly against racism.[59] As for the press, although Britain has not been immune to Islamist terrorism and there have been other problems such as the sexual exploitation of vulnerable white girls by groups of Asian men, on the whole the press has behaved responsibly in relation to such events within Britain. The migrant crisis allowed the right-wing press and the Brexit movement generally to tap into latent Islamophobia discreetly in order to bolster their case for leaving the EU. The chaotic attempts of the EU to manage the crisis, like the euro crisis before it which was then entering its final stages, played into the hands of the Eurosceptics.

7.3   THE 2015–16 EUROPEAN MIGRANT CRISIS

The United Nations refugee agency, the United Nations High Commissioner for Refugees (UNHCR), reported in 2016 that at the end of 2015 a record number of 65.3 million people in the world were either refugees, asylum seekers or internally displaced persons. Despite the huge focus on Europe's migrant crisis, 86% of the world's refugees were being sheltered in low and middle income countries. Turkey was the biggest host country for refugees worldwide, with 2.5 million people, followed by Pakistan and Lebanon.[60]

EU member states received over 1.2 million first-time asylum applications in 2015.[61] The flow of migrants was the biggest movement of people into Europe since World War II[62] and no other rich countries had ever faced a bigger surge of refugees.[63] The rush of migrants into Europe had been foreseeable, as Syrian refugees had been building up on its doorstep in Turkey, Jordan and Lebanon for years. Europe had pretended not to see it.[64] Most of the migrants crossed the Mediterranean from the Middle East and North Africa. In 2015–16, the largest number came across the eastern Mediterranean from Turkey to the Greek islands; previously most had come across the central Mediterranean to Italy.[65]

The main flow of migrants in 2015 who arrived in Greece made their way northwards through the western Balkans heading for Austria, Germany and Sweden. By the summer of 2015 the flow of refugees along the western Balkans route had swelled to a flood and the strain on border control and reception facilities in the transit countries was severe; aid agencies were providing indispensable help, as were ordinary members of the public offering food and drink to the travellers in the endless column.[66]

At the end of August, a large number of refugees had built up in Budapest where they were being stopped by the Hungarian government from boarding trains to Austria and Germany. The Prime Minister, Mr Orbán, wanted the migrants returned to Greece, the country of first entry into the EU which under the EU's "Dublin rules" was officially responsible for their asylum applications. Hungary was building a fence on its border with Serbia. After consultation with her Austrian counterpart the German Chancellor, Angela Merkel, broke the logjam by announcing that Germany would take in the stranded migrants. They received a warm welcome from Germans who thronged Munich railway station to meet them holding welcome banners and handing out toys and sweets to the children. On 13 September 2015, however, Mrs Merkel was forced to change course because of internal disagreements about her policy and the pressure of handling the huge numbers of migrants in such a short space of time. Germany introduced controls on its southern border to restrict entry to genuine refugees.

A staggered closure of the Balkan route followed. Starting with Hungary the other countries along the route, from Slovenia and Croatia in the north-west to Serbia and Macedonia in the south-east, one by one closed their borders or restricted the passage of refugees across them.[67] The border closures worsened the situation in Greece, at least temporarily.[68] Nevertheless, from its peak of over 10,000 a day in October 2015 the flow of migrants fell and by March 2016 it was down to trickle, as an agreement with Turkey to stem the flow of migrants at source began to take effect.

The total number of migrants who applied for asylum in Germany in 2015 while the Western Balkans route was open was 890,000; for Sweden the figure was 160,000 and for Austria 90,000. In January 2016 Austria introduced an annual cap on the asylum seekers it would accept.[69] Mrs Merkel, too, under pressure from members of her own party and its long-standing coalition partner the Bavarian CSU party promised that the 2015 level of refugees would not be repeated, and in the coalition negotiations after the 2017 general election she committed herself to a limit of 200,000 asylum seekers per year.[70]

While the numbers of refugees crossing the central Mediterranean were much smaller than those crossing the Aegean to Greece in 2015, this route is more dangerous and in early 2015 more attention was focussed on it than on Greece and the Balkans because of an increased number of migrants being drowned when overcrowded unseaworthy boats frequently capsized.[71] The first action of the EU in the crisis was directed at this serious situation.

7.3.1   The EU's Fragmented Response

The EU's response to the migrant crisis of 2015–16 was chaotic and piecemeal. Thanks to Mrs Merkel it just about avoided disaster. Should and could the EU have done better? Clearly, yes. The problem cried out for a cooperative European solution, but the EU was not able to do more than take holding action to deal with the immediate crisis and step up its work on a system to manage migrant flows better in the future. The case showed that without at least the beginnings of a consensus on how to respond to a crisis and a legal basis for joint action, "the EU" in the sense of a cohesive unit is as nothing.[72] As it was, the EU member states were split into three camps: the frontline states Greece and Italy receiving the bulk of the migrant arrivals, supported by member states like Germany, Austria, Sweden and Finland and a few others willing to take a considerable number of those migrants, if possible under a European-wide quota scheme as proposed by the European Commission and the president of the European Council Donald Tusk; a group of central and eastern European countries who were vehemently opposed to taking any irregular migrants at all;[73] and finally the rest of the member states, which paid lip service to solidarity but in practice because of a sensitive political situation regarding immigration back home were happy to keep their heads down and let Greece and Italy and a coalition of the willing led by Germany carry the burden alone.[74] Britain was in the third camp, sheltered by the barrier of the Channel, the border controls it maintained because it was outside Schengen and its opt-out from the common asylum policy.[75]

When the migrant crisis struck in 2015 the EU's asylum policy was still work in progress. Indeed, while the crisis was unfolding new legislation was just entering into force and the Commission was publishing new proposals that had been under preparation for some time.[76] Development of the "Common European Asylum System" had started in 1999 under the Amsterdam Treaty and had achieved a partial harmonization of standards for reception conditions and asylum procedures, criteria for determining whether an asylum seeker qualified for recognition as a refugee, a "Eurodac" database for recording the fingerprints of newly arrived asylum seekers, and criteria for determining the member state responsible for examining asylum seekers' applications, the "Dublin rules," which, however, were no longer fit for purpose.

The emergency meeting of the European Council held in April 2015 to deal with the acute humanitarian crisis in the central Mediterranean led to a tripling of funding for rescue operations and to a clamp down on people smugglers.[77] The rate of losses at sea decreased but still totalled 3700 for the year compared with 3200 in 2014.[78]

In February 2015 the EU Commission had put forward the first proposal to relocate migrants from Greece and Italy, where they had first arrived, on an equitable basis between member states. An expanded quota scheme was proposed in May 2015 as part of the Commission's comprehensive framework for developing asylum policy, the "European Agenda on Migration."[79] In September 2015 a "second implementation package" from the Commission set out a series of further measures to tackle the crisis, including a proposal to turn the overburdened reception facilities in Greece and Italy into so-called "hotspots" in which national officials would be assisted by EU agencies including the Border and Coast Guard service Frontex and Europol.[80] In October, on the initiative of Mrs Merkel, a special meeting of the leaders of countries along the Western Balkans route and Austria and Germany was convened to defuse tensions and better coordinate the handling of refugees.[81]

Progress was made in fits and starts; original proposals could not be agreed and were redrafted countless times. The main measures that have been implemented in some form or are still pending are as follows.

- After several failed efforts to gain voluntary agreement on the scheme to relocate a limited number of the asylum seekers from the "frontline" countries Greece and Italy, the scheme was pushed through in the Council of Ministers by a majority vote in September 2015. The

Czech Republic, Slovakia, Hungary and Romania voted against and were later joined in their opposition by Poland, which had had a change of government. The distribution key was based on population, Gross Domestic Product (GDP), level of unemployment and numbers of refugees already in the country. Although the numbers of asylum seekers allocated to the central and eastern European countries, from a total of 160,000, were small, they nevertheless refused to comply with the decision and Hungary and Slovakia unsuccessfully appealed against the decision to the European Court of Justice. Prime Minister Orbán of Hungary held a referendum on the subject in which on a small turnout a majority opposed compulsory quotas. However, the scheme was dogged by bureaucratic delays which slowed the relocations, even to countries that supported the measure. At a European Council meeting in June 2018, the EU dropped compulsory quotas for the time being.[82]

- The reception facilities for migrants in Greece and Italy have been improved through first reception "hotspots" at which migrants are identified, registered and fingerprinted before being considered for relocation to member states under the 2015 quota decisions. The reception centres are staffed by both national and EU staff working together. Previously the Greek and Italian authorities were overwhelmed by the numbers of arrivals and many migrants were not registered but just waved through.[83] The EU is providing humanitarian aid to pay for migrants' food and housing in the countries that host large numbers of migrants.[84]

- Financial help is being provided to Jordan and Lebanon to improve the conditions of the Syrian refugees being hosted by the countries.[85] Of the 6 million people displaced from Syria by the war, Lebanon is hosting 1.5 million (a third of its normal population), Jordan 1.3 million, and Turkey 2.5 million. A donor conference was held to help Jordan, Lebanon and Turkey deal with the Syrian refugees in February 2016.[86]

- An agreement with Turkey was signed in March 2016, after negotiations in which Mrs Merkel, the Commission Vice-President Timmermans and the European Council President Tusk were heavily involved.[87] Under it, Turkey is preventing migrants attempting to cross the Aegean to Greece and taking back migrants that manage to do so in return for the EU taking one Syrian refugee from Turkey for every migrant returned to Turkey. The EU is providing up to €6bn to support Syrian refugees in camps in Turkey. Part of the agreement was the removal of the visa requirement for Turkish citizens travelling to Europe from June 2016 and relaunching of the negotiations on Turkey's accession to the EU which had been suspended since a slow improvement in human rights and democracy in Turkey had started to go into reverse under President Erdogan. Despite misgivings about the efficacy and morality of a deal with Turkey, the agreement succeeded in stopping the flow of refugees across the Aegean and in ameliorating to some extent the conditions of Syrian refugees in camps in Turkey.[88] Visa-free travel to Europe for Turkish citizens, intended to start in mid-2016, has not yet been granted, although negotiations are ongoing.[89] As far as Turkish accession in concerned, in June 2018 the EU Council of Ministers was forced to conclude that the negotiations were at a standstill, and that Turkey had in fact been moving further away from the EU.[90] The European Parliament has also voted in favour of suspending the negotiations in view of the unsatisfactory human rights situation in Turkey.

- To stem the flow of migrants from Africa, the EU, under an agreement with a group of African countries, is providing finance to help address the causes of migration at source, such as the lack of economic development, employment opportunities, training, and provision for internally displaced persons. The finance is being channelled through an Emergency Trust Fund for Africa.[91] Projects are also being funded in Libya.[92] In these agreements, the EU was able to learn from the experience that Spain had built up with bilateral agreements with African countries of origin.[93]

- Legislation to strengthen the EU Border and Coast Guard Agency Frontex with a broader mandate and much increased staff and equipment is well underway. It is planned to build up the staff of the agency to a standing corps of 10,000 operational staff; they will work alongside national border control agencies. Member states would still have to give their consent to the deployment of the EU border and coast guard. The Commission originally proposed a virtual federal border force which it would have been able to deploy as of right without permission from the member state.[94]

- Conversion of the European Asylum Support Office set up in 2010 into a fully fledged EU Agency for Asylum with a strengthened mandate to provide services to national authorities is proceeding. The Agency could be a stepping stone towards a Europeanization of the handling of asylum applications, but that is some way off.[95]

- The necessary reform of the obsolete but politically highly sensitive "Dublin rules", which determine the state responsible for handling asylum applications from irregular migrants, is still in abeyance. Under the current rules, the country responsible is the member state in which an asylum seeker first lands on EU territory. However, if the asylum seeker has family members in another member state or another member state has previously issued the asylum seeker with a visa, then that member state is responsible. Should a migrant apply for asylum in a member state other than that in which he or she first landed in the EU (unless one of the above exceptions apply), the second member state can return him or her to that first member state. The Dublin rules are clearly unsuited to the typical modern situation in which arrivals of irregular migrants are concentrated in particular countries, because only land or sea routes are open to them (airlines are obliged to turn away passengers without visas or entry documents for the country of destination.)[96] In their current form, the Dublin rules severely disadvantage "frontline" countries. To deal with surges in migrant arrivals equitably would require other member states to take a share of such migrants.[97] The current draft proposal leaves the "first entry" rule unchanged except when there is a surge in arrivals in a particular country, in which case other member states would have to take over some of the asylum-seekers under a compulsory allocation scheme. Not only central and eastern European countries oppose it; so do the countries the current rule benefits, namely those far away from the main points of arrival of refugees in southern Europe, like the UK.[98]

This catalogue of action on many fronts shows that however chaotic its response to the migrant crisis may have been, and however imperfect the result, the EU managed to get an acute and dangerous situation under control and to stabilize it to a large extent. The management of migrant flows across borders in the southern extremities of the EU was improved through better coordinated and better funded systems on the borders and through agreements with third countries. The death toll in the Mediterranean was brought down and action taken to curb people smugglers exploiting the migrants. The EU-Turkey agreement has held, despite failure to fulfil the commitment to remove the visa requirement for Turkish citizens or advance the accession negotiations, though this was not for want of trying. And financial aid from the EU and wider aid efforts by the international community have helped improve the living conditions of Syrian refugees accommodated in Turkey, Jordan and Lebanon.

European cooperation has, if not prevailed, at least not broken down. True, there have been instances where EU action has been too slow for the fast-changing situation, especially on the Western Balkans route, leading member states to take unilateral action in building fences and temporarily reintroducing border controls within the Schengen area, disrupting free movement and trade. There was a wholesale revolt by a caucus of central and eastern European countries against quotas and relations between Balkan countries frayed nearly to breaking point. But one way or another it was possible, as in the euro crisis with leadership from Germany supporting the EU institutions, to agree collective action to contain the worst effects of the crisis and simultaneously to continue developing the common policy framework necessary to deal with migration in the future. Although there is still a long way to go, and although the divisions about migration between member states remain strong and have to some extent been exacerbated, the experience of dealing with the crisis and confronting divisions in open and often acrimonious debate has shown that cooperation can achieve more than national action. Refugees and irregular migration are an international phenomenon and require international solutions.

The Schengen system of border-free travel and transport throughout most of Europe[99] did not collapse under the strain of temporary restoration of checks at some internal borders as many had feared and some Eurosceptics had hoped.[100] Member states are too conscious of the economic and social advantages of Schengen to consider reintroducing controls on a permanent basis.

The million-plus migrants received in Germany, Sweden, Austria and other countries during the crisis are having their claims processed and those successful are gradually being assimilated into society.[101] There have been setbacks like the New Year's Eve attacks on women in Cologne,[102] terrorist incidents, and arson attacks by right-wing extremists on immigrant centres.[103] The influx has also fostered distrust in governments' ability to control borders, feeding anti-immigrant sentiment, causing governments to respond with tighter restrictions on immigrants, and bringing anti-immigrant parties to power or into government in Italy, Austria, Denmark and Sweden and into state and federal parliaments in Germany.[104] In time, however, despite the difficulties and the cost, the new wave of immigrants should settle down and come to be accepted as useful and welcome members of the community, just as central and eastern European migrants now seem to have become more accepted in Britain since the EU referendum.[105]

7.3.2 Was Merkel's Open Door Policy an Act of Compassion or "Misguided Altruism"?[106]

Ms Merkel was widely praised for her action to open the door to the masses of asylum seekers streaming towards Germany through Hungary. It was a compassionate response to a humanitarian crisis. To critics within Germany, she said: "If we have to start apologizing for showing a friendly face in response to emergency situations, then this is not my country." The US magazine TIME designated her as its "person of the year" for asking more of her country than most politicians would dare, and for providing moral leadership in a world where it was in short supply.[107] President Obama, too, said her stand on refugees was "courageous." *The Economist* called her "the indispensable European" for being the only national leader willing and able to assume the leadership of Europe in a crisis.[108] Some, however, maintained her humanitarian gesture was unnecessary,[109] that she should have sought out the European middle ground,[110] and even that her offer of an open door was largely posturing for domestic consumption, which is a ludicrous, given the opposition it was bound to arouse.[111] It is undeniable, however, that by announcing that the migrants stranded in Hungary were welcome to come to Germany she sent a signal that encouraged lots more migrants, including non-Syrians, to head for Europe.[112] Philip Stephens in the *Financial Times*,[113] and *The Economist*,[114] strongly defended her action. She was not the cause of the onrush of migrants: they were coming anyway; she acted to avert a humanitarian disaster; and her critics had offered no plausible alternative. I am firmly on the side of Stephens and *The Economist*. Ivan Krastev argues that it was inevitable the pendulum would swing back to reclosing the borders after the migrant surge, in order to protect indigenous majorities, who feel their identities threatened by immigration.[115] The reversal of policy in late 2015 was probably necessary in order to digest the unprecedented influx which was causing political instability. On the other hand, if rich European countries fail to show compassion to refugees and pull up the drawbridge immediately, they will both elevate the far right and its principles at home and encourage extremism on Europe's borders.[116] Nor will turning one's back on refugees and immigration halt Europe's demographic and political decline—rather the reverse.[117]

However, clearly there are good reasons for people fleeing conflict situations to be accommodated close to their home country, if possible, because that makes it easier for them to return which most would like to do. Rich countries should be generous in helping the host countries provide refugees with decent living conditions, schools for their children and if possible employment, but should also be willing to accept refugees who wish to seek a completely new life elsewhere because the wait is protracted or the conditions intolerable, or because return is not possible for the individuals concerned.[118]

7.4   Coverage of Immigration and the 2015–16 European Migrant Crisis in the British Press and Its Effect on the EU Referendum

Thanks to its geographical position, to not being in Schengen and consequently being able to carry out identity checks at its borders, to having an opt-out from arrangements like the quota scheme but at the same time a right to deport asylum seekers who entered the EU through another country (under the "Dublin rules"), and thanks to its partners' forbearance given the prospect of the referendum in which immigration was a highly sensitive subject, Britain was spared involvement or responsibility in the migrant crisis. In relation to the migrant crisis, therefore, Britain, as it had been during the euro crisis, was largely an observer watching from the sidelines—or from behind the ramparts—as the drama unfolded. Britain committed itself to take in 20,000 Syrian refugees over five years from camps in the Middle East and to accept an additional 3000 unaccompanied children from among the migrants already in Europe, but such figures appeared miserly and hard-hearted when compared with the huge numbers Germany and Sweden, for example, were taking.[119] On the credit side, however, Britain had attracted considerably more migration from the EU under free movement than other countries and this was contributing to a fast population increase and a strain on services, making another source of mass immigration politically problematic. Secondly, the government had objections of principle to anything that could act as a "pull factor" to mass irregular migration, including, at its most heartless, opposing sea rescues of boat people in the Mediterranean. It preferred supporting refugees close to their home countries, a policy it actually practised as one of the biggest donors to Syrian refugee camps in Turkey, Jordan and Lebanon.[120]

But most of the problems Britain had with mass migration were of its own making. As seen in Sect. 7.2 above, successive governments had created highly flexible labour markets offering low or minimum-wage jobs that were highly attractive to migrant workers from countries where wages were much lower. The Conservative-led governments after 2010 had also allowed pressure on services and housing to become a political issue by failing to invest in the regions mainly affected by migration. Finally, to appease a strongly anti-immigrant press and neutralize the growing support for UKIP the government had boxed itself into an unrealistic net immigration target, which was impossible to meet even without taking in extra asylum seekers. The government was thus on the defensive over immigration and was afraid of appearing over-generous, of giving too much away to the EU, with which it was trying to negotiate restrictions on free movement, or of toning down its hostile rhetoric towards illegal immigrants, both those already in Britain and those camped in Calais waiting for a chance to cross over.

Therefore, during the run-up to the EU referendum and in the referendum campaign itself, Remain supporters had their backs to the wall on immigration. First, David Cameron had made reform of freedom of movement to reduce EU migration into the main plank of his renegotiation on Britain's terms of membership of the bloc, but in the end the concessions he achieved in the form not of an unconditional emergency brake on the numbers of EU migrants coming, but only of restrictions on their eligibility for non-contributory in-work benefits for four years, were disappointing.[121] Secondly, there was the migrant crisis playing out in mainland Europe, and the potential it offered for, on the one hand, stirring up fears of Islamist terrorism and further mass immigration—including from Turkey—despite Britain's being relatively sheltered from such developments by the Channel and not being in Schengen, and, on the other hand, for denigrating the EU's chaotic efforts to manage the crisis.[122] Despite the difficulties, however, it was probably a strategic mistake by the Remain campaign not to engage with the public more vigorously on migration or to defend free movement.[123]

Being virtually unopposed on this issue, the Leave politicians and the Brexit-supporting press exploited the discontent among the population about immigration and their anxiety about terrorism and crime to the full; they mounted a veritable "Project Fear" of their own. The *Financial Times*, *The Economist* and *BBC News* as usual provided the most comprehensive coverage on the migrant crisis, as the references in the previous section testify, and were serious and balanced. So, too, were the *Guardian* and the *Times*. Of the Brexit papers, the *Mail, Express* and *Sun* were true to their anti-EU colours in exploiting both EU migration and the migrant crisis mercilessly in the interests of the dogged campaign of their proprietors or editors to get Britain out of the EU, though the *Mail* occasionally made a show of compassion for the refugees, for example in campaigning for the UK government to do more to help unaccompanied children. The *Telegraph* was, as noted in Sect. 7.2, more nuanced on immigration generally, no doubt because of its links to business, but on the European migrant crisis it used the problems it posed for Europe as a further stick with which to attack the EU and beat the drum for Brexit.

Here are a few examples of the relentless onslaught of scare stories and misinformation that appeared in our Brexit-supporting newspapers during the referendum debate. The "stop Brexit" and "People's Vote" organization *InFacts* has also published a collection,[124] which also clearly shows that different Brexit newspapers repeated the same stories as part of a concerted campaign.

7.4.1   Security, Terrorism and Crime

Con Coughlin in the *Daily Telegraph* of 3 February 2016 stirred fears that "scores" of Islamist terrorists would slip into Europe with the crowds of migrants,[125] just as Nigel Farage had predicted in the European Parliament the previous year.[126] That this was a genuine threat was undeniable: several of the perpetrators of the Bataclan theatre attack in Paris on 13 November 2015, for example, were found to have re-entered Europe along with refugees and one had a Syrian passport, though most were French and Belgian. But the risk of infiltration of the migrants with terrorists was never as great as made out.[127] There was a lively debate during the referendum campaign about whether leaving the EU would improve or worsen Britain's security. The balance of opinion among the experts was that it was better to stay in,[128] and the final position of the May government regarding the future relationship was that it should try to maintain the close security cooperation and participation in data-sharing arrangements the country has with the EU currently.[129]

The *Mail Online* on 30 March 2016 quoted the Brexit campaigner Dominic Raab comparing the number of non-EU nationals stopped by British immigration authorities from entering the UK at borders with the number of EU citizens they stopped. The figure for non-EU nationals was ten times higher than that for EU nationals. Raab was comparing apples with oranges, however, because EU citizens cannot be stopped on suspicion of being illegal immigrants, whereas that is a frequent reason for stopping people arriving from outside the EU. The newspaper's headline describing the people stopped as "terror suspects" made the original misleading comparison worse. The clear implication was that EU freedom of movement made it harder for the UK to stop terrorists entering the country. The figure did not show this but would be further confirmation of the view most *Mail* readers had obtained from earlier coverage of the topic.[130] Two stories in *Daily Telegraph* of 6 and 17 February 2016, one about the daughter-in-law of the Islamist preacher Abu Hamza and the other about criminal offences committed by EU migrants in Britain, also misrepresented facts or figures. In the former, the Independent Press Standards Organization (IPSO) confirmed that the *Telegraph*'s story was "significantly misleading" and the newspaper published a correction, but only nearly three months later and only on page 2.[131]

Finally, the *Sunday Express* of 17 April 2016, in a story about the 4000 EU migrants serving sentences in British prisons, conflated this with a claim by Vote Leave that foreign offenders were using EU freedom of movement laws to enter Britain "despite being convicted of serious crimes."[132] The implication that the bulk of the 4000 EU citizens in British jails, at British taxpayers' expense, were there because of crimes committed elsewhere in Europe was ludicrous, because criminals from EU countries who have committed crimes there and are apprehended in Britain would be returned under European Arrest Warrants.[133] In fact, most of the 4000 EU citizens in British jails were presumably there for crimes committed in Britain, and—as the government reportedly stated when asked to comment—they too can be removed. The story also implied, without the slightest evidence—not even a cursory reference to crime statistics—that British people were relatively more at risk from foreign criminals than from British-born ones. The message: EU freedom of movement comes at a "deadly cost" of higher crime, on top of the high financial cost of accommodating EU criminals in our overfilled jails.[134]

7.4.2 Turkey: The Second Big Lie

Charles Moore, in a powerfully worded piece in the *Daily Telegraph* of 7 May 2016 about the EU's agreement with Turkey, combined a panoply of pet hates and grievances English conservatives feel towards the European

Union with anxiety about the Islamization of Europe.[135] The German-led, undemocratic, bureaucratic EU, having failed to control the flow of Middle Eastern migrants across its borders, saw the answer, as usual, in more centralization, "more Europe." The agreement with Turkey, Mr Moore averred, was putting Mr Erdogan "in charge of Europe's supply of Muslims," and Germany, with its long-standing, close ties with Turkey, was "shaping the future demography of Europe," which he suggested could turn out to be "Hell." Mr Moore's criticisms of President Erdogan and his comments about the need of Islam to fit into pluralist societies may be widely shared. The Enoch Powell-like doom-mongering about Islamization and the criticism of German hegemony in Europe when Britain itself has for a long time just looked away from Europe's problems are not. It is a travesty to say Mrs Merkel "unilaterally invited" a million migrants into her country and hypocritical to criticize the EU for its management of a major migrant crisis when Britain itself cannot even handle the threat posed by a "bunch of migrants"[136] camped across the Channel. A jibe at the Muslim Mayor of London, Sadiq Khan, suggesting he might somehow exploit the situation was uncalled for.

The promise of the EU to reactivate the accession negotiations with Turkey as part of the agreement to stem the flow of migrants across the Aegean gave the Leave campaign a golden opportunity to pretend that Turkish accession was imminent and that Britain would soon be swamped with Turks, Albanians and others, taking British jobs. This was the second big lie perpetrated by Leave—after the £350 million a week—that helped swing the referendum vote. They knew very well it would be many years before Turkey would join, because accession negotiations are never hurried and after 11 years of negotiations only one chapter out of 33 had been agreed and Turkey was further away than ever from meeting the criteria for democracy, human rights and press freedom that are a condition for joining. Subsequent events have shown how mendacious this claim was.

A piece by Michael Gove in the *Daily Mail* of 30 April 2016 featured a photograph of Albanian refugees clambering off a ship that had just arrived in Italy. The picture was from 1991, after Albania had got rid of its communist dictator, the banner headline, "Think the EU's bad now? Wait until Albania joins." Albania and not Turkey was mentioned in the headline probably because the *Mail* had a graphic photograph of Albanians swarming off a ship handy and they had a bad reputation for crime and mafia activity. But the real target was obviously the much bigger Turkey. The article referred to the strain EU migration was putting on the NHS, schools and housing and said that with four Balkan countries and Turkey set to join the EU, which would give their 88 million citizens the right to move to other EU countries where wages are much higher, the pressure on services in Britain would intensify. He quoted appreciatively his fellow Brexiteer Frank Field MP, who had spoken about the pressure migrants were putting on services, and his cabinet colleague Mrs May, who in a Remain-backing speech had questioned whether further enlargement to poor Balkan and Middle Eastern countries was wise at the present time. Mr Gove implied the UK would not have a veto on the new countries' membership, because somehow the Cameron renegotiation had weakened Britain's right to veto Turkish membership. This was untrue, but it became part of the Turkish accession lie that was afterwards repeated endlessly by other Brexiteers. In fact, no new country can ever join the EU without every existing member agreeing. He also expressed outrage at the pre-accession aid the EU was providing the candidate countries to prepare them for membership, giving the impression that this "Balkan bonanza" was for some kind of hand-outs, whereas in fact such pre-accession financing is for building infrastructure and institution and capacity building. The Leave campaign knew very well that nothing angered ill-informed British voters more than the thought of foreigners ripping them off. The £350 million was the same type of highly effective stimulus. The punch line about the pre-accession aid was that this money—partly from British taxpayers—was not only helping Albanians and Montenegrins in their own country, but was *qualifying* them for accession and thus to be able to come and access the UK's public services as well. Gove avoided saying when Turkey would join (in later speeches he said it would be around 2020), but the impression he conveyed was that it was imminent. This untruth was defended to the hilt until the end of the campaign, just like the £350 million figure was—and still is. In an interview in the *Daily Telegraph* of 7 May 2016, Mr Gove repeated his warnings about a poorer health service and worse schools in Britain should the country vote to remain in the EU and the future accession of the four Balkan countries and Turkey gave 88 million people access to the UK and its public services under freedom of movement.[137]

The Sun ran similar stories about Turkey joining and Britain paying huge sums to prepare it for accession. On 21 and 22 June 2016 it quoted both the Vote Leave chief executive Matthew Elliott and Iain Duncan Smith insisting that Turkey was definitely joining the EU and that Cameron was lying in denying it.[138] The paper insinuated that the fact that pre-accession aid was already being paid and that negotiations would be resumed almost immediately after the British referendum were proof that accession was imminent. The fact is, however, that pre-accession pro-grammes typically run for ten years or more before accession takes place, and negotiations sometimes take longer than that, and in Turkey's case, given the country's human rights situation, they were likely to take a very long time indeed.

Two years later, on 16 July 2018, *The Sun* hypocritically reported that Michael Gove appeared to regret the dubious claims he had made about Turkey and other matters like the 350 million, citing Tom Baldwin's book *Ctrl Alt Delete: How Politics and the Media Crashed our Democracy.*[139]

The proposal to grant visa-free travel to Turkish citizens by mid-2016—a realistic prospect at the time, unlike the myth of imminent Turkish accession—was also easy to exploit to stoke up fears of mass migration and infiltration by terrorists and make it into another reason for leaving the EU. Visa-free travel meant that Turks would no longer have to be fingerprinted at EU borders. The EU openly admitted that abolition of the visa requirement would bring an increased security risk. The *Daily Telegraph* was happy to report such concerns and to quote Brexit campaigners like Iain Duncan Smith and Sir Richard Dearlove, a former head of British intelligence services, expressing alarm at the development. Sir Richard said it would be like "storing gasoline next to the fire."[140]

The *Daily Express*[141] warned that the "75 million Muslims from Turkey" soon to be granted the right of visa-free travel across the EU would have to stop at Calais for now because Britain had had the foresight to opt out of the Schengen open borders agreement; but in future, the paper claimed, it would be possible for them to be issued with EU passports by Schengen countries, giving them "free entry to Britain and access to our welfare system, hospitals, schools, doctors and dentists."

It is debatable whether EU migrants are to blame for pressure on services, or whether it is not at least partly the government's fault for not expanding services enough in areas with high immigration. In health and social care services, at least, migrants are not to blame for the strain on these services, for they contribute much more in financial resources and work than they consume in services, as shown in Sect. 7.2. But true or not, the argument that EU migrants are to blame for the pressure on services and housing is part of the Brexit movement's stock in trade, another of those stimuli guaranteed to produce outrage at Johnny Foreigner again taking advantage of us. Applying the argument to Turks entering Europe for a stay of up to 90 days and then somehow becoming EU citizens and gaining the right to enter Britain was far-fetched, however. Was the paper deliberately confusing visa-free travel and EU accession? Only the latter would result in Turks getting EU passports and free movement. The article referred to Turkey as an Islamic state, alluding to the same fears of Islamization as Charles Moore's article in the *Telegraph*. The *Express'* naming of its long-standing Brexit campaign as a "crusade" and the nationalist symbolism of the Cross of Saint George on the crusader's shield, which is the badge of the campaign, make it clear what it wants its readers to think about immigration and European cooperation.

The *Sunday Express* of 17 April 2016 had a brief report about the European Parliament voting for Turkish to become an official EU language, "as the Islamic nation draws ever closer to being admitted as a member state."[142] It quoted "infuriated" critics (UKIP MEPs?) saying the proposal to make Turkish an official EU language was proof that Turkey's accession was "all but guaranteed." The report was, of course, premature and false. The Commission clarified that there were no plans to make Turkish an official language and that such a decision could only be taken unanimously by the European Council. But denials of fake news are rarely effective. The 90-word article was an object lesson in hitting multiple xenophobic panic buttons.

7.4.3   The EU's Management of the Migrant Crisis

Con Coughlin, in a column in the *Daily Telegraph* of 28 October 2015[143] about crowds of refugees including women and children stuck at Balkan country borders as winter approached, expressed compassion for the refugees' plight, but used it as a stick with which to beat the EU. The "rank ineptitude" of "Europe's political elite" in failing to devise an efficient system for processing the refugees was leading to a humanitarian crisis, he wrote, just as its divisions had contributed to the Rwandan genocide and the Srebrenica massacre.

The piece alluded to flaws in the EU's strategy, such as the fruitless discussions on quotas, but showed no understanding of the difficulties. The traditional "fierce national rivalries," he referred to, "particularly between major powers such as Germany, France and Britain," were not in evidence during this crisis. Germany and France were not at odds, though France was passive; Britain was simply keeping its head down and its nose clean. The real problem was an unprecedented, three-fold and partly doctrinal split between member states over the issue of immigration, as described earlier.

Coughlin did not take a position on Mrs Merkel's intervention, unlike Charles Moore. Was she right to open her borders? However, he did criticize the "armies of Eurocrats"[144] wasting their time in interminable discussions with member states. Presumably, they should have been manning the reception facilities and border posts instead.[145] How else do you coordinate the response to a crisis other than through talking? Does not a British Cobra committee meet regularly during a civil emergency instead of the ministers and their civil servants joining the firefighters? And had the EU really "all but washed its hands of the [Syrian] conflict?" As to Srebrenica and Rwanda, while the EU's success in agreeing common foreign policies and coordinated interventions in conflict situations is mixed, largely because the big member states have independent foreign policies which the EU can only try to coordinate, the EU has not such a bad record on peace-keeping operations overall.

An article by Fraser Nelson in the *Daily Telegraph* of 3 February 2016 about Sweden's difficulties in trying to look after vastly increased numbers of unaccompanied child migrants arriving in the country shows that the paper is sometimes capable of making the case against EU membership without invective or distortion of facts.[146] The apparently reluctant Brexiteer writes sympathetically of abandoned children roaming Stockholm streets, and of small tragedies like the young aid worker stabbed to death by a 15-year-old refugee. Sweden is desperate, he said: it wants a new system under which the EU would distribute refugees to countries deemed able to take them, including the UK. He makes the unsubstantiated claim that Britain would lose its leverage to resist pressure to join in the quota scheme should it vote to stay in the EU. Why should it? There was no evidence for this. Otherwise, the article was well-reasoned and based on easily verifiable facts.

In an article also about unaccompanied child refugees, the *Daily Mail* of 30 April 2016 took the opposite line and argued that Britain should take in some of the unaccompanied child refugees in Europe, for example from the camps in Calais, despite the government's argument that this would encourage others to put their lives at risk with people traffickers.[147] The article was unusual in not taking the opportunity to blame the EU for the crisis.

The *Daily Express* of 13 April 2016, too, turned its anger on the government rather than the EU in protesting at the high cost of resettling the 20,000 refugees the government had promised to take from Syria over five years. However, it interpreted the EU's change of tack in the migrant crisis towards stopping migrants from leaving Turkey as a vindication of Mr Cameron's approach of prioritizing the improvement of conditions for refugees in the countries close to Syria over accepting them as immigrants. Next to this article was another about the never-ending procession of refugees arriving in overcrowded boats in Malta and Italy. This pressed the fear button with a quote from Paul Nuttall of UKIP warning of terrorists slipping in amongst the refugees.[148]

Images of refugees streaming northwards across Europe, or maps showing the routes they were following and detailing the huge numbers involved, could get their message across about the risks arising from the crisis with scarce need for comment. For example, the *Daily Mail* of 16 April 2016 printed colourful maps and tables with a short article about migrants paying smugglers to lead them along old Alpine donkey paths to sneak into northern Europe, and possibly Britain.[149]

Nigel Farage's "breaking point" billboard for UKIP and Leave.eu that he unveiled on 16 June 2016, the same day as the Labour MP and Remain campaigner Jo Cox was murdered, was another image that conveyed directly without the need for comment the Brexit message of Britain being invaded. It showed a column of refugees snaking along a road in the Balkans with Nigel Farage in the foreground under the words "Breaking Point" and with a caption saying that the EU had "failed us all" and it was time to take back control.[150] Members of the official Leave campaign protested that the poster had gone too far, but in fact there was little difference between it and the picture of Albanians scrambling off a boat to shore alongside Michael Gove's article in the *Mail* of 30 April 2016. Both were intended to stir up xenophobia and fear of mass migration and both served the Leave campaign's purpose equally well.

The xenophobic tone of much the Brexit campaign on immigration was instrumental in a rise in hate speech against foreigners after the referendum and does not bode well for a calmer debate about immigration post Brexit.

7.4.4 EU Bureaucracy and Constant Power Grabs

Con Coughlin wrote in a *Daily Telegraph* column on 4 May 2016 about an asylum seeker who had committed suicide while in detention awaiting removal from Britain.[151] The asylum seeker had worked as a translator for the British army in Afghanistan and had not been granted leave to come to Britain after British troops left the country and ex-translators had become targets of the Taliban. Mr Dawoodzai had made his own way to Europe, arriving in Italy, where he had been fingerprinted. From there he had paid people smugglers to get him into Britain. However, the British Home Office had decided to deport him back to Italy under the "Dublin rule" whereby the country of first entry of a refugee into the EU is supposed to handle his asylum request. Mr Coughlin blamed "the EU's treatment of this deserving migrant" for his suicide. He had fallen foul of the "dead hand of the EU's bureaucracy." "Thanks to the EU," he had been denied the chance of making a better life for himself.

This misrepresented the facts. It was the British Home Office that had decided to deport the Afghan. It could have exercised its discretion to waive application of the "Dublin rule" (just as Mrs Merkel had done in September 2015 when she allowed 800,000 refugees first registered in Greece to continue their journey to Germany), and as Britain itself had regularly done for migrants entering the EU through Greece since 2011. No "Eurocrat" had had any part in the UK's decision. Britain was the Dublin rule's biggest fan, because it allowed the UK to get rid of some "illegal immigrants" that found the way to its shores after landing in southern Europe, and it was resisting the Commission's proposal to relax the rule to relieve pressure on the "frontline" countries bearing the brunt of irregular migration to Europe. Even the *Mail* correctly laid the blame for the Afghan's suicide while in a British detention centre squarely on the British Home Office. Mr Coughlin threw in a further warning about Islamic State terrorists entering Europe as a result of the planned relaxation of the visa requirement for 75 million Turkish citizens, which he said was going to happen "today," that is, 4 May 2016. (It still hasn't.) He concluded by claiming that as a member of the EU Britain was "subjugated to the will of Brussels" as to who can, or cannot, reside in our country. There might have been a grain of truth in this if the EU had had any part at all in the decision on such cases, but it did not.

Articles in the *Daily Express* on 7 and 8 March 2016, while not like Con Coughlin's distorting the context of EU rules and unfairly shifting blame for applying them on to the EU, returned to the familiar Brexiteer theme of Brussels power grabs. The articles attacked proposals by the Commission to expand the EU border and coast guard force and centralize asylum applications under an EU agency.[152] Besides both reports being premature, as the subsequent slow progress of the proposals through the Council of Ministers and European Parliament shows, they falsely claimed that the new arrangements would apply to Britain, despite its opt-out from the common asylum policy. The articles mentioned the opt-out, but cast doubt on government assurances that it would hold.

The *Daily Telegraph* of 22 April 2016 referred to the EU Border and Coast Guard proposal as "one of the biggest transfers of sovereignty since the creation of the euro" and claimed the member states' interior ministers had "agreed the plans," which was false.[153] The "transfer of sovereignty" probably referred to the proposal that the Commission would be able to deploy the border force in a member state without its agreement. As noted in the previous section, this proposal has been taken out of the current version of the draft legislation.

7.4.5 *"Uncontrolled" EU Migration Causing Strain on Public Services Highlighted, Controlled Non-EU Migration Running at a Similar Level Ignored*

The Brexit press and the Leave campaign were keen to inflate the extent of migration, especially "uncontrolled" migration from the EU. They avoided talking much about non-EU migration which the government did control, because net migration from outside the EU was running at around the same or above the level of the uncontrolled variety, so drawing attention to it would raise the question whether regaining the ability to control EU migration the same way as it already did with non-EU migration would actually have much effect on the total level.[154] Rather, it is likely that the British low-wage, low-productivity labour market will remain a strong pull factor, and until that changes reducing overall migration will hurt the economy.

The *Daily Telegraph* and *Daily Express* of 13 May 2016 both had front-page splashes of revelations about the "true" EU migrant figure which they said was between two and three times the official figure.[155] The "official" net migration figure was compiled from data on long-term migrants, defined as those staying for more than a year. The papers took the official figure for long-term net migration over the five years 2011–15 and compared it to a figure comprising the official long-term migration figure plus the number of short-term EU visitors who had come to the UK over the same period, which they claimed was the "true" figure. Short-term visitors are defined as those who come for under a year.

Adding the two figures together is nonsense since short-term visitors leave within a year. Allison Pearson, the *Telegraph*'s columnist, justified this by saying that while "Piotr the plumber" might have had no intention of staying on beyond a year, he might change his mind and stay after all. But this was not a valid argument because the long-term migration statistics are already adjusted by the Statistical Office of take account of the "switchers" she had in mind. She then repeated the stock refrain of blaming EU migrants for the pressure on services and housing—kids not getting into secondary schools of their choice, young people not getting on to the housing ladder, and pregnant women being turned away from maternity units. Such claims were sharply qualified by the Migration Advisory Committee when it investigated them for its 2018 report in which it made recommendations to the government for the future immigration policy (see Sect. 7.2 above).

The articles were thus an attempt to raise readers' anger level about migration from the EU and about the EU itself and fortify any reader who might be wobbling in their resolve to vote Leave. To do so they juggled figures to show EU migration as higher than it really was, ignored migration from Commonwealth countries or elsewhere in the world which, though completely under the government's control, was running at a similar level to EU net migration, and blamed the pressure on services and housing entirely on the former, the Poles, Romanians and Latvians, and not on the Indians, Australians and Chinese.

An article in the *Daily Mail* of 16 April 2016 played a similar trick with figures. Iain Duncan Smith was reported to have said in a campaign speech that:

> In the 12 months to the end of September last year [2015], there were 323,000 more arrivals than departures—up 31,000 in the year. Of the arrivals, 257,000 were from the EU.

If you go back to the migration statistics which are the source of the figures reportedly given by Mr Duncan Smith, the following picture emerges. That total net migration for EU and non-EU combined had been 323,000 was correct. It was also true that this was 31,000 up on the year up to September 2014, though the article failed to mention the fact that the figure had actually *fallen* by 13,000 since the peak of 336,000 in the year from June 2014 to June 2015. The really misleading part came in the final sentence, however.

The only other figure given in the article with which the reader would tend to compare the 257,000 figure was 323,000, the figure for the excess of arrivals over departures for both EU and non-EU migrants, or total net migration. The reader would conclude from this that the bulk of net migration, 257,000 out of 323,000, was from the EU. But this was not so. Net migration from the EU had been only 172,000 of the 323,000, not 257,000; the rest had been from outside the EU. This statistical sleight of hand thus inflated EU net migration by 50% and more than halved non-EU net migration, in order to prove to *Mail* readers—if further proof were needed—that the EU is mainly to blame for new immigration.[156]

A report in *Mail Online* on 3 April 2016, followed the next day by a similar story in the *Daily Mail*, also attributed the strain on medical services one-sidedly to EU migrants. The NHS was nearly "at breaking point" with General Practitioners having had to take on 1.5 million extra patients in just three years. The headline avoided saying the 1.5 million increase was *due to* the "massive influx of EU migrants," but this was the clear implication. After the fact-checking website *InFacts* complained that the implication of the headline was false as the facts did not support it, the *Mail* withdrew the article and republished a corrected version with a new headline attributing the misinterpretation solely to the Leave campaign. The original headline was wrong because the source of the figures, the Health & Social Care Information Centre, did not record the nationality of patients, so how many of the increased number of patients were EU migrants, new non-EU migrants, or older British-born or immigrant patients who were nowadays living longer, was not known.[157]

A story in the *Daily Mail* of 16 April 2016 was about "health tourism," another favourite theme strongly but not exclusively associated with the EU.[158] It reported several problems arising from EU visitors getting health care in Britain which were due to its lack of a requirement for identity cards. EU visitors who get health care in Britain might well have come to the country on holiday and have fallen ill, and thus not be "health tourists" who have come specially to sponge off the NHS, so the term in the headline of the article was a misnomer.

The first of the problems with EU visitors getting NHS treatment is that such visitors cannot be required to produce a European Health Insurance Card or other identification when they register with a GP where this is not required of other patients, as it would be discriminatory. Once they have registered with a doctor they can get free treatment from an NHS hospital. This leads to a second problem: if the EU patient does not have an EHIC card or other identification, the NHS after treating him or her will be unable to claim back the cost of treatment from his or her country of origin. The result is that the NHS only claims back around £50 million a year from EU countries for treating their citizens, whereas other EU countries claim back £750 million from Britain for treatment of Brits who fall sick abroad, because they have to show identification. All EU countries except, Britain, Ireland and Denmark require ID cards. Frank Field, campaigning for Leave, told the paper Mr Cameron had not raised this in his renegotiation, suggesting that it was an EU problem. But it is a purely British one. The article also reported a scam the paper had investigated the previous year whereby EU visitors could come to Britain, obtain a British EHIC card and then use the card to obtain free treatment in their home county, with the hospital then claiming the cost of the treatment from Britain.

Most people skimming through the article or just glancing at the headline and subhead would conclude this was another case of Britain being ripped off by the EU. The quote from Frank Field referring to the Cameron renegotiation confirmed this misleading impression. It has nothing to do with the EU. It has everything to do with Britain's nonsensical aversion to identity cards.

The Sun had made its position on what Cameron should be negotiating from the EU regarding immigration with a threatening front-page splash on 18 December 2013. It featured a huge red line across Europe between Britain and the Continent and warning Cameron to "stop the flood—OR ELSE."[159]

7.5   OUTLOOK—IMMIGRATION POLICY AFTER BREXIT

Immigration was part of the potent brew of dissatisfaction that led to Brexit. It combined with rapid changes in society due to globalization and a long period of austerity which had hit living standards and choked off investment in public services. Many in the old industrial heartlands, coastal towns and rural areas of England and Wales felt abandoned and ignored by the government. The EU was a scapegoat for this dissatisfaction, groomed for this role by years of propaganda by a right-wing press pursuing a long-term Brexit agenda. Increased immigration from Europe had turned up as a convenient further issue with which to steer public discontent and anxiety against their target.

Dissatisfaction about immigration appears to have abated since the referendum,[160] probably because the campaign is over and neither Brexiteer politicians nor the press see the need to hype up the issue anymore,[161] and also because there are fewer EU migrants around with less arriving and more leaving, and the old ones still there have settled down and become more accepted.

Assuming Brexit takes place, the country has an opportunity to reshape its immigration policy. The government has set the process in train, but the debate has hardly begun.[162] With Brexit out of the way, the Conservative party and the right-wing press will no longer have an axe to grind and could potentially play a constructive part. The *Telegraph* already reflects both sides of the debate—the needs of the economy including science and technology and the creative industries, which militate for a continued supply of immigrants, on the one hand, and social cohesion and stability arguing for restriction, on the other. The other right-wing newspapers will have a much harder job to rebalance their output towards a fairer discussion of the pros and cons of migration. If they decide to stick with the nationalism and xenophobia they fostered during the referendum, the debate will again be fraught and emotional. If a sensible policy is to emerge, the public conversation about immigration must cease to be so polarized. The Migration Advisory Committee's report is a good basis but its conclusions and recommendations and the Government's proposals in the White Paper need to be properly discussed in the press, in parliament and between think tanks taking opposite sides of the argument, on the basis of evidence, not dogmatism and preconceptions.

The main issues seem to be balancing the needs of the economy with social cohesion, including ensuring public investment in communities and improving education and training for the indigenous population.[163] Quantitative targets have not proved practical or sensible and must go.[164] Students must be taken out of the figures. The issue of maintaining a supply of lower-skilled migration where it is still needed will be difficult.[165] A more tolerant administrative environment towards all immigrants, regular, irregular, and refugees, must be developed.[166] The handling of settled status for EU migrants already here will be a test. Britain has absorbed refugees and immigrants smoothly before and can do so again. The nettle of ID cards needs to be grasped.[167]

In the event Britain does not leave the EU, it should consider what it could do better in future to control EU migration. There are plenty of things it could do within the present rules and probably there will be more scope for reforming free movement in a cooperative spirit than David Cameron found possible in the adversarial atmosphere that prevailed during the renegotiation.[168] There needs to be a discussion of free movement within the EU in any case. Reconciling the different interests of the send-ing and host member states in free movement could help overcome the polarization of attitudes towards irregular migration and refugees. The same two sets of countries are on opposite sides in relation to both issues.

When the migrant crisis in Europe broke in 2015, the Hungarian-born American business magnate and philanthropist George Soros reminded us that the world had dealt with big movements of refugees before:

> After the 1956 Soviet invasion, 200,000 Hungarians fled to Austria and Yugoslavia; within months almost all had been resettled in countries as far flung as the US, Australia, Brazil and Tunisia. A generation later, when war scattered millions in Indochina, the international community resettled 1.3 million. In the 1990s, the Balkan conflicts displaced almost 4 million people, and again the world helped.

He called for a remaking of the EU's migration system to reflect a more collective and generous spirit, and one that is more faithful to European values.[169]

Almost every nation in Europe has once been refugees. Europe has long been an exporter of people to other continents as well as an uninvited colonizer. Migration has been and still is a two-way street. And we are an ageing and demographically declining continent. Migrants and refugees should not be seen as a problem but as a wanted resource.

The British population is as racially mixed as that of any other country. Some ancient Britons had dark to black skin.[170] Roman Britain was ethni-cally diverse.[171] Our linguistic heritage, too, is varied. Britain has minority languages that have retreated into enclaves, multiple regional variants of English, and languages introduced by recent immigrants. Diversity is nothing to be afraid of.

NOTES

1. Office of National Statistics. 2018. Overview of the UK population. November 2018.
2. Office of National Statistics. 2018. Annual Population Survey 2018; see also *The Economist*. 2018. Enoch Powell, race and migration—Fifty years down-river. 21 April.
3. Davidson, Ruth. 2017. *Daily Telegraph*. 8 August.
4. Migration Observatory. 2018. Impact of migration on UK population growth. 24 January. Past migration also influences natural change (differ-ence in births over deaths).

5. *Financial Times.* 2017. May renews pledge to lower immigration below 100,000. 9 May.
6. Migration Observatory. 2018. Net migration in the UK. 24 August.
7. The ONS had forecast that only 5000–13,000 would arrive each year.
8. *The Economist.* 2017. Immigration: Return journey. 16 September; Clegg, Nick. 2017. Squaring the Brexit circle on freedom of movement. *Financial Times.* 4 July; *The Guardian.* 2015. How immigration came to haunt Labour: the inside story. 24 March.
9. *The Economist.* 2017. Immigration: Return journey. 16 September.
10. *Financial Times.* 2016. City urges 'open' philosophy on immigration. 5 October; *The Economist.* 2018. Enoch Powell, race and integration: Fifty years down-river. 21 April.
11. Sproul, David. 2017. Best and brightest must be welcome post-Brexit. *Daily Telegraph.* 27 June; *Financial Times.* 2017. 26 May.
12. *Daily Telegraph.* 2017. Hunt: keeping EU workers in NHS is top priority. 16 June.
13. *London Evening Standard.* 2017. East Europeans vital to UK economy, says ONS report. 10 July.
14. In a letter to the *Daily Telegraph* published on 13 April 2017 a reader sarcastically notes that with an 86% activity rate among EU migrants aged 16–64, compared with 75% for the UK population as a whole, the latter rate will surely drop once "all those lazy EU migrants are sent home."
15. *Daily Telegraph.* 2017. Officials lose quarter of a million migrants each year. 16 June.
16. Migration Observatory. 2018. Net migration in the UK. 24 August; *Financial Times.* 2017. UK business fears labour crunch as Europeans head home. 26 May; *Daily Telegraph.* 2017. Eastern Europeans shun UK after Brexit vote. 26 May; Evans-Pritchard, Ambrose. 2017. Migration is yesterday's concern now eastern Europe is booming. *Daily Telegraph.* 6 July.
17. *Financial Times.* 2017. Homeward bound: Polish ministers predict a rush of returnees. 26 April.
18. MacShane, Denis. 2017. *Brexit, No Exit: Why (In the End) Britain Won't Leave Europe*, 199. London: Bloomsbury; reader's letter to *Financial Times*, 26 October 2017; interview with Gordon Ramsay. *Daily Telegraph.* 2017. 10 October.
19. MacShane, ibid., 196–199.
20. *Financial Times.* 2017. Reader's letter: CEE suffers as EU skims off its best and brightest. 6 July.
21. Clarke, Harold D., Matthew Goodwin and Paul Whiteley. 2017. *Brexit: Why Britain Voted to Leave the European Union.* Cambridge: Cambridge University Press.

22. *The Economist.* 2018. 21 April, op. cit.
23. See Hirsch. Afua. 2018. *Brit(ish).* On Race, Identity and Belonging, 25, 119–125. London: Vintage; and the comments of the ex-Liverpool and England footballer John Barnes on BBC 1's *Question Time* of 21 February 2019 about Liam Neeson's confession of feelings of racial hatred.
24. Heath, Allister. 2017. *Daily Telegraph.* The Conservatives must not let Britain's jobs miracle turn sour. 18 May; *Financial Times.* 2017. May renews pledge to lower immigration target to below 100,000. 3 May.
25. *The Guardian.* 2015. 6 October, editorial. See also letter from Dr David Webster to the *Financial Times.* 2017. 15 November, saying that large-scale and sudden migration flows can destabilize a country socially and politically.
26. *The Times.* 2017. May forced to weaken key target on migrants. 20 April, and 2018. Pressure on May over 'migrant' students. 3 January.
27. *The Economist.* 2018. Identity crisis. 5 May; Ganesh, Janan. 2018. Measured May succumbs to tawdry migrant pose. *Financial Times.* 24 April. A "dehumanized" approach towards immigration enforcement continued under Mrs May's own government, illustrated by the "Windrush" scandal and rushed deportation decisions that were frequently overturned on appeal: *Financial Times.* 2018. Union hits out at 'dehumanised' Home Office approach to migration. 18 May; *The Economist.* 2018. Bagehot: A hostile environment. 28 April; *Helsingin Sanomat.* 2018. Heti ulos Britianniasta, jossa asuit 50 vuotta ("Get out of Britain, where you've lived for 50 years"). 21 April.
28. Migration Advisory Committee. 2018. EEA Migration in the UK: Final Report. September.
29. Ibid., Executive Summary, paras 17 and 25.
30. Ibid., Executive Summary, paras 22–23.
31. Ibid., Executive Summary, para. 24.
32. Ibid., Executive Summary, para. 20.
33. Ibid., Executive Summary, paras 26–28.
34. Ibid., Executive Summary, para. 18.
35. Ibid., Executive Summary, paras 7–8. See also Brown, Gordon. 2016. *Britain: Leading, not Leaving: The Patriotic Case for Remaining in Europe*, 260–261. Selkirk: Deerpark Press.
36. Migration Advisory Committee. 2018. EEA Migration in the UK: Final Report. September, Introduction, paras 23–24.
37. Speech to the Conservative party conference, 5 October 2015.
38. See Chap. 5, Sect. 5.3.4.
39. For example, the European Globalization Adjustment Fund, see UK Government. 2013. Review of Balance of Competences, Cohesion Policy, paras 132–133. Whether the new EU Asylum, Migration and Integration

Fund will fare any better in Britain remains to be seen. At least it has been publicized: Gov.UK website, 19 December 2018.

40. Kaufmann, Eric. 2018. *Whiteshift: Populism, Immigration and the Future of White Majorities.* London: Allen Lane.

41. Goodhart, David. 2017. *The Road to somewhere: The populist revolt and the future of politics.* London: Hurst; also Goodhart, David. *Financial Times.* 2016. May promises a bit more state and a little less 'anything goes'. 10 October, and *Daily Telegraph.* 2016. Britain won't heal its divisions as long as the clever are too powerful. 11 October. See also Luce, Edward. *Financial Times.* 2017. 6 July.

42. Dr Anna Rowlands and Shelina Janmohamed on BBC- Radio 4, *Sunday,* 30 December 2018, special edition on immigration and religion.

43. *The Economist.* 2016. Integration nation. 21 May. *Daily Telegraph.* 2017. Editorial: UK is a good place to be an immigrant. 11 October.

44. Freedland, Jonathan. 2017. The Road to Somewhere by David Goodhart—a liberal's right-wing turn on immigration. *The Guardian.* 22 March; Taylor, Paul. 2018. How Britain made me a citizen of nowhere. *Politico.* 16 May; Ganesh, Janan. *Financial Times.* 2018. Measured May succumbs to tawdry migration pose. 24 April; letter of Dimitris Vayenas to *Financial Times,* 29 June 2017, hoping "that [the UK] will not sacrifice its noblest of values and most precious—albeit impossible to quantify—assets, such as soft power, on the altar of transient populism and pettiness." See also O'Toole, Fintan. 2018. *Heroic Failure: Brexit and the Politics of Pain,* 148. New York: Apollo.

45. Moore, Charles. 2017. This country has come through many a crisis, but this one is a true shemozzle. *Daily Telegraph.* 24 June.

46. Pearson, Allison. 2017. *Daily Telegraph.* 24 June. Whether all these nurses back in the good old days of 1972 were all British-born is another question, however: many were immigrants from the Windrush generation. But at least they were not all called Magda and from Riga!

47. As in its editorial of 11 October 2017: UK is a good place to be an immigrant.

48. See *Daily Telegraph.* 2018. Million new EU citizens get UK rights. 10 April. The article reported that a total of 995,000 immigrants had been granted the citizenship of EU member countries in 2016. Some 90% of them were from non-EU countries or were stateless. For 150,000 of the new EU citizens the citizenship they had been granted was that of the UK, so presumably they were already living in Britain. Certainly, the remainder granted the citizenship of other EU countries had thereby acquired the freedom of movement right to live and work in the UK. But that they would do so was no more likely than that the 440 million original inhabitants of the other 27 member states would come to Britain.

49. Davidson, Ruth. 2017. It is time to give the British people a mature debate on immigration. *Daily Telegraph.* 8 August.
50. Evans-Pritchard, Ambrose. 2017. Migration is yesterday's concern—now eastern Europe is booming. *Daily Telegraph.* 6 July; Heath, Allister. 2017. The Conservatives must not let Britain's job miracle turn sour. *Daily Telegraph.* 18 May. See also *Daily Telegraph* editorial, 11 October 2017, referred to above.
51. *The Economist.* 2018. Bagehot: A hostile environment. 28 April.
52. Individual journalists, however, have not shrunk from raising sensitive issues, for example Islamisation: Melanie Phillips, the *Mail* and *Times* columnist, in her 2007 book. *Londinistan: How Britain is Creating a Terror State Within.* New York: Encounter Books.
53. *Mail Online.* 2014. Your benefits system is crazy. 14 February; *Daily Express.* 2014. Kick out all foreign benefit cheats. 28 August; *The Sun.* 2013. EU are kidding—Brussels: UK's 600,000 benefit tourists is no problem. 21 October. *The Sun* subsequently issued a correction to this story admitting that the 600,000 figure was wrong; its editor said that the paper was pro positive immigration—its chairman Rupert Murdoch was an immigrant: see *The Guardian.* 2013. Sun benefits tourism gaffe may have resulted from a subbing error! 13 November.
54. Migration Observatory. 2014. Costs and 'Benefits': Benefits tourism, what does it mean? 21 February.
55. *Mail Online.* 2016. Curbing benefits paid to EU workers is unlikely to lead to a dramatic reduction in migration, a report claims today. 4 May.
56. Migration Watch UK's announcements, like those of the Brexit tabloids and UKIP, sensationalize the issue, such as its warning that a million EU nationals could come to Britain during a two-year transition period (*Financial Times.* 2018. 1 February), or that current rates of migration are equivalent to having to build a city the size of Birmingham every four years. The Migration Advisory Committee put the latter figure into perspective by saying it is the same as two extra people coming to live on a 100-person street over a period of five years (Migration Advisory Committee. 2018. EEA Migration in the UK: Final Report. September, Introduction, para. 21).
57. In 2016, the AfD adopted an explicitly anti-Islam policy, *BBC News.* 2016. 1 May, taking over from the popular "Pegida" ("Patriotic Europeans against the Islamization of the West") movement in eastern Germany: *BBC News.* 2015. 6 January; *Financial Times.* 2015. The Pegida people are reshaping German politics. 16 February. In the September 2017 general elections AfD became the third-biggest party in the *Bundestag* with 92 seats: *Financial Times.* 2017. A test of compassion. 20 September, and 2017. Wrath of the eastern periphery. 30 September.

58. See *The Economist.* 2015. Terror and Islam, 24. 17 January. Nigel Farage has been accused of hate speech by a Roma MEP: *Observer.* 2014. 22 June. In 2018 UKIP, under their new leader Gerard Batten, veered towards an anti-Islam position, adopting a policy similar to Trump's of screening all Muslim immigrants for Islamic extremism: *Sky News.* 2018. 21 September. The former far-right English Defence League activist Tommy Robinson had become associated with the party: *BBC News.* 2018. 23 November. Nigel Farage has since left the party and founded a new one, the "Brexit Party."

59. *The Guardian.* 2018. Sayeeda Warsi calls for inquiry into islamophobia in Conservative party. 4 July.

60. *BBC News.* 2016. Refugees at highest ever level, reaching 65m, says UN. 20 June.

61. Eurostat, Asylum Statistics.

62. *BBC News.* 2016. Some 885,000 migrants crossed from Turkey to Greece and 150,000 from Libya to Italy. 20 June.

63. *The Economist.* 2016. Special Report on Migration, 7. 28 May. See also Kingsley, Patrick. 2017. *The new Odyssey: the story of Europe's refugee crisis.* London: Guardian Faber.

64. *The Economist.* 2016. Special Report on Migration, 3. 28 May, and 2015. Charlemagne: Best served cold. 10 October. However, the EU had made proposals in reaction to warning signs as early as 2010: EU Commission, IP/11/532.

65. According to the UNHCR in 2014 170,000 refugees arrived in Italy but only 43,300 in Greece: UNHCR. 2015. The sea route to Europe: The Mediterranean passage in the age of refugees. 1 July.

66. For example, in Croatia, *Financial Times.* 2015. Growing migrant crisis threatens to raise old ghosts of Balkan wars. 6 November. The acts of kindness of the ordinary population of Hungary towards the refugees contrasted with the hard-heartedness of their government.

67. *BBC News.* 2016. Schengen: Controversial EU free movement deal explained. 25 January. Controls were also reintroduced on the Denmark-Sweden border: *The Economist.* 2015. Charlemagne: Bridge of sneers. 5 December.

68. Thousands of migrants were camped on the northern border with Macedonia, which had erected a fence to stop people crossing, and on the island of Lesbos there was no medical treatment for newly arrived refugees who were sick including babies, women and young children: *BBC News.* 2015. Migrant crisis: Greece denies Schengen threat from EU. 3 December; *Financial Times.* 2016. Europe turns its back on Greece over refugees (editorial). 29 February.

69. *Reuters.* 2017. Asylum requests in Austria more than halved in 2016. 15 January. See also *BBC News.* 2016. Migrant crisis: Austria's Plan B to cap

influx of refugees. 21 January, and *Financial Times*. 2016. Brussels criticizes Austria for capping asylum applications. 19 February.

70. *Financial Times*. 2015. Schäuble warns of refugee 'avalanche.' 13 November; *The Economist*. 2016. Charlemagne: An ill wind. 23 January; *The Guardian*. 2017. Germany: Merkel agrees to 200,000 refugee cap in bid to build coaltion. 9 October.

71. *The Economist*. 2015. Europe's boat people. 25 April. In April, 800 boat people were drowned off Libya in a single incident. It was claimed that the scaling down in search and rescue efforts after the replacement of the Italian Mare Nostrum scheme by the more limited Triton operation run by the EU border agency Frontex had contributed to the increase in deaths. Some EU member states including Britain had been against expanding search and rescue operations on the ground that they encouraged people to risk the dangerous crossing. See also *Financial Times*. 2015. EU migration chief urges member states to share burden of refugees. 6 May.

72. BBC's Europe editor Katya Adler's dispatches on the migrant crisis posted on *BBC News* voiced her frustration at the inability of the EU to act quickly to prevent severe hardship being suffered by refugees on their journey and to provide relief to national authorities bearing the brunt of the influx while other countries looked away. See, for example, 16 June 2015, "EU solidarity damaged by splits on migrants and Greece;" 19 October 2015, "Long winter ahead for migrant crisis;" 27 February 2016, "Why Europe is in a 'Scream'." The frustration was justified but unfortunately the underdeveloped legal framework limited the EU's means of action. Appealing to member states' good will or trying to knock heads together in such a situation is not always enough. See *The Economist*. 2015. Charlemagne: A walk down solidarity street. 13 June.

73. See *Financial Times*. 2015. Big read: Migration. Barbed rhetoric. 27 November.

74. France stood aside, for fear of attack by Marine Le Pen of the anti-immigrant National Front party: *The Economist*. 2015. Charlemagne: The dispensable French. 7 November. It took only 24,000 migrants.

75. Britain has an opt-out from the Justice and Home Affairs provisions of the Lisbon Treaty which covers asylum policy. However, it has opted into the "Dublin rules" which lay down the principle that the country in which an asylum seeker first enters EU territory is responsible for dealing with his asylum application and that other countries to which the asylum seeker makes an asylum request can return him to the first country. With most asylum seekers from the Middle East and Africa entering the EU through southern Europe by land or sea, the Dublin rule reduces the number of applications the UK needs to deal with. Since 2003 the UK

has been able to return 12,000 migrants to other EU countries by virtue of the "Dublin rule": *BBC News*. 2016. Cameron faces refugee 'burden' battle as EU draws up new scheme. 20 January.

76. In May 2015 the Commission issued a "European Agenda on Migration," and in May and June 2016 two further packages of legislative proposals to advance the "Common European Asylum System" (CEAS). See the useful guide in European Parliament. 2019. Fact Sheets on the European Union, Asylum Policy; see also European Commission. 2018. Managing Migration: Possible areas for agreement at the June European Council. June.

77. *BBC News*. 2015. Mediterranean migrant crisis: EU to hold emergency summit. 23 April; European Council. 2015. Special meeting on Mediterranean, 23 April 2015; *The Economist*. 2015. Briefing: Europe's boat people. 25 April.

78. In 2018 the assumption of power by a new government in Italy brought the situation in the central Mediterranean back into the limelight, with the populist interior minister from the anti-immigrant League party Matteo Salvini refusing to let rescue ships dock in Italy and calling for migrant processing centres away from Italy. *BBC News*. 2018. Migrant crisis: Mediterranean crossings deadlier than ever—UNHCR. 3 September.

79. *The Economist*. 2015. Charlemagne: Small boats, choppy seas. 16 May.

80. COM (2015) 490 final. See *Financial Times*. 2015. Juncker plan on migrants deserves full backing (editorial). 10 September.

81. European Commission. 2015. Western Balkans Migrant Route. 25 October. *Financial Times*. 2015. Growing migrant crisis threatens to raise old ghosts of Balkan wars. 6 November.

82. European Council, meeting of 28–29 June, 2018, Conclusions. In defence of quotas Daniel Gros, Centre for European Policy Studies, Brussels, letter to *Financial Times*, 29 September 2015. *The Economist* was sceptical of the quota plan because the numbers of migrants to be relocated were irrelevant seen against the total scale of arrivals and not worth the bad blood they were causing: *The Economist*. 2015. Charlemagne: Small boats, choppy seas. 16 May; 2015. Charlemagne: The birth-pangs of a policy. 25 July; 2015. Charlemagne: Point taken, Mr Orban. 26 September; 2016. Special Report on Migration, 16. 28 May.

83. European Parliament. 2018. Briefing: 'Hotspots' at EU external borders. June 14. In response to the refusal of the new Italian government that took office in May 2018 to accept asylum seekers arriving from Africa, the European Council at a meeting on migration on 28–29 June 2018 agreed to the idea of member states setting up "controlled centres" on a voluntary basis, which unlike the "hotpots" would be enclosed. For the same

purpose, the European Council also agreed to explore the possibility of EU-funded "regional disembarkation platforms" in North Africa: European Council, meeting of 28–29 June 2018. See *The Economist*. 2018. Charlemagne: For those in peril on the sea. 15 September.

84. A three-year €700m package: *The Economist*. 2016. 5 March.
85. EU Commission, EU Regional Trust Fund in Response to Syrian Crisis, 17 December 2018. A letter to *The Economist* from a reader in Beirut compared the situation of Lebanon hosting a number of refugees equivalent to a third of its previous population with the infinitely better resourced Europe struggling to take a million, 0.2% of the population. See also Peter Sutherland, UN Special Representative for International Migration and former member of the EU Commission and director-general of the WTO, *Financial Times*. 2016. Europe has turned a tragedy into a needless political crisis. 22 May.
86. *The Economist*. 2016. Special Report Migration, 13. 28 May; *Financial Times*. 2016. Leaders pledge billions in aid to alleviate migration crisis. 5 February; *BBC News*. 2017. Who really gives the most to help Syria? 10 February.
87. European Council, 18 March 2016, EU-Turkey statement, press release 144/16. *The Economist*. 2016. A messy but necessary deal. 12 March; 2016. All quiet on the Aegean front. 16 April; 2016. Visa liberalization: Europe's murky deal with Turkey. 28 May; *BBC News*. 2016. EU-Turkey migrant deal: A Herculean task. 18 March. Critical: *BBC News*. 2016. Turkey has EU over a barrel. 17 March; and letter from Alan Sked, former leader of UKIP, to *Financial Times*. 2016. 22 March.
88. See European Commission, EU-Turkey Statement. Two years on, April 2018. However, child labour is widespread, *Financial Times*. 2017. A day on the factory floor for a young refugee. 20 September, and the amount of aid provided for education is tiny by western standards: *BBC News*. 2017. Who really gives the most to help Syria? 10 February. The living conditions of migrants on the Greek islands in 2016 were hardly better: *The Guardian*. 2016. Pope follows thousands of volunteers to Greek island at frontline of migrant crisis. 16 April; *The Guardian*. 2016. Greek islands feel the heat in Europe's migrant crisis. 29 August.
89. Turkey still does not meet a number of conditions that the EU set, in particular amendment of its restrictive anti-terrorism law introduced after a failed coup attempt in 2016. It is feared that Turks, or Syrians that have acquired Turkish passports, could enter the EU without visas and then apply for asylum. *The Economist*. 2016. Visa liberalization: Europe's murky deal with Turkey. 28 May; *Financial Times*. 2016. Turkey faces tough obstacles in EU visa talks. 2 May.
90. Council of the European Union, General Affairs meeting on 26 June 2018.

91. European Commission, International Cooperation and Development, EU Emergency Trust Fund for Africa; *BBC News*. 2015. Migrant crisis: Swedish border checks introduced. 12 November.
92. EU External Action, EU-Libya Relations, 9 November 2018. *BBC News*. 2017. Migrant crisis: EU summit seeks action plan with Libya. 3 February.
93. *The Economist*. 2015. Forward defence: How Spain deals with migrants. 17 October; *The Economist*, 2016. Special Report Migration, 16. 28 May.
94. Council of the European Union, press release 20 February 2019 announcing finalization of the legislation in the Council of Ministers and the start of negotiations with the Parliament. Cf. original proposal, *Financial Times*. 2015. Brussels plans new force to police external borders. 11 December; *The Economist*. European borders: A real border guard at last. See also Soros, George. By failing to help refugees Europe fails itself. *Financial Times*. 2015. 27 July.
95. See European Commission, State of the Union 2018, A reinforced European Agency for Asylum, 12 September 2018. See also George Soros, op. cit.
96. Since 2010 Sweden, Germany and the UK had in practice not been returning asylum seekers to Greece because of the unsatisfactory conditions there and national courts in most member states and the European Court of Human Rights had accepted appeals against planned returns to Greece: *Financial Times*. 2010. Migrant crisis in Greece strains EU open borders. 21 December, and 2011. EU migration: Asylum can test policy on borders. 22 January. See also *Helsingin Sanomat*. 2013. EU:lta puuttuu maahanmuuttolinja ("EU lacks migration policy"). 25 August.
97. Readings from Hans Rosling (Rosling, Hans. 2018. *Factfulness: Ten reasons we're wrong about the world and why things are better than you think*. London: Sceptre, Hodder and Stoughton.) on BBC Radio 4, 2–6 April 2018.
98. Were it to stay in the EU, the UK would be faced with the difficult choice of agreeing to the reformed Dublin rules, involving compulsory quotas in some circumstances but possibly retaining the right to deport asylum seekers arriving elsewhere, or opting out of the new Dublin rules completely, which would mean losing its present right of deportation which it uses extensively. Since 2003 the UK has been able to return 12,000 migrants to other EU countries by virtue of the "Dublin rule": *BBC News*. 2016, Cameron faces refugee 'burden' battle as EU draws up new scheme. 20 January. See also *Financial Times*. 2016. Brussels plans radical asylum overhaul. 7 March, and 2016. Dublic regulation: EU states face charge for refusing to take refugees. 4 May. The UK has sometimes invoked the "Dublin rule" to keep migrants out of the UK even when they have relatives in Britain: *Daily Telegraph*. 2016. Calais migrants can join siblings in UK. 27 January.

99. Countries belonging the Schengen area—that is, all EU Member States except the UK, Ireland, Bulgaria, Romania and Croatia, but including the non-EU countries Norway and Switzerland—no longer carry out checks on persons crossing the border to another country within the Schengen area.

100. *The Economist*. 2015. Europe starts putting up walls. 19 September; 2015. After Paris, drawbridges up? 19 September; *Financial Times*. 2015. Europe heads for jam over loss of passport-free travel. 27 November; *BBC News*. 2015. Paris attacks: The crisis of Europe's borders. 18 November.

101. *Financial Times*. 2015. Merkel studies lessons of past influx to integrate newcomers. 18 September; *The Economist*. 2015. Integrating refugees in Europe: More toil, less trouble. 12 December; 2015. German immigration: All down the line. 19 December; 2016. Educating refugees: Learning the hard way. 2 January; 2016. The economic impact of refugees: For good or ill. 23 January; and 2016. Special Report Migration, 8–10. 28 May; *Financial Times*. 2015. German employers pessimistic about the chances of finding work for low-skilled refugees. 27 November; *BBC News*. 2015. How one city in Germany is coping. 10 November.

102. *Guardian Weekly*. 2016. Refugee crisis: Dial down the rhetoric. 29 January.

103. *Financial Times*. 2015. Arson raises fears of upsurge in anti-refugee prejudice. 13 April; 2016. Welcome wears thin. 30 July; 2017. Nearly 10 attacks a day on migrants in Germany. 29 February; *The Economist*. 2015. Is Tröglitz everywhere?. 18 April; 2016. Integration panic. 20 August; 2016. Attack in Berlin: The spectre of terror. 24 December.

104. *The Economist*. 2015. Briefing: Terror and Islam. 17 January; 2015. Anti-immigrant populism: The march of Europe's little Trumps. 12 December; 2016. Special Report Migration, 6. 28 May; *Financial Times*. 2016. Hard-headed humanity can save Merkel. 29 January, in which Philip Stephens speaks of the danger of leaders appearing to have lost control of events, when refugees can come to be equated with terrorists. Readmission agreements with the countries of failed asylum seekers are part of gaining control and regaining confidence: *The Economist*. 2015. Charlemagne: The birth-pangs of a policy. 25 July.

105. *BBC News*. 2019. Crossing Divides: Has the UK changed its mind on immigration? 4 March.

106. Which it was according to the former Australian prime minister Tony Abbott, see *BBC News*. 2015. Ex-Australian PM Abbott tells Europe to close borders. 28 October.

107. *TIME*, 21 December 2015.

108. *The Economist*. 2015. The indispensable European. 7 November.

109. For example, Collier, Paul. 2016. Merkel's open door has harmed those it was meant to help. *Financial Times*. 5 February, and Münchau, Wolfgang. 2016. The EU sells its soul to strike a deal with Turkey. 21 March.
110. Rachman, Gideon. 2016. Merkel's power is unravelling across Europe. *Financial Times*. 15 March.
111. Paul Collier, op. cit.
112. *The Economist*. 2015. Charlemagne: Refugee realpolitik. 24 October.
113. *Financial Times*. 2015. Do not blame Merkel for the refugees. 2 October.
114. *The Economist*. 2015. Exodus, and Charlemagne: Leading from the front. 12 September; 2015. The indispensable European. 7 November; 2016. Briefing: Europe's migrant crisis: "Only Mrs Merkel appears to think beyond the constraints of national politics." 6 February. See also *BBC News*. 2015. 8 October, reporting Mrs Merkel's address to the European Parliament, in which she called on everyone to "see immigrants as people."
115. Krastev, Ivan. 2016. Fear and loathing of a world without borders. *Financial Times*. 7 April, an argument similar to those of Kaufmann and Goodhart. Krastev, Ivan. 2017. *After Europe*. Philadelphia: University of Pennsylvania Press.
116. Sutherland, Peter. 2015. Europe has turned a tragedy into a needless political crisis. *Financial Times*. 22 May; and *The Economist*. 2015. Exodus. 12 September.
117. *The Economist*. 2015. Migration and labour markets: More vacancies than visitors. 19 September; *Financial Times*. 2015. EU claims refugee influx will boost growth. 20 November.
118. *BBC News*. 2017. Who really gives most to help Syria? 10 February.
119. *BBC News*. 2016. Cameron faces refugee burden battle as EU draws up new scheme. 20 January; and 2017. Who really gives most to help Syria? 10 February.
120. David Cameron was instrumental in getting the EU to boost spending on the World Food Programme, the UN refugee agency and aid to Syria's neighbours: *The Economist*. 2015. Charlemagne: Point taken, Mr Orban. 26 September. *BBC News*. 2017. Who really gives most to help Syria? 10 February.
121. And not a complete ban on EU workers receiving non-contributory in-work benefits for four years but only a graduated phasing-in of their eligibility for such benefits, and the restriction would apply to EU workers arriving over only the next seven years and not the 13 he had asked for: *BBC News*. 2016. What Cameron wanted and what he got. 20 February.
122. *The Economist* predicted that the migrant crisis and the EU's—a slightly harsh judgment, this—"mismanagement" of it would make the case for

staying in the EU harder: 2015. Europe's migrant crisis: Shooting Schengen. 19 September; also 2015. The indispensable European. 7 November.

123. See Shipman, Tim. 2017. *All Out War: The Full Story of Brexit*, 366 *et seq.* London: William Collins.

124. Piras, Annalisa. 2016. Read all about it! Brexit press coverage skewed. *InFacts.* 23 May, and Lythgoe, Luke, and Hugo Dixon. 2016. Press' hateful 8 stories from Brexit debate. *InFacts.* 19 May. A survey by the Oxford Reuters Institute of Journalism found that pro-Leave stories carried by the newspapers exceeded pro-Remain articles by 45% to 27%.

125. "Our spies can no longer keep track of terrorists: Brussels must tighten checks on migrants, not lecture member states on taking more of them."

126. Nigel's figure was half a million, however: *BBC News.* 2015. Nigel Farage: EU asylum plan could let in extremists. 29 April.

127. The *Daily Telegraph.* 2016. Open borders let Isil into Britain, warns US spy chief. 29 April, had a similarly misleading story, which was repeated in *Mail Online* and the *Daily Express: InFacts.* 2016. Press' hateful 8 stories from Brexit debate. 19 May.

128. *BBC News.* 2016. EU referendum: Brussels attacks spark UK security debate. 24 March, and 2016. Row as ex-intelligence chiefs say EU membership protects UK security. 8 May.

129. See Political Declaration setting out the framework for the future relationship between the European Union and the United Kingdom, Part III: Security Partnership.

130. *InFacts.* 2016. Press' hateful 8 stories from Brexit debate. 19 May, *Mail Online* story headlined "Britain could stop ten times more terror suspects from entering the country if it leaves the EU, justice minister says as he blasts EU rules for allowing terrorists to 'waltz into Britain.'"

131. *InFacts.* 2016. Press' hateful 8 stories from Brexit debate. 19 May, *Daily Telegraph*, 6 and 17 February 2016, "The daughter-in-law of Abu Hamza cannot be deported from Britain despite a criminal past because of human rights laws, an EU law chief has ruled," and "More than 700 offences are being committed by EU migrants every week, official figures suggest." On the *Telegraph's* breach of the IPSO code see *Press Gazette*, 3 May 2016. The European Court of Justice's ruling on the Abu Hamza daughter-in-law deportation case in September 2016 turned out to be broadly in line with the advice of its Advocate General. It found that Britain could not automatically deport a non-EU national who was the carer of a British child because the child had rights as an EU citizen; however, even then deportation was possible if the British courts considered the convicted individuals to be a danger to society: *The Times.* 2016. Britain will rule on kicking out Hamza's daughter-in-law. 14 September. The *Mail Online* of

14 September typically misrepresented the ECJ ruling as arbitrary meddling in British affairs by its "unelected judges" and said it was a further reason for Mrs May to accelerate Britain's departure from the EU. Michael Gove cited the Abu Hamza's daughter-in-law case in an interview with the *Daily Telegraph* of 7 May 2016, "Gove: We will make Britain safe after Brexit," as a case of intervention by the EU's "rogue court" despite there not being a final ruling ECJ ruling at that stage.

132. *Sunday Express.* 2016. 250 EU migrants serving life sentences in Britain. 17 April.

133. Had they come to Britain deliberately in order to escape the harsher conditions in continental jails—a sort of "jail tourism," like "benefits tourism" and "health tourism"?

134. And of course there are no British-born criminals in continental jails at their taxpayers' expense! This story is an evergreen in the *Express*. It came again in 2018: see *Euractiv*. 2018. Brexiteers cry foul over EU prisoner figures. 12 April.

135. "We should resist Turkey's thin-skinned president rather than pander to him: Germany is putting the future security of the EU in the hands of an anti-Western Muslim autocrat."

136. Mr Cameron's words in reaction to Jeremy Corbyn visiting the camp in Calais and saying they should be allowed into Britain: *BBC News*. 2016. Government's partial answer to migrant criticism. 28 January. See also discussion on BBC 1's *Question Time* on 29 January 2016.

137. *Daily Telegraph*, 2016. The British people will suffer if we stay in the EU. 7 May.

138. *The Sun*. 2016. Turkey swizzlers. Brits are forking out £675 million to help Turks join EU … even while Cameron insists they won't. 21 June; 2016. Will Turkey be next? David Cameron 'lying' about Turkey joining EU as talks will take place just days after referendum. 22 June.

139. Could *The Sun* be in the process of converting to Remain? I doubt it. It is more likely to be trying to shift the blame for Brexit on to the campaigners and away from the mouthpieces: *The Sun*. 2018. "GOVE AND TAKE: Top Brexiteer Michael Gove says Leave campaign was WRONG to spread fears about Turkey joining the EU in order to win the referendum. 16 July. See Baldwin, Tom. *Ctrl Alt Delete: How Politics and the Media Crashed our Democracy*, 210. London. Hurst, quoting Gove as admitting coyly that "We didn't always get everything absolutely right," and Dominic Cummings being a little blunter: "If Boris [Johnson] and Gove had not picked up the baseball bat marked Turkey/NHS/350m with five weeks to go then 650,000 votes would have been lost."

140. *Daily Telegraph*. 2016. Visa-free travel deal imminent for Turkey. 3 May, and 2016. Visa-free Turkey 'terror threat'. 17 May.

141. *Daily Express.* 2016. Slap a sticker in window. 16 April.

142. *Sunday Express.* 2016. Turkish to be EU language. 17 April.

143. *Daily Telegraph.* 2015. Refugees aren't to blame for the chaos. 28 October.

144. I would be surprised if more than 250 EU officials were working on the migrant crisis. The EU Commission's Directorate General for Migration and Home Affairs has a total staff of 550.

145. According to the European Commission (The EU and the Migrant Crisis, July 2017), in 2015 it deployed 1550 officers to support member states and their 100,000 or so national officials at external EU borders. Few of these officers would have been permanent officials working in the EU administration.

146. Nelson, Fraser. 2016. Sweden is a good example of how not to handle the Great Migration. *Daily Telegraph.* 3 February.

147. *Daily Mail.* 2016. Thirty Tory MPs set to rebel on child refugees. Ministers forced to reconsider letting youngsters in. 30 April.

148. *Daily Express.* 2016. Anger over UK's £589m bill for Syrian refugees— Alarm at Libya migrant surge. 13 April. An editorial in the paper ("Ever more child migrants") argued against taking unaccompanied child refugees: charity should begin at home.

149. *Daily Mail.* 2016. Migrants pay £160 to take Alps donkey paths into northern Europe. 16 April. Images of refugees snaking their way through Europe or arriving in boats on Greek shores also increased support for Mme Le Pen before regional election in late 2015 without her having to murmur a word: *The Economist.* 2015. Charlemagne: The dispensable French. 7 November.

150. See Banks, Arron. 2017. *The Bad Boys of Brexit: Tales of mischief, mayhem and guerrilla warfare in the EU referendum campaign,* 290–291. London: Biteback.

151. *Daily Telegraph.* 2016. Turkey doesn't deserve this huge visa reward. 4 May.

152. *Daily Express.* 2016. EU seeks control of our coasts. 7 March, and 2016. Now EU wants asylum control: Madness as Brussels plots to tell us who can come and stay in our country. 8 March—both examples from *InFacts,* 19 May 2016, "Press' hateful 8 stories from Brexit debate."

153. *Daily Telegraph.* 2016. Aegean migrant deal is working, claim EU and Nato. 22 April.

154. Heseltine, Michael. 2017. The Tories need a coronation, not a contest, to anoint their next leader. *Daily Telegraph.* 20 June, reminding readers that half of Britain's net migration comes from outside Europe and "we are already free to control it, limit it, or stop it in any way our sovereign interest demands."

155. *Daily Telegraph*. 2016. The gap between the official migrant figure and the truth is as wide as the Grand Canyon. We are owed an apology, by Allison Pearson. 13 May, and *Daily Express*. 2016. Britain's 1.5 million hidden migrants. 13 May, critiqued in *InFacts*. 2016. Press' hateful 8 stories from Brexit debate. 19 May. See also the article by the same *Daily Telegraph* columnist on 14 June 2017, referred to in Sect. 7.2 above.

156. *Daily Mail*. 2016. Britain cannot cut migration unless we quit the EU, warns IDS. 16 April. See Office of National Statistics, Migration Statistics Quarterly Report, 25 February 2016.

157. *InFacts*. 2016. Press' hateful 8 stories from Brexit debate. 19 May, critiquing the misleading *Mail Online* article of 3 April 2016. The new headline was "Figures show strain on NHS as doctors take on 1.5 million extra patients in just three years—with Vote Leave campaigners blaming rise on EU migrants."

158. *Daily Mail*. 2016. Health tourists' NHS loophole: EU nationals don't need special card—or even any ID—to get free treatment, minister admits. 16 April.

159. *Huffpost*. 2013. The Sun's front page on immigration with massive red line across Europe is branded 'xenophobic'. 18 December.

160. *BBC News*. 2019. UK migration: Increase in net migration from outside the EU. 28 February; *Full Facts*. 2019. EU immigration to the UK. 18 March; *BBC News*. 2019. Crossing Divides: Has the UK changed its mind on migration? 4 March; Samuel, Juliet. 2018. Britain must pay the price for living off the fruits of cheap EU workers. *Daily Telegraph*. 6 February.

161. *BBC News*. 2019. 4 March, thought the "remarkable change" in attitudes to migration might be because the national debate on immigration during 2017 elections and the Brexit referendum may have focussed people's minds on the social, practical and economic trade-offs involved in cutting migrant numbers, resulting in a more nuanced response to the issue. That might be so, but there might be a different explanation, namely the ceasefire in xenophobic rhetoric against immigration by politicians and newspapers after the referendum.

162. *Gov.UK*. 2018. The UK's future skills-based immigration system. 19 December; Davidson, Ruth. 2017. It is time to give British people a national debate on immigration. *Daily Telegraph*. 8 August.

163. *The Economist*. 2018. Essay on Liberalism: Immigration in open societies, 45–46. 15 September.

164. See Cllr Alan Law's letter to *Daily Telegraph* of 15 June 2017: "Immigration controls are dubious at best when it actually comes to reducing numbers. Our past performance over that part of immigration

we do control—relating to arrivals from outside the EU—has been pretty ineffectual."

165. Samuel, Juliet. 2018. Britain must pay the price for living off the fruits of cheap EU workers. *Daily Telegraph*. 6 February.

166. Whitworth, Damian. *The Times*. 2017. Welcoming migrants was part of our culture. We've lost some of that (interview with Ian Hislop). 17 June.

167. *The Economist*. 2018. Bagehot: A hostile environment. 28 April; 2018. Identity cards: Big bother. 5 May.

168. Clegg, Nick. 2017. Squaring the Brexit circle on freedom of movement. *Financial Times*. 4 July, and readers' letters *Financial Times*, 6 July 2017 (Jonathan Faull) and 15 November 2017 (David Webster). Heseltine, Michael. *Daily Telegraph*. 2017. The Tories need a coronation, not a contest, to anoint their new leader. 20 June.

169. Soros, George. 2015. By failing to help refugees Europe fails itself. *Financial Times*. 27 July.

170. *The Guardian*. 2018. Britons had 'dark to black' skin, Cheddar Man DNA reveals. 7 February.

171. *Daily Telegraph*. 2017. Roman row erupts as Mary Beard defends black cartoon character. 11 June.

PART III

Conclusion

CHAPTER 8

Conclusion

This book is about the negative reporting about the European Union (EU) practised by the bulk of British print media over the past 25 years, which can fairly be described as "propaganda" given its consistently one-sided and remorseless nature. The misinformation was one of the factors that induced a No vote in the referendum for it had long helped to form the attitudes of British voters towards Europe. The degree of animosity towards Europe shown by the British—or rather English—Brexit-supporting press is unique in Europe. The book debunks the myths at the heart of the misinformation about sovereignty, money and immigration propagated by the Brexit movement and its newspapers by comparing the myths with verifiable facts.

The EU referendum taught us a lot about our country. I do not think all of it had to do with the EU. The dissatisfaction and desire for change had deeper causes which would have had to be tackled in any case. The "burning injustices" Mrs May talked about in her first speech as Prime Minister from the steps of Downing Street are real for large sections of the population: poverty, lack of opportunity, deteriorating public services, alienation, hopelessness, violence, abuse, mental health problems. Brexit is a red herring and a distraction from tacking such problems. This should be a government's main job, but the government and parliament are having the energy sucked out of them by the all-consuming priority of Brexit, and everything else is on hold. Brexiteers say it will come good in the end. Once the economy is freed from the dead hand of Brussels and is

© The Author(s) 2019

F. Rawlinson, *How Press Propaganda Paved the Way to Brexit*,
https://doi.org/10.1007/978-3-030-27765-9_8

again striding the world stage confidently as an independent country, the story goes, there will be more money to invest in services and everyone will be better off.

Yet the signs of a miraculous improvement in ordinary people's lives from Brexit are not promising. All but the most rose-tinted economic forecasts point to a fall of economic activity and a loss to public finances, not a Brexit dividend. Immigration was ostensibly a major reason for people voting out, and there were real grievances behind the dissatisfaction, but it is still in doubt whether having the theoretical power to control immigration will automatically cause net migration to fall in practice. The pull factors will not change unless, besides changes to immigration rules, there are major reforms to the labour market itself. Nor will the investment come to communities in the Midlands and North of England, the run-down coastal towns like Blackpool and Clacton, the South West and Wales, without some redirection of resources into regional development, something that the EU was doing but the *laissez-faire* Conservative government had little interest in because it would mean higher taxes and fiscal transfers.

The fact that in this book I do not go into the problems and challenges the EU itself faces, apart from the migrant crisis, does not mean I deny they exist. It is just that they are not the focus of this book. Brexit is mainly a British—and a Conservative—problem. Brexiteers say that if only the EU had changed to accommodate the UK's wishes, Brexit would not have happened, so it is the EU's fault: the EU has shown it cannot reform. This is not true. The EU is constantly reforming itself. It is always work in progress. What the Brexiteers want is for the EU to fundamentally change direction to suit the UK, to recreate itself in the UK's image. Why should it? The UK does not have all the answers.

The lessons I personally would draw from the referendum are unconnected to the EU or the effect of leaving on the economy and Britain's place in the world. Only time will tell who was right. The more important and worrying messages the referendum throws up for me are about education, democracy and the press.

Britain is a divided, still class-ridden society and part of the problem is its education system. The well-off educate their children privately; private education is considered a passport to the best universities and to employment in many sectors, so it is natural parents should want it for their children if they can afford it. It delivers privileges. The state schools that 93% of children attend are starved of funds and have a fraction of the resources of independent schools. Their quality can vary from good to poor, largely depending on the catchment area. Parents move house to get into the catchment area of a school of their choice. In some areas grammar schools, which are reputedly better than normal comprehensives but by no means always so, are a magnet.

Educational and social mobility charities like the Sutton Trust try to increase permeability between the privileged independent school sector and the state sector and to improve the access of state school pupils to Oxbridge, but they consider that the independent school sector is too entrenched and its supporters too powerful for any government to envisage a fundamental reform. Instead, they advocate pulling the state sector up by its bootstraps to something like the level of the private school sector. That requires investment. But investment in education is not forthcoming in a climate of financial austerity. Mrs May's recipe of expanding grammar (i.e. selective) schools in the state sector is not a solution. A bigger selective system perpetuates the division into a two-class structure, one for the fortunate selected few and another, lower standard for the many who will be denied the same chances. The latter will include many gifted children who will thereby be blocked in a less challenging school environment. Such an education system ends up failing very many children. A single state system giving every child the same chance is preferable. The gulf between grammar school and Secondary Modern back in the 1950s when I was at school was huge. It was a bad system for the majority of children who missed out. Today's system is better but with the recent lack of investment it cannot maintain that improvement, but is bound to slide back. There are other problems, too, that need attention such as the whole question of league tables and the exclusion of difficult or underperforming pupils, who become tomorrow's jail inmates, gang members and homeless.

Assuming the money that schools need is forthcoming, I would have two priorities to spend some of it on: foreign language learning and applied mathematics. People who do not speak any foreign languages cannot imagine the pleasure it gives to be able to communicate with people more easily in their own language and how it furthers mutual understanding and trust. You put yourself on the same level as your interlocutor and discover how alike you are as human beings. The distrust of Europe would not be as great, and Brexit would not have happened, if more British people had known the rudiments of French, Italian or German. But at Secondary Modern schools in the 1950s and 1960s foreign languages were not on the curriculum. Today, foreign languages seem to have become something of a taboo subject in many circles in Britain, including in the BBC, World Service excepted. It is as if knowing a foreign language was somehow unpatriotic or unfair to monoglot colleagues. This should change.

In foreign language teaching all pupils should be taught the international phonetic alphabet, which is as vital to knowledge of languages, even one's own, as music notation is for music education. Understanding how sounds are produced by the speech organs and how to write the sounds down in a standard transcription is a huge help in learning foreign languages, which all have different sounds than English and require training in producing those sounds. It also demystifies posh accents like Jacob Rees-Mogg's Eton-and-Oxford to show they are really just dialects of equal value to Dennis Skinner's homely Derbyshire. Eloquence, of course, is an entirely different matter, and Jacob Rees-Mogg is certainly a highly articulate and accomplished speaker. Accent snobbery is akin to racism and is still prevalent in Britain, much more so than in Germany or Finland. Foreign language learning helps by relativizing the differences within one's own language.

In mathematics, analysing the figures in statements put out by government should be included in the curriculum. Governments now use figures to pull the wool over the eyes of voters. For example, a minister might say the government has increased the funding it is putting into schools by x amount but omit to mention the amount y it has taken away from school budgets by making them responsible for teachers' pensions or some other financial burden previously assumed by the Department of Education. If voters—or radio presenters, for that matter—were trained to detect such ruses by politicians and to challenge and embarrass them on such statements, politicians would begin to take voters more seriously as adults and not just potential votes.

This takes us on to populism. It is politicians' job to explain complex issues to voters in simple terms, not because voters are stupid, but because the subject matter is difficult or unfamiliar to non-experts. Populists, however, oversimplify to the point of distortion, by omitting relevant facts or qualifications, or indeed lying. Another characteristic of the populist is endless repetition of the same distorted message, lie, half-truth or bullshit and the use of slogans, mantras, cues and dog whistles to get the audience fired up against an opponent, who soon becomes the enemy. Farage and Johnson were the master populists in the referendum campaign, almost the equal of Trump, a bit softer at the edges in Johnson's case but essentially the same.

If the populist slogan-parroting had stopped after the referendum it would not be so depressing, but it did not. May and her ministers kept trotting out the "taking back control" slogan, despite knowing it obscures a much more complex reality. No doubt, they felt obliged to keep up the pretence as Brexit was based on it, but it has reduced politics and democracy to a very low level when the government feels a need to infantilize voters to this extent. There must be honesty in politics or democracy is no longer worth having because we will be electing demagogues and heading for a dictatorship. Modern political campaigning has become the science of mobilizing voting fodder and social media is further mechanizing the process. It is a travesty of democracy. Politics must rediscover the art of persuasion through calm, reasoned, honest argument.

The referendum showed British politics at its worst, from Cameron's cynical strategy for winning the referendum by first acting tough with the EU, negotiating a few concessions, and then supporting Remain on the platform of a "reformed" relationship; through Johnson and Gove's lies about the £350 million and Turkey; to Farage's "Breaking point" poster and other inflammatory rhetoric on immigration. British political scientists and commentators seem to think British populism is of a milder variety than the extremist Continental sort and Britain could never be afflicted with this scourge to the degree Germany, France and Italy now are. After the referendum, I am not so sure. If referendums are to be part of Britain's parliamentary democracy in future, they have to be better regulated to ensure fairness.

The long-standing campaigns of denigration of the EU by the majority of British newspapers ensured that the referendum could not be fair. A third of British voters already had their minds made up long before the campaign started, according to Dominic Cummings of Vote Leave. Without any doubt, most of these die-hard Leavers were readers of the right-wing press which had long been agitating for Brexit. Britain has a free press, but it is accountable to no one (IPSO is a fig leaf), and so does not have to behave responsibly; it is powerful and not afraid of using its power and governments and other media like the BBC fear its ruthlessness. The Fourth Estate should not see itself as an alternative seat of power, committed to one-sidedly pushing the agenda of a particular faction of the Establishment against any government that dares to stand up to it. For a free press to throw its weight around as a virtual alternative government is just as bad as a controlled press kowtowing to a dictatorship. Substituting itself for government is not the press' role. The press should keep to its role in a democracy of holding government to account, defending the weak and righting injustices. Campaigning for a change in the long-term political orientation and constitution of a country, like leaving the EU, is legitimate in a free press, but not at the cost of abandoning its journalistic principles of objectivity and fact and ignoring its role in educating readers, and instead manipulating them to do its will. The British right-wing press, which counts some of the world's best journalists and political commentators in its ranks, betrayed the principles of journalism in Brexit.

Index[1]

[1] Note: Page numbers followed by 'n' refer to notes.

© The Author(s) 2019
F. Rawlinson, *How Press Propaganda Paved the Way to Brexit*,
https://doi.org/10.1007/978-3-030-27765-9

CPI Antony Rowe
Eastbourne, UK
February 06, 2020